D0454881

Short-term Counseling

SHORT-TERM COUNSELING

Guidelines Based on Recent Research

IRVING L. JANIS

Yale University Press   New Haven and London

Portions of this book have been published in slightly different form in
Counseling on Personal Decisions, ed. Irving L. Janis (New Haven: Yale
University Press, 1982).

Designed by Nancy Ovedovitz and set in ITC Garamond type.
Printed in the United States of America by Murray Printing Company,
Westford, Massachusetts.

Library of Congress Cataloging in Publication Data

Janis, Irving Lester, 1918–
    Short-term counseling.
    Bibliography: p.
    Includes index.
    1. Short-term counseling. I. Title.
BF637.C6J36 1983 158'.3 83-3488
ISBN 0-300-03102-5
ISBN 0-300-03125-4 (pbk.)

10 9 8 7 6 5 4 3 2 1

To Marjorie—the best counselor I have ever encountered

Contents

Preface

Within the rapidly expanding universe of professional helping relationships, this is the age of short-term counseling. The trend toward using brief forms of treatment designed to aid people to make and carry out sound personal decisions has become dominant in psychological consultation centers, family service agencies, and vocational counseling facilities. The same trend is apparent in medical clinics and hospitals as well as among all sorts of private practitioners in the fields of mental and physical health. The guidelines for short-term counseling presented in this book are intended to be applicable in all such settings.

The main guidelines emphasized throughout the book are ones that my colleagues and I have carefully investigated in counseling clinics during the past 15 years. Most of the research involved carrying out systematic investigations designed to control for the influence of extraneous variables and for methodological artifacts, in order to test prescriptive hypotheses about ways of increasing the effectiveness of short-term counseling. Those hypotheses form the bases for the recommended guidelines. They, in turn, were derived from two general theoretical frameworks, discussed in chapters 2 and 6. One of the frameworks gives an account of how a supportive helping relationship can be built up within a single counseling session and thereafter used effectively when a counselor is attempting to facilitate adaptive changes in a client's behavior. The other framework, which can be used in conjunction with the first one, outlines a general strategy for counseling any client who seeks help at a time when he or she is facing an acute personal dilemma, such as what to do about a health problem or an unsatisfactory career or marriage. It is particularly applicable when the client is considering the possibility of making a major change in life-style but feels extremely ambivalent about it.

The present book draws heavily upon an extensive research monograph that I edited (*Counseling on Personal Decisions: Theory and Research on Short-term Helping Relationships* [1982]), which reports on 23 field experiments carried out at Yale University with my collaborators. Lengthy excerpts from the theory section of that monograph are included in the first three chapters. Briefer extracts and rewritten summaries of the research findings and their implications from other sections of the monograph are presented in the remaining chapters of this book. The last two chapters, which deal with special problems of decision counseling, present substantive material from three prior publications: chapter 3 of the 1982 monograph cited above, *Decision making* by Janis and Mann (1977), and *A practical guide for making decisions* by Wheeler and Janis (1980).

I have rewritten most of the pertinent material from the 1982 research monograph and from the other prior publications in a way that I believe will be most valuable for practitioners. For example, I have highlighted the steps a counselor can take to make full use of the practical implications of the theoretical framework for preventing unsound decision making and to apply the new techniques of decision counseling that I have found to be effective. Also, in order to meet the needs of practitioners, I have added a great deal of new material on related or supplementary guidelines suggested by recent research by other investigators. But in summarizing the research findings, whether my own or those of others, I have omitted the technical details about experimental design, research procedures, and data analysis—all of which can readily be found by consulting the appropriate references. Nevertheless, I have tried to present sufficient information in my summaries of the research so that the reader can see how the recommended guidelines follow directly as practical implications of the findings.

Whenever I recommend a standard counseling procedure or a new technique for special problems, I present sufficient details so that practitioners, whether novices or experts, will know how and when to apply it. For example, in the chapters on building an effective client–counselor relationship, I include considerable information about how to elicit the optimal amount of self-disclosure at the outset of the initial session, how to express acceptance and give related kinds of positive feedback, how to make specific recommendations at the appropriate time to facilitate changes in clients' behavior without evoking resistances, and how to terminate counseling treatment in a way that will help clients maintain favorable changes in attitudes and behavior. The chapters on decision counseling include details about how and when to carry out new procedures to overcome clients' resistances that interfere with realistic appraisal of the pros and cons for alternative courses of action and to prepare them psychologically to cope with the stresses of subsequent setbacks that might interfere with either the initial steps of implementation or long-term adherence to the decision.

This book does not, however, purport to give full coverage to all the practical issues that counselors need to be familiar with in selecting and assessing clients, implementing an appropriate counseling strategy, giving homework assignments to clients, and evaluating their progress. Although most of the guidelines I present are intended to be broadly applicable to a wide variety of client problems—including depression, phobias, sexual inhibitions, drug addictions, delinquency, learning disabilities, obesity, physical defects, career dissatisfactions, shyness, bereavement, family discord, and divorce—I do not include the technical details to be found in the extensive clinical literature on how a counselor might attempt to deal with each of these special problems.

In short, this is not a comprehensive textbook or a handbook covering all the strategies and tactics that a professional counselor might want to have in his or her repertoire for dealing with all sorts of psychological problems and distressing circumstances. But I believe that it can be a useful supplementary textbook in courses on the fundamentals of counseling. I have tried to write this book in a readable style with numerous illustrative examples so that it might be an easily mastered guide for trainees and novices. I hope it will also be a source of fresh ideas for experienced counselors, whether they generally adhere to one of the behavioral, cognitive, psychodynamic, humanistic, or eclectic approaches.

Acknowledgments

Eighteen psychologists collaborated with me in carrying out a large series of field experiments at Yale University on the effectiveness of various counseling procedures and in preparing the original research reports that I have drawn upon in this book. I wish to express my deep appreciation to Dr. Donald Quinlan, who as codirector of our research project was my main collaborator, and to all the others: Ms. Virginia Bales, Dr. Elaine Blechman, Dr. Edward S. Conolley, Dr. Mary Ellen Colten, Dr. Murdo M. Dowds, Jr., Dr. Les R. Greene, Dr. David Hoffman, Dr. Michael F. Hoyt, Ms. Debra Kimes, Ms. Donna-Maria LaFlamme, Dr. Ellen Langer, Dr. Leon Mann, Dr. William L. Mulligan, Dr. Carla Nowell, Dr. John H. Riskind, Dr. Arthur D. Smith, and Dr. John A. Wolfer. Excellent suggestions for improving certain chapters in this book were made by my daughter, Ms. Charlotte Janis, and by Dr. Judith Isroff, Dr. Elaine Sofer, and Dr. Richard A. Wessler. For a critical review of the entire manuscript, with extensive suggestions used in the final revision, I want to thank my wife, Marjorie Graham Janis.

1 Problems of Short-term Counseling

SCOPE OF THE BOOK

This book deals mainly with when, how, and why counselors can be effective in just a few sessions with clients who seek help when they are making vital decisions concerning their health, career, marriage, or other aspects of their personal lives. The theoretical analyses and the conclusions derived from the research studies summarized in the chapters that follow provide the basis for the guidelines I shall present. These guidelines are tentative because the evidence is suggestive, not definitive. But they might be useful for increasing the effectiveness of all sorts of professional counselors and therapists, irrespective of whether their interview procedures and treatment repertoires are based on behavior therapy, cognitive-behavior modification, biofeedback, psychodynamics, stress and crisis theory, or any other approach. Many of these guidelines may apply equally to the work of the large numbers of men and women in other professions who have had no training in counseling but nevertheless sometimes find themselves in the role of adviser to clients who ask them what they should do.

In order to highlight the need for guidelines based on systematic research, this chapter presents a brief overview of the main issues that require investigation and the current state of knowledge (or lack of it) in the field of counseling. This overview also provides the background for the theoretical framework outlined in chapter 2 and for the research strategy used in the series of 23 naturalistic field experiments summarized in chapters 3 to 7, which were carried out in my research program at Yale University on the effectiveness of counseling interventions in various clinical settings.

A recurrent phenomenon concerning counseling effectiveness, widely observed in studies of clients who seek professional help for marital difficulties, health problems, and other personal dilemmas, is emphasized in a review of cogent research on career counseling by Holland, Magoon, and Spokane (1981). The phenomenon—which causes some consternation among those noneclectic counselors who would like to believe that the particular strategy or set of procedures they use is clearly superior to all others—is that *systematic evaluations of a wide variety of counseling treatments generally show that almost all of them are effective to some extent, and no one of them is consistently better than the others.* As Holland, Magoon, and Spokane put it, there is a "general failure to find different effects for different treatments, which demonstrates a large hole in our understanding" (pp. 285–86). The systematic evaluation studies of career or vocational counseling, these authors suggest, "imply that the beneficial effects are due to the common elements in these divergent treatments" (p. 285). They surmise that four common elements run through the treatments given by counselors employing different approaches and different kinds of interventions with clients seeking help for career dilemmas:

1. Providing the client with social support
2. Giving pertinent information about alternative choices
3. Helping the client to clarify his or her personal objectives and potentials by eliciting cognitive rehearsals of aspirations and images of the future
4. Encouraging the client to develop a cognitive structure to organize information about himself or herself in relation to available alternative choices (pp. 285, 298).

All four elements are typical components of the treatments given by marital counselors, health counselors, and all sorts of other counselors who deal with people facing difficult decisions. The first component looms very large and perhaps is crucial for clients whose difficulties lie in the sphere of sustaining a high level of motivation when carrying out an arduous course of action. Prime examples would be men and women in mid-career completing a demanding training program in order to change to a new occupation, overweight persons having trouble maintaining self-control in sticking to a weight-reduction diet, and long-time addicts wishing to abstain from nicotine, alcohol, or other drugs. Chapters 2–5 focus mainly on guidelines for providing effective social support when trying to help clients who have such problems.

The other three components are especially pertinent when clients are undecided about what to do about some important aspect of their lives that distresses them and seek help in resolving the decisional conflicts. These components become prominent in the discussion of decision counseling in the final two chapters of this book—especially when I describe new types of intervention, such as the balance-sheet procedure and emotional role playing, which stimulate clients to seek pertinent information about feasible choices, to clarify their personal objectives, and to reorganize their cognitions about their own capabilities and goals in relation to the expected demands and probable outcomes of available alternatives.

ROOM FOR IMPROVEMENT

Actually, much of the counseling on personal decisions that goes on in America and throughout the Western world is carried out by persons who themselves might benefit greatly by consulting a specialist in the psychology of counseling. Many of them have never read even a single book on helping relationships. They include the vast numbers of physicians, attorneys, personnel managers, stockbrokers, accountants, teachers, clergymen, and other professionals whose primary expertise lies elsewhere than in counseling. Nevertheless they are the ones to whom people most often turn for guidance on important decisions.

The various professional advisers to whom I have been referring generally give counseling on a short-term basis—that is to say, they see each client for only a few sessions, usually only one or two. Large numbers of educational guidance and career counselors are also providing brief forms of counseling. Often their counseling is limited to one well-structured session (Radloff, 1977). Among professional psychologists short-term counseling is also becoming a widely prevalent type of helping relationship (see Garfield, 1971).

It is difficult to estimate how effectively these professionals are functioning as counselors. Professionals who give health-care counseling have been studied more intensively than the other professionals in this regard, and the evidence indicates that there is vast room for improvement.

Numerous studies indicate that physicians often fail to influence their patients to do what they recommend (See reviews of the literature by Kasl, 1975; Kirscht & Rosenstock, 1979; Sackett, 1976; Stone, 1979.) For example, follow-up studies on patients who were given standard prescribed medications for their illnesses in first-rate medical clinics have revealed that about half the patients failed to take the medications in accordance with the physicians' instructions (Sackett, 1976). Similarly, in a number of studies, 20–50 percent of medically ill adults failed to keep scheduled appointments for the standard medical treatments that were recommended (Kirscht & Rosenstock, 1979). Reviews of the large number of studies of compliance with well-qualified physicians' recommendations report wide variation in different circumstances, with noncompliance rates ranging from 15 to 93 percent (Davis, 1966; Sackett & Haynes, 1976).

These and many related findings reveal that physicians' instructions or recommendations concerning what to do about serious health problems frequently go unheeded. We have no clear indications, however, as to how often their lack of success as counselors is primarily attributable to insurmountable resistances of the patients or to defective communications by the physicians. Health-care practitioners may fail to communicate their recommendations clearly enough to avoid being misunderstood by the patients. Or they may fail to motivate their patients sufficiently to overcome surmountable resistances arising from the unpleasantness and other costs of adhering to the recommendations. If for any reason the patients do not follow the medical advice they are given, the physicians' skills in diagnosing the illness and prescribing appropriate treatments or regimens are of no use whatsoever. Similarly, attorneys, financial consultants, and other professional persons who advise large numbers of clients on personal decisions fail to fulfill their primary functions effectively insofar as their clients misunderstand what they are recommending or remain unmotivated to adopt the recommended course of action.

In recent years the gap between what medical patients are told to do by their physicians and what the patients actually do has been narrowed somewhat by the newly developing profession of health counseling. Hospitals and medical clinics have begun to employ specially trained psychologists as well as social workers and nurses to function as health counselors in order to deal with the behavioral problems posed by the large numbers of patients who fail to comply with medical recommendations. These counselors also contribute to public health by helping people who are not ill (but are at risk) to carry out preventive courses of action.

The lack of adherence to personal decisions that promote health is becoming increasingly recognized as a major social problem because of the impressive medical evidence that has accumulated on the major causes of premature death and disability. Until recently the main kinds of serious illness were the infectious diseases. But in the last few decades premature death and disability have been caused mainly by cancer and heart or cardiovascular diseases, which are at least partly a consequence of life-style. Thomas J. Stachnik (1980) points out that the major chronic diseases affecting people under the age of 65 "are in part a product of how we live, that is, what and how much we eat and drink, how we exercise, how we deal with daily stresses, whether or not we smoke, and so on." The same point is made in a widely cited Surgeon General's report (Richmond, 1979). In short, the most serious medical problems that plague the majority of Americans and Europeans today are not primarily medical problems at all; they are behavior problems, requiring the alteration of personal habits, preferences, or decisions. Thus they fall squarely within the domain of health counseling.

The tasks confronting health counselors are not easy. A high incidence of failure has been well documented in studies of the effectiveness of counselors in clinics that offer professional help to heavy smokers and to overweight men and women. In the United States some of these clinics are part of a profitable industry. Each year hundreds of thousands of new consumers and repeaters pay for their services, but most of their successes appear to be short-lived. A high percentage of those who go to the clinics do cut down on cigarette smoking or lose weight for a few weeks, but most of them fail to adhere to the prescribed regimen after supportive contact terminates (see Atthowe, 1973; Henderson, Hall & Lipton, 1979; Leventhal & Cleary, 1980; Lichtenstein & Danaher, 1976; Sackett &

Haynes, 1976; Shewchuk, 1976). In a review of the literature on the effectiveness of clinics for heavy smokers, Hunt and Matarazzo (1973) found that, just like heroin addicts and heavy drinkers, many smokers respond well to whatever counseling treatment they receive, but a very high percentage relapse within a month or two after starting the program. More recently, Leventhal and Cleary reviewed studies of treatments for heavy smokers and again concluded that the long-term results are poor: "Initial cessation rates are high, but so is the rate of return to smoking. . . . Whereas most backsliding occurs within 6 months, it continues with inexorable force for months [after that]" (Leventhal & Cleary, 1980).

The low rates of cure, however, do not necessarily mean that people who are heavy smokers, or obese, or addicted to alcohol have such a bad prognosis that it is futile for them to attempt change. Suggestive findings from small samples of two different communities seem to show that a very high percentage (60% or more) of persons with such disorders are successful in curing themselves (Schachter, 1982). If this finding is confirmed by additional samples, the low incidence of cures among clients who seek professional treatment may be attributable to the intractability of the "self-selected, hard-core group of people who, unable or unwilling to help themselves, go to therapists for help, thereby becoming the only easily available subjects for study of recidivism and addiction"; furthermore, "the inferences drawn from studies of therapeutic effectiveness . . . based on single attempts to cure some addictive state or other . . . [may be in error because] people do try to quit repeatedly . . . [and] it may be that success rates with multiple attempts to quit are greater than single attempts to do so" (Schachter, 1982, p. 437).

Consequently, the outlook for most cases of obesity, heavy smoking, opiate addiction, and other such "addictive-appetitive disorders" now no longer seems bleak, as it was until the recent data suggesting high rates of self-cures among untreated cases became available. If this new optimistic outlook continues to be substantiated by studies of men and women who have attempted to cure themselves, it will be good news for most people who are overweight or addicted to nicotine or other drugs. The prognosis for such persons will no longer appear to be so poor as to warrant feelings of pessimism about their capacity to sustain long-term cures. But if it is true that most people with addictive-appetitive disorders who go to clinics for professional help are hard-core recalcitrants, as Schachter surmises, the new outlook will not necessarily make it much easier for counselors to cure the majority of their clients.

The hypotheses and conclusions about effective short-term counseling discussed in this book appear to have a good chance of being applicable to a large majority of therapists and advisers, whether they give short-term or long-term counseling, and including many who do not consider themselves professional counselors. The new theory and research that are presented about when, how, and why clients are helped in short-term counseling may also increase the understanding and skill of even the best qualified practitioners. I expect the guidelines to be useful not only to novices but also to those who have been well trained as clinical psychologists, psychiatrists, or social workers, or who have had extensive experience as marital, career, or educational guidance counselors and know a great deal about the psychology of helping relationships.

DIVERSE FORMS AND STYLES OF COUNSELING

I use the term *helping relationships* in the plural because they come in many different forms and styles, varying in the degree of directedness and other dimensions. At one extreme is the form practiced by clinicians who consistently follow the principles of "client-centered" counseling. At each session, conducted once or twice a week over a period of several months, the counselor listens attentively to what the client says about personal problems and consistently responds in an accepting and empathic manner, reflecting the emotional content of the client's statements. The counselor carefully abstains from offering any advice or specific recommendations as to what the client should do. Carl Rogers (1951), who developed the client-centered approach, proposes that essentially the same nondirective procedures that are used in conducting psychotherapy with people who seek relief from anxiety attacks or other neurotic symptoms should be used in counseling people who seek help in making a vital personal decision. He acknowledges, however, that counseling may involve asking more questions and giving more information than psychotherapy, with fewer attempts to give psychological interpretations of the latent content of what the client is saying. Other practitioners argue that psychotherapy differs in more fundamental ways, both in objectives and in effective techniques, from counseling. They assert that counseling generally requires an educational and a supportive stance in order to help people deal with specific dilemmas (see Brammer & Shostrom, 1968; Corsini, 1968).

At the opposite pole from the nondirective approach of Rogerian client-centered counseling is the authoritarian-directive approach, which frequently characterizes the counseling given by large numbers of professionals, such as physicians, attorneys, and financial advisers. These counselors generally listen to the client's statement of the problem at the start of the first session and then use their expertise to decide on the best course of action. Before the first session is over, the client is usually told exactly what to do. If the client returns to discuss any complication that has arisen, the authoritarian counselor once again tells the client, in the same directive manner, what to do about it.

Other types of counseling fall somewhere between the two poles of completely nondirective and completely directive. One intermediate type, often practiced in health clinics for people who want to quit smoking or to lose weight, involves giving supportive guidance for executing and sticking with a difficult decision (see Bandura & Simon, 1977; Cormier & Cormier, 1979; Krumboltz, 1966). The client already knows what he or she would like to do but seeks help in carrying out the intended course of action. In one or two sessions the counselor offers direct suggestions, sometimes in an authoritarian manner (e.g., "You should follow carefully every day all the rules of this 1200-calorie diet") and sometimes not (e.g., "You may find it helpful to spend about 10 minutes every day in meditation about your reasons for dieting"). Usually in this type of supportive counseling the counselor also offers information and persuasive arguments to reinforce the decision that the client has already tentatively arrived at before coming to the first session (e.g., by presenting medical facts about the potentially harmful effects of remaining overweight).

Another intermediate type is a relatively new form of decision counseling, which involves the joint work of the counselor and the client in diagnosing and improving the latter's decision-making efforts (see Broadhurst, 1976; Janis & Mann, 1977). The counselor attempts to help the person resolve realistic conflicts that arise when he or she is facing a difficult choice, such as whether to be married or divorced, to switch to a different career, or to undergo elective surgery. This type of decision counseling is usually nondirective with respect to substantive issues involved in the decision: The counselor abstains from giving advice about which course of action the client should choose and even avoids suggesting in any way that he or she regards certain choices as good or bad. Instead, the decision counselor tries to help clients make the fullest possible use of their own resources for arriving at the best possible decision in terms of their own value systems. Much of the counselor's work consists of making clients aware of the decision-making procedures that they are using and of alternative procedures that they are not using. The counselor may be somewhat directive, however, in suggesting where to go for pertinent information, how to take account of knowledge about alternative courses of action, how to find out if deadlines need to be taken at face value or can be negotiated, which risks might require preparing contingency plans, and the like.

Among counselors in many different types of settings there appears to be a trend away from the traditional "tell-them-what-they-should-do" approach toward the type of decision counseling just described (see Cormier & Cormier, 1979; Egan, 1975; Greenwald, 1973). In the five-county area around Syracuse, New York, for example, a new Regional Learning Service, funded by the Carnegie Corporation, offers decision counseling to adults who want more education in order to upgrade their job qualifications or to change to a new vocation. According to an account in *Carnegie Quarterly* (Radloff, 1977), the counselors in this organization do not attempt to sell clients on making any particular choice or on going to any one of the 15 institutions of higher education in the area, but function mainly as resource persons. Instead of telling clients what they are best qualified to do, as many career guidance counselors do, these counselors help the clients answer for themselves, "What is the next thing I want to do with my life?" More than 70 percent of the 9,000 clients seen during the period from 1974 to 1977 were given only one session; the rest were given somewhat more counseling in a series of individual sessions or in group counseling workshops. The testimony of some of the most satisfied clients suggests that interacting with the counselor provided them with more than just useful information to pilot them through the maze of available educational pathways. One client reported that he benefited from talking to "somebody who really believed in me" because until then "I wasn't sure I could make anything of my life." Another said, "There are a lot of people like me . . . all we need is a little information and a lot of support." Recognizing the importance of the social-support dimension, the directors of the counseling organization selected their 20 part-time counselors from more than 400 applicants by giving priority to "personalities that were warm, resourceful, and 'naturally helping' " (Radloff, 1977).

Decision counseling is currently used to some extent as a component in the treatments offered by psychotherapists, marital counselors, career counselors, and other clinicians who deal with people at a time when they are making important personal decisions (see Baudry & Wiener, 1974; May, 1969; McClean, 1976). It is also similar to an approach that is becoming popular among consultants whose work with executives in large organizations is oriented toward trying to improve the quality of policy-making decisions (see Schein, 1969; Hackman & Morris, 1975).

This book deals primarily with the two types of counseling I have just described: short-term guidance for carrying out a difficult decision and short-term decision counseling to help people arrive at a vital choice. The guidelines and new procedures presented may also prove to be relevant across the entire spectrum of counseling approaches and perhaps in many forms of psychotherapy.

COUNSELING AS AN ART

In 1968 Corsini pointed out that "all varieties of symbolic helping relationships," including all types of counseling as well as standard forms of psychotherapy, are "currently an art, not a science" (p. 1113). Taking account of the few systematic research investigations that have been carried out in recent years, one might modify that harsh conclusion slightly by saying that at present *counseling is more of an art than a science*. The bulk of the scholarly literature on helping relationships is by psychotherapists or counselors who tell us about their hard-won guiding principles based on long years of clinical experience. Most of them provide practically no evidence that could withstand the challenges of skeptical critics and, instead, rely almost exclusively on what is presumed to be tacit knowledge. Much of the alleged wisdom in books and papers on career counseling, marital counseling, educational guidance, and case work may strike the critical reader as being either untested, implausible generalizations or nothing more than common sense. Like Polonius, they occasionally give us strikingly brilliant jewels ("To thine own self be true . . .") that all too often are lost in a sandpile of platitudes. However, not all their homilies deserve to be discarded. Edith Hamilton (1958), in commenting on the seeming truisms uttered by the chorus of wise old men in Aeschylus's *Agamemnon,* says, "But truisms are truths when they are first discovered, and become trite only because they are so true" (p. 161). One might add the truism that some old sayings embody bits of wisdom that can be eye-openers when first encountered by the young in each successive generation. The same might be said of some of the platitudes uttered by the wise old men and women who today write many of the psychology books and articles on how people can be helped by change agents.

Examples of valuable truisms are presented in a fresh, untrite manner in an essay on "The art of being a failure as a consultant," by Quentin Rae-Grant (1972). The essay is directed to consultants in the field of mental health, including clinical psychologists, psychiatrists, and social workers. Rae-Grant points out that the dice are so heavily loaded in favor of the prestigeful mental health expert that it is difficult to fail unless he or she unwittingly works hard to do so. The blueprint that Rae-Grant lays out contains four fundamental rules for anyone who wishes to cultivate the art of failing as a consultant in any mental health clinic; all four can be applied equally to counseling individual clients. The consultant or counselor must (1) present himself or herself as knowing all the answers, which means ignoring the clients' ideas, desires, and goals and never hesitating to use his or her professional status to deal devastatingly with anyone who raises skeptical questions or offers an alternative point of view; (2) carefully avoid learning any facts about the clients so that his or her interventions are unencumbered by any knowledge about their needs, their available resources, and their limited capabilities, such as their inability to understand the impressive technical jargon he or she enjoys spouting; (3) insist upon complete reliance on his or her authority as an expert; (4) seize on every opportunity to function as a crusader for redressing whatever personal grievances or for promoting whatever social causes he or she is inclined to put on a hidden agenda, which should always be arrived at and implemented as a one-person "conspiracy" (p. 74).

These four essential components of a self-defeating strategy have a number of important corollaries that counselors should heed, according to Rae-Grant, if they want no unexpected forward-sliding despite their best efforts to prevent clients from making progress. When not busy dazzling the client with dynamic interpretations, the would-be unsuccessful counselor should tell the client exactly what line of action to carry out. The counselor must guard against allowing any decisions to be brought up or elaborated by the client lest the client become committed and implement the decision successfully. The consultant "can take those solutions proposed by the consultee and gently, or not so gently, indicate their inappropriateness, naiveté, superficiality, or lack of dynamic relevance." When the client reports that he or she dutifully did what the counselor recommended but it did not work, the counselor need not be at a loss to exploit the ambiguities in whatever words of advice were given by showing how the client had misunderstood or had failed to do it in the right way. Similarly, if the client reports having succeeded in trying out something on his or her own, the counselor can deal with the alarming situation by claiming that the client has no reason to feel proud or take credit for it because the idea was an obvious implication of what the counselor had been proposing all along.

Above all, according to Rae-Grant's strategy for failure, counselors must avoid the development of warm and trusting personal relationships because this would make it difficult for them to avoid empathizing with their clients and would incline them to take seriously the clients' sincere complaints or other forms of feedback that invite honest self-appraisal and modification of counseling procedures. But I must add that the counselor who avoids building up such a relationship is by no means guaranteed that his or her work will be worthless. On the contrary, under certain conditions (which we are just beginning to learn about) a counselor who makes no attempt to build up a warm and trusting relationship in short-term counseling may end up being more helpful than one who does.

(This very complicated matter is discussed in detail in chapter 4 and comes up again in chapter 5.) For the present it suffices to point out as another corollary to Rae-Grant's rules that one of the subtlest ways for a counselor to court failure is to rely upon spontaneous warmth and empathy to the exclusion of any special counseling techniques that might better aid his or her clients to work out solutions to their dilemmas.

Even the most gifted relationship-builders who are successful in helping most of their clients might find that on the average it will take fewer sessions to achieve the goals of their counseling work if they follow the research literature and add the new techniques that have been tested and found to be effective (see Blechman, 1977). And, of course, not all counselors are capable of developing the type of relationship that will have positive motivating effects for the vast majority of their clients. For these less talented counselors, using fairly well validated techniques—such as the counseling procedures recommended in chapters 3 to 7 on the basis of recent research findings—might enable them to get much better results with many of their clients, whereas if they ignore the new techniques they are likely to continue to have a high rate of failures.

THE ILLUSION OF SUCCESS

A further point about the blueprint for failure is that the consultant runs the risk of being rated as successful despite careful adherence to all the fundamental principles set forth by Rae-Grant for achieving failure. The reason is that the process of evaluation is so poorly worked out that a completely unsuccessful consultant or counselor is likely to be rated favorably by colleagues, potential clients, and the community at large if he or she is not outrageously obnoxious. In fact, it is very easy for the counselor—or any therapist dealing with problems of physical or mental health—to have the illusion of being a great success in those instances when the clients would do just as well or perhaps somewhat better if they had never come for help. Neal Miller and Barry Dworkin (1977) point out that the vast majority of people with any type of problem fluctuate in the intensity of their discomfort or suffering over a period of several weeks or months. They generally come for help only when they are in one of the recurrent low points in the cycle, at a time when they feel most miserable, demoralized, depressed, inhibited, or lacking in whatever they think it takes to gain control over the causes of their distress. If a large number of sufferers who come for help were to receive no professional treatment of any kind but were to be reexamined after several days, weeks, or months, most of them would no longer be at their lowest point.

This source of error is extremely difficult to eliminate. It would still be there even if counselors or therapists kept careful records to avoid memory distortions in their favor and even if they tried to prevent other sources of bias when evaluating their own effectiveness by using behavioral measures and blind ratings by outside observers along with their clients' ratings. The results of a series of carefully documented case studies using objective measures of successful or unsuccessful outcomes would still greatly overestimate the percentage of cases who benefit from the treatment.

The main way to determine accurately whether favorable changes observed in the clients can be attributed to a counseling treatment is to carry out a controlled field experiment in which half the people who come for help are randomly assigned to the specific counseling treatment and the other half do not receive that particular treatment but otherwise are given the same information, recommendations, and auxiliary procedures (see Fiske, Hunt, Luborsky, Orne, Parloff, Reiser, & Tuma, 1970). Almost all the recent studies described in this book use this type of experimental design.

TRANSFORMING AN ART INTO MORE OF A SCIENCE

Rudimentary knowledge about social influence has slowly been accumulating to the point where the time may now be ripe for a major effort to transform the art of helping others into more of a science. Obviously, this requires stepping up two types of scholarly enterprises, both of which are in a very early stage of development. First, the theoretical schemas that practitioners claim to be useful either for explaining what goes on in successful counseling or for suggesting promising new techniques must be explicitly formulated in terms of the conditions under which a helping relationship allegedly will be effective. This is an enterprise to which we can expect Kurt Lewin's well-known adage to apply: *Nothing can be so practical as a good theory.* Second, systematic empirical research is required to examine the testable implications of the theoretical formulations and to discover whatever can be learned about what goes on when the outcome of a helping relationship is successful as against when it is unsuccessful. We need dependable evidence on the effectiveness of various counseling procedures that practitioners claim to be successful. For this phase of developing a rudimentary science, the reverse of Kurt Lewin's adage might also prove to be true: *Nothing can be so theoretical as good practice.*

The research summarized in this book represents an attempt to move ahead on the twofold task of formulating testable theoretical ideas and obtaining systematic evidence bearing on them. In my research program at Yale I give priority to selecting as research sites those counseling situations that allow us to obtain clear-cut criteria of the effectiveness of a helper's interventions—such as a dieting clinic, where weight loss can be objectively measured, and a career counseling clinic, where behavioral measures of the degree to which the clients carry out the recommended information-seeking activities can be obtained unobtrusively.

The ultimate purpose of the research described in this book was to try to increase our understanding of how and why the influence of one person operates in a constructive way to help another person achieve his or her own goals. The main objective was to test hypotheses concerning the conditions under which talking with a professional counselor or some other type of helper will aid a person to choose and adhere to a difficult course of action, such as giving up smoking, going on a diet, or switching to a new career. Typically such a decision is difficult because it entails suffering short-term losses in order to attain long-term gains.

More specifically, the studies were intended to enable us to explain and predict when only one or a few sessions with a counselor will succeed in helping a client to arrive at and adhere to a recommended course of action that appears to both participants to be in the client's best interests, with a minimum of postdecisional backsliding and regret. The findings, as I have already suggested, may prove to have practical applications for improving the effectiveness of all sorts of face-to-face counseling in a variety of community settings—wherever psychologists, social workers, lawyers, physicians, nurses, professional counselors, or paraprofessional interviewers talk with people and give them advice about their personal decisions in an effort to help them achieve long-term goals of improving their competence, health, or welfare.

There are, of course, some practical and ethical constraints on the types of intervention that can be used in a setting that is committed to providing a genuine clinical service. One obvious ethical constraint is that no new procedure can be tried out for which there is reason to suspect any potentially adverse effects. Another less obvious one is that everyone who participates in a study as a client in a clinic must be given some genuine help. This requires us to set up a baseline control condition in which we use procedures that, in light of existing knowledge, are expected to help the clients achieve whichever of their goals the clinic is designed to facilitate. But these constraints have not prevented us from investigating the effects of various innovative psychological treatments that, on the basis of a theoretical analysis, we believe could prove to be more effective than the tried-and-true treatment given to the baseline control group.

In our naturalistic field experiments, my associates and I have investigated hypotheses concerning the mediating processes that may account for the effects of two basic types of intervention: (1) *relationship-building* interventions, such as inducing self-disclosure and responding with explicit acceptance, which influence the client's attitude toward the counselor and motivation to follow the counselor's recommendations; and (2) *decisional process interventions,* such as inducing the client to make contingency plans for anticipated postdecisional setbacks, which can introduce qualitative changes in the way the person arrives at, implements, and sustains his or her personal decision.

AN IRREPLACEABLE CORE OF ART
IN APPLYING GUIDELINES

In extracting and highlighting what seem to be the most important practical implications of recent research bearing on both types of intervention, I have been constantly mindful of the rich but controversial lore on the art of counseling based on detailed case studies and impressionistic observations. Although I do not attempt to provide an exhaustive survey of the clinical literature, I do try to show how the guidelines I present fit in with (and occasionally modify) the counseling strategies and tactics recommended by clinicians who are regarded as outstanding practitioners of the art of counseling.

Even when the guidelines for using a counseling strategy or tactic are based on accumulated evidence from well-designed field experiments as well as clinical reports by astute practitioners, they obviously will be of little value unless they are applied with sensitivity to the needs and capabilities of each client. The guidelines are prescriptive hypotheses that are expected to be beneficial *sometimes* for counseling *some* clients, not necessarily always with all clients. They are *not* intended, as Cormier and Cormier (1979) put it in their textbook on counseling addressed to advanced trainees, to be used like many medical prescriptions—

> automatically and without thought or imagination.... [Any] one counseling strategy may not work well for all clients. As your counseling experience accumulates, you will find that one client does not use a strategy in the same way, at the same pace, or with similar results as another client. In selecting counseling strategies, it is helpful to be guided by the documentation concerning the ways in which the strategy has been used. But it is just as important to remember that each client may respond in an idiosyncratic manner to any particular approach. (Cormier & Cormier, 1979, p. 8)

Nevertheless, if applied with discretion, the general guidelines and the specific interventions described in the chapters that follow could prove to be valuable additions to the repertoire of anyone who practices the art of counseling.

2 Helping Relationships: A Theoretical Framework

The theoretical framework presented in this chapter pertains to the powerful social incentives that influence a person's actions when he or she interacts with a professional counselor or with anyone else who takes on the role of helper. Under what conditions are a helper's suggestions or recommendations most likely to be accepted? What interventions can a helper introduce to build up an effective relationship? First, these questions will be examined from a novel perspective based on the social psychology of interpersonal influence. I shall focus especially on the problem of how counselors, who have no power to prevent their clients from firing them any time they wish, come to have sufficient motivating power to exert a positive influence on many people who seek their help, sometimes enabling the clients to carry out burdensome decisions that they cannot implement on their own. Then I shall introduce explanatory theoretical concepts in the context of analyzing two closely related problems: What are the crises that typically jeopardize the outcome of a helping relationship? What does it take to surmount these crises successfully? To answer these two questions we must draw upon both clinical psychology and social psychology.

THE SOCIAL POWER OF SUPPORTIVE HELPERS

The present theoretical analysis takes as its point of departure some well-known assumptions about one of the primary bases of social power, as described by social psychologists: becoming a "significant other," a reference person whose signs of approval and acceptance are highly rewarding. The widely used typology by French and Raven (1959) designates *referent power* as a major determinant of social influence. A person with referent power is able to induce genuine internalized changes in attitudes, values, and decisions (see Tedeschi & Lindskold, 1976).

18

The concept of referent power can be applied directly to the social influence of professionals when their signs of approval have positive effects on their clients as incentives for adhering to the courses of action they prescribe. Professionals are most likely to have referent power when their clients perceive them not only as useful and likable but also as benevolent, admirable, and accepting.

French and Raven (1959) contrast referent power with four other bases of social influence that are effective in inducing acquiescence but are much less likely to create sustained change or internalization: coercive power, reward power, legitimate power, and expert power. In a review of systematic research bearing on these postulated bases of social influence, Tedeschi and Lindskold (1976) conclude that the evidence supports a number of relatively independent dimensions pertaining to one person's influence on another, five of which correspond roughly to the French and Raven typology. Two additional components suggested by the empirical evidence are trustworthiness and credibility, which can be regarded as supplementary to the knowledge and skill components of expert power.

From a social psychological viewpoint, how would we character ize the power that a counselor typically exerts over the attitudes and actions of his or her clients? Of the various factors that have emerged from social psychological research, the one least pertinent to the helping relationship is coercive power, which pertains to the use of threats and punishments to induce compliance with authoritarian demands (see Strong & Matross, 1973). Many professional counselors also avoid introducing material rewards as inducements for compliance with their recommendations, although proponents of behavioral intervention techniques point to research indicating impressive successes from reinforcing desired actions with external rewards, such as special privileges in an institutional setting (see Bandura, 1969; Nay, 1976). Those who are opposed to offering any material rewards generally rely upon social rewards of a symbolic nature, which are embodied in their reassuring, empathic verbal statements and in their friendly gestures, smiles, eye contact, and other nonverbal communications, all of which augment referent power.

To some extent, all professional counselors take advantage of the expert and legitimate bases of their power to influence clients (e.g., by displaying their credentials and their affiliations with legitimizing professional associations). Most of them also conduct themselves in a forthright manner conducive to creating an authentic image of themselves as trustworthy and credible, which may contribute to their referent power as well as their expert power (see Strong & Schmidt, 1970).

BECOMING A SIGNIFICANT OTHER

What are the primary means available to a counselor for acquiring social influence as a significant reference person? According to social psychological research on interpersonal attraction there are several ways in which counselors (or anyone else) can build the type of relationship that results in their becoming significant reference persons for the people they deal with (Bennis, Berlew, Schein, & Steele, 1973; Berscheid & Walster, 1978; Byrne, 1971; Levinger & Breedlove, 1966; Newcomb, 1961; Strong & Matross, 1973; Tedeschi & Lindskold, 1976). One way is to make salient the *similarities* between themselves and their clients, particularly with regard to beliefs, attitudes, and values. Another way is to give *contingent praise* for specific accomplishments, actions, or intentions that are in line with the goals of the counseling sessions. Suppose, for example, that a woman who comes for help with shyness says she is not sure she can get herself to carry out a homework assignment recommended by the counselor—to talk with her boss about undesirable working conditions that she feels are unnecessarily making her daily life at the office miserable—but she adds that she will try. The counselor might say, "It's good that you intend to make a real effort to do it because if you were to continue to avoid raising the issue you can't expect to improve your work situation or to achieve your goal of overcoming your shyness."

A third way is to talk and act in a manner that conveys a *benevolent attitude* toward the client, an unselfish willingness to provide help out of a genuine sense of caring about the client's welfare (see Carkhuff, 1972; Truax & Mitchell, 1971). Still another extremely powerful way, which may overlap somewhat with the third way, is to give empathic *noncontingent acceptance* statements. Such statements bolster the client's self-esteem by conveying that he or she is held in high regard as a worthwhile person despite whatever weaknesses and shortcomings might be apparent (see Goldstein, 1975; Rogers & Dymond, 1954; Truax & Carkhuff, 1967). For example, in a career counseling clinic, if a client says something unfavorable about himself when reporting a distressing incident to illustrate his lack of self-confidence, the counselor might respond with an empathic comment that conveys continued acceptance, such as "You seem to have a good grasp of that serious problem of yours, which is an important first step toward finding a way to solve it." Counselors can attempt to build up each client's self-esteem by consistently expressing the sincere belief that the client has whatever it takes to succeed at changing in the direction he or she wants. To do so, counselors can adopt an apporoach that many psychotherapists use: viewing every client as a worthwhile person and focusing in an open-minded way on the person's assets that could represent real potentialities for change (Cormier & Cormier, 1979; Okun, 1976). This approach is facilitated by an empathic set such that the counselor constantly makes "an attempt to think *with* rather than *for* or *about* the client" (Brammer & Shostrom, 1968, p. 180).

There are, of course, marked individual differences among counseling practitioners in the degree to which they use one means or another of building up their motivating power and also in the extent to which they rely upon the other sources of social influence. For example, the nondirective approach of client-centered counselors in the Rogerian tradition relies most heavily on expressing "positive regard," which is equivalent to the fourth type of means (noncontingent acceptance) for building up their motivating power; in contrast, behavioral interventionists are likely to make relatively little use of that means and instead to rely primarily on contingent praise and external rewards. Some client-centered counselors, especially those who practice long-term psychotherapy, attempt to give insight-inducing interpretations in a way that conveys empathic noncontingent acceptance, including "advanced empathic" responses that formulate what the client seems to be getting at but is leaving unsaid (Carkhuff & Pierce, 1975; Cormier & Cormier, 1979; Egan, 1975). In short-term counseling, however, they are likely to rely much less on their inferences about the latent content of what the client is saying but communicate empathic noncontingent acceptance by reflecting feelings and attitudes expressed in the manifest content.

The bases of social influence that professional counselors rely upon in general differ from those used by mutual helpers who participate in a buddy system of the sort pioneered by Alcoholics Anonymous. Buddies lack the credentials that give the professionals a head start in expert and legitimate power, have somewhat more difficulty conveying benevolent intent to each other, and usually do not realize how or why noncontingent acceptance can be used effectively. But they may find it much easier than the professionals to build up motivating power as a significant reference person by highlighting the similarities of their current frustrations, concerns, hopes, and aspirations (see chap. 3).

Some counselors fail to do anything at all to build up their influence as a significant reference person. For example, some attorneys, physicians, nurses, and social workers concentrate narrowly on their professional tasks. They tell their clients what they ought to do without paying much attention to the clients' psychological resistances. A few are so businesslike that they do not openly show any concern about the client's current plight or future welfare. Such counselors, in effect, rely heavily on legitimate, expert, and reward power but neglect the potential increase in their ability to influence clients that could come from acquiring referent power as well.

Even if a businesslike counselor is using the other sources of power to the very limit, his or her effectiveness would be expected to increase by adopting one of the means of acquiring social power as a significant reference person in the life of each client. By adding referent power to the other bases of social power, according to the foregoing analysis, a counselor would become an even more highly esteemed helper with whom the clients are more likely to identify. Then his or her recommendations would not only meet with less initial psychological resistance but would also be more likely to be internalized and conscientiously adhered to long after the counseling sessions have come to an end.

SOCIAL REINFORCEMENTS

A considerable body of social psychological research on affiliative behavior indicates that when people face actual or anticipated situations of stress, they generally become motivated to affiliate with others in order to satisfy a number of important psychological needs, which include seeking social comparison, obtaining reassurance, and bolstering self-esteem (Darley & Aronson, 1966; Dittes, 1959; Festinger, 1954; Helmreich & Collins, 1967; Janis, 1968; Radloff & Helmreich, 1968; Schachter, 1959; Zimbardo & Formica, 1963). People are likely to be under stress whenever they are trying to arrive at or to implement a decision that they know will require them to undergo short-term deprivation in order to attain long-term gains—as when people decide to obtain training in a new speciality in order to improve their career prospects or to accept a physician's recommendation to stop smoking or to take other preventive actions in order to improve their health in the future (see Janis & Mann, 1977). Given the strong affiliation motivation of persons in stressful dilemmas who seek help from a decision counselor, the question of whether they will develop strong affiliative ties depends largely on the degree to which they receive positive social reinforcements, as Berscheid and Walster (1978) point out.

Of the four ways of building reference power via social reinforcement, three are part of the conventional wisdom of our times. Popular books, magazine articles, and soap operas repeatedly tell us that if we want to win friends and influence people we should try to talk about things we agree about rather than dwell on disagreements, we should give plenty of praise whenever someone deserves it, and we should always be considerate in a way that shows we really care about what happens to any person we want as a friend. Except for the relatively small number of people with personality defects or trained incapacities, these three types of social reward are commonly used spontaneously by persons who take on the role of helper, whether as friend, teacher, or professional counselor. But the fourth type—giving noncontingent acceptance—is not part of the conventional wisdom of the Western world and is not very popular among the vast majority of counselors, despite the best efforts of Carl Rogers and his followers to make it so.

One reason people do not use noncontingent acceptance even when they have been trained in how to do it is that it seems to violate powerful social norms involving social justice and equity (see Walster, Berscheid, & Walster, 1976). Noncontingent acceptance is often seen as giving verbal rewards to someone who does not deserve them. Most counselors, like most middle-class people, can be expected to have a sense of social equity and to be reluctant to violate norms asserting that social rewards should be given only to those who have earned them or who are likely to reciprocate.

Another reason professional counselors may refrain from giving noncontingent acceptance is that it is not easy to do so in an effective way. It requires the counselor to take account of the clients' point of view and to empathize with their feelings in order for his or her positive comments to be impressive and believable. But this is difficult for anyone, no matter how well trained, when a client is weak, miserable, and lacking in self-control. And yet this is the way most clients appear to be. Frank (1972) points out that the majority of clients come for professional help only as a last resort, when they are depressed and demoralized about not being able to help themselves and have exhausted all possibilities of getting help from others in their social networks.

Aside from the problem of empathy, exceptional skill is needed to avoid the pitfalls of using noncontingent acceptance. Clients are just as aware of the norms of social equity as counselors are, and they are likely to be suspicious when given unearned praise or compliments. The attempts of counselors to use noncontingent acceptance can have a boomerang effect if they lay it on so thick, from the standpoint of their clients, that they are presumed to be either habitually insincere or attempting to ingratiate with hidden manipulative intent (see Jones, 1974). Nevertheless, it probably is done quite effectively by some counselors, especially those who have gone through well-monitored practicum training.

Working with clients assigned to the buddy system in a weight-reduction clinic, Nowell and Janis (1982) observed that the partners remained uncomfortable and inept in their attempts to use noncontingent acceptance even after they had been given special training, including modeling by a staff psychologist and practice trials followed by critiques and more coaching. Obviously, a brief training session is not sufficient to enable novices to become skilled at giving noncontingent acceptance, and if they remain inept it can do more harm than good. But perhaps large numbers of professional counselors could become more effective if they were to obtain the type of training recommended by Carl Rogers (1967). He emphasizes the importance of cultivating empathy and skill in presenting genuine and credible statements that convey unconditional positive regard.

The theoretical analysis of critical phases in helping relationships, to which we now turn, is intended to add something to our understanding of how a professional counselor or any other kind of helper can influence clients to attain their own goals. It attempts to answer the following question: What does it take, besides positive social reinforcement and the other factors already discussed, for a helper to build up his or her motivating power and use it effectively?

PHASES IN HELPING RELATIONSHIPS

Where do the theoretical ideas come from? Mainly from my own clinical observations in a variety of counseling settings. In an effort to learn something more about the way professionals build up their referent power—or fail to do so—in their interactions with clients, I functioned as a professional counselor in many kinds of clinics where clients seek help—about marital problems, choosing or changing their careers, giving up smoking, going on a diet, or undergoing disagreeable medical treatments recommended by a physician. I met with each client once or twice a week for several weeks, usually from 3 to 12 sessions. Sometimes, as in the case of the dieting clinics, the goal of counseling was to help the clients carry out a difficult course of action in the face of temptations to backslide; in other clinics, the goal was to help the clients arrive at their own decisions concerning marriage or career by encouraging them to go through the necessary steps of exploring alternatives, seeking pertinent information, and making unbiased appraisals.

After comparing successful and unsuccessful cases in an impressionistic way, I tried to evaluate the plausibility of my inferences from these observations in light of the clinical and social psychological literature on social influence. The main hypotheses that emerge are consistent with findings from systematic studies indicating how social support from a significant person or group can facilitate marked changes in behavior (Cartwright & Zander, 1968; Garfield & Bergin, 1978; Hare, 1976; Shaw, 1971).

The hypotheses to be presented pertain to crises that typically arise in helping relationships. These hypotheses specify a number of variables in addition to the more familiar ones pertaining to social power and positive social reinforcements that I have just discussed—variables that are often overlooked by many professional counselors, but that nevertheless can affect the extent to which a client will be favorably influenced.

The key variables are listed in Table 2.1, organized according to critical phases. The variables are formulated in a way that makes it easy to see how they could be subjected to experimental investigation. (The list in Table 2.1, in fact, includes the principal variables investigated in the series of studies summarized in the next three chapters.)

Each of the variables shown in Table 2.1 should be understood as representing a *moderate* range of values. For example, the first variable refers to encouraging (*versus* not encouraging) clients to make self-disclosures that are well below the upper limit with regard to the amount and intensity of disclosure the client feels to be appropriate and tolerable in the here-and-now social situation. Encouraging a moderate amount and a moderate depth of self-disclosure, for reasons to be discussed shortly, is expected to contribute to the development of a positive relationship to the counselor. But attempts by a counselor to induce very high levels of self-disclosure could have unfavorable rather than favorable effects (see Cozby, 1973; Jourard, 1971; Tedeschi & Lindskold, 1976).

My observations suggest that there are three critical phases in almost every helping relationship. When these crises are surmounted, people are most likely to benefit from the attempts of a counselor to help them arrive at or adhere to a difficult decision.

Phase 1: Acquiring Motivating Power

The first critical phase involves overcoming the usual tendency toward reticence, suspiciousness, and defensiveness that prevents a person from trusting someone who purports to be trying to help change his or her behavior. Fears of being exploited, dominated, or rejected by the stranger who is supposed to be a professional helper constitute initial bases for ambivalence. On first contact, the client cautiously appraises the competence and trustworthiness of the would-be helper: "Does this person know what it's all about?" "Does this person tell the truth or is the person trying to sell something?" When

Table 2.1 Critical phases and key variables that determine the motivating power of counselors as change agents

Phase 1: Building up motivating power	1. Encouraging clients to make self-disclosures *versus* not doing so 2. Giving positive feedback (acceptance and understanding) *versus* giving neutral or negative feedback in response to self-disclosure 3. Using self-disclosures to give insight and cognitive restructuring *versus* giving little insight or cognitive restructuring
Phase 2: Using motivating power	4. Making directive statements or endorsing specific recommendations regarding actions the client should carry out *versus* abstaining from any directive statements or endorsements 5. Eliciting commitment to the recommended course of action *versus* not eliciting commitment 6. Attributing the norms being endorsed to a respected secondary group *versus* not doing so 7. Giving selective positive feedback *versus* giving noncontingent acceptance or predominantly neutral or negative feedback 8. Giving communications and training procedures that build up a sense of personal responsibility *versus* giving no such communications or training
Phase 3: Retaining motivating power after contact ends and promoting internalization	9. Giving reassurances that the counselor will continue to maintain an attitude of positive regard *versus* giving no such reassurances 10. Making arrangements for phone calls, exchange of letters, or other forms of communication that foster hope for future contact, real or symbolic, at the time of terminating face-to-face meetings *versus* making no such arrangements 11. Giving reminders that continue to foster a sense of personal responsibility *versus* giving no such reminders 12. Building up the client's self-confidence about succeeding without the aid of the counselor *versus* not doing so

clients have not been coerced into attending the clinic but come on a voluntary basis, these initial hurdles are usually passed with flying colors by a counselor who conveys by professional manner, as well as by office setting with framed licenses on the wall, that he or she has all the proper credentials. The client may be only vaguely aware of processing information about the counselor when making these appraisals.

In addition to evaluating the counselor's competence and trust-worthiness, the client also assesses the counselor's readiness to give social rewards in the form of approval and acceptance, which can profoundly enhance the client's self-esteem. Whether he or she uses a directive or a nondirective approach, the counselor's influence on the clients increases as soon as they develop an image of the counselor as a genuine helper (see Barrett-Leonard, 1962; Luborsky, 1976). The crucial questions the clients raise in their own minds are: "Does this person think well of me?" "Does this person really care about me?" To make these judgments, clients attend to verbal and non-verbal cues indicating whether the counselor has genuine positive regard for them and takes a personal interest in their welfare. Once a client decides that the helper really does care and can be counted on to express positive regard, his or her self-esteem is raised and the helper acquires a considerable amount of motivating power (see Tedeschi & Lindskold, 1976). Serious complications can arise, however, from the client's sensitivity to possible signs of disapproval by a counselor, especially at a time when the person has just taken the first step to obtain professional help, which requires admitting personal weaknesses and inability to handle one or more serious problems with his or her own resources.

At the very beginning of a relationship with a trustworthy person, as Bennis, Berlew, Schein, and Steele (1973) have pointed out, a man or woman starts to reveal personal defects and "bad" aspects of his or her self "in small increments, tentatively waiting for a response. If the response is disapproval or rejection, the relationship freezes at that point, is terminated, or the testing begins anew. If each [self-] exposure is met with acceptance, there is a continual buildup of trust . . ." (p. 135). According to these authors, practically everyone is highly sensitive to signs of acceptance or rejection even from the very beginning of an initial encounter with a stranger because, as a result of socialization experiences early in life, he or she has acquired a chronic concern about "bad" aspects of the self, which makes for low self-esteem and fear of being unacceptable to others: "Maintaining self-esteem is a life-long concern for most of us, and for many of us the possibility of even a single instance of rejection by another presents a terrible threat and one to be carefully guarded against" (p. 131). Many other behavioral scientists agree with the assumption that self-esteem maintenance is a basic feature of interpersonal relations and depends upon signs of acceptance, both verbal and nonverbal (see Becker, 1968; Rogers, 1961; Marlowe & Gergen, 1969; Wylie, 1961). Becker (1968, p. 328) goes so far as to formulate a "principle of self-esteem maintenance" which asserts that all persons strive in their interactions with others to feel "good" about themselves. He proposes this as a "universal principle for human action akin to gravitation in the physical sciences."

In line with these assumptions about self-esteem dynamics, one would expect that the quality of the helper–client relationship depends to a substantial degree on how the helper responds to whatever self-disclosures are elicited. In a weight-reduction clinic, for example, when clients are asked to discuss their eating problems they often make self-critical statements about their appearance, such as "Look how fat and ugly I am," and about their lack of self-control, such as "I'm such a pig I just can't resist rich desserts." After a client has started to reveal some personal weaknesses to a counselor, a major consequence of being given verbal and nonverbal acceptance responses that convey positive regard is marked improvement in the client's self-regard, which makes for strong motivation to continue the relationship, with high reliance on the helper as a respected model (see Carkhuff, 1972; Goldstein, 1975). From this point on, the helper becomes a significant reference person for the client and has the potentiality of acquiring as much social power to influence the client's actions as the most cohesive of normative reference groups (see Collins & Raven, 1969). But there are some emotional hurdles the client has to get over before the helper can succeed in using his or her newly acquired social power to foster adherence to a difficult course of action.

One complicating factor to which Bennis and his collaborators (1973) call attention is the hope for *unconditional* acceptance. They

assume that from early in life on, everyone has a longing for unconditional love: a wish for a loving caretaker or friend who will be
uncritical and undemanding, who can always be counted on to be
accepting and affectionate no matter what one does or says or thinks.
The concept of unconditional love, they assert, is acquired from early
socialization experiences and persists into adult life, even though it
is rarely, if ever, attained. All adults, however, have learned that love
is conditional, that one is treated affectionately and accepted at certain times and not at other times, depending on whether one's actions are good or bad in the eyes of the person whose acceptance
is being sought. And yet, coexisting with reality-testing and ego-
autonomous mastery motives in most people is a latent hope of
finding someone who will supply them with something approxi-
mating unconditional acceptance.

Carrying the analysis by Bennis and his collaborators (1973) one
step further, I assume that if a counselor encourages clients to disclose personal feelings, aspirations, troubles, or weaknesses and
consistently responds to the self-disclosures with statements of noncontingent acceptance, the clients tend to develop an image of the
counselor as an unconditional accepter, which at least temporarily
increases their self-esteem by producing a gratifying sense of moral
worth and heightened self-confidence about solving whatever personal problems are under discussion. The important point is that a
counselor will acquire much more social influence as a significant
reference person when a client sees the counselor as a dependable
source of self-esteem enhancement.

When a professional counselor gives conditional acceptance from
the outset, making it apparent that acceptance responses must always
be earned, clients may nevertheless come to like the counselor if
he or she expresses attitudes similar to their own, continues to be
affable, gives approval when the person has met the required demands, and limits disapproval for failing to do so to specific criticism
of the client's actions without implying total rejection of the client
as a person. All of these are considerate ways of giving contingent
acceptance, and they contribute to the influence of the counselor as
a significant reference person. Counselors who use this pattern,
combining contingent acceptance with consistent respect for each
client, presumably will attain much more social influence than those

who withhold approval when it is deserved or who give contingent approval but also use threats, ridicule, or other humiliating punishments when their clients do or say the wrong thing, which markedly lowers their self-esteem.

Whenever a contingent accepter gives praise for a desirable action, the client's self-esteem is temporarily enhanced. But whenever the contingent accepter gives justified criticisms or disapproval in response to the client's disclosures of failure to do what is expected, the client's temporary feelings of low self-regard remain low and may plummet much lower. Consequently, even the most consistently respectful contingent accepters will be perceived by clients as *undependable* sources of self-esteem enhancement.

In contrast, the noncontingent accepter who is consistently respectful of clients will usually be perceived as a *dependable enhancer.* That is to say, such a counselor will generally be seen by clients as someone who can always be counted on to raise their self-esteem if he or she consistently responds by making statements and nonverbal gestures of acceptance, not only expressing approval about the "good" things the clients report but also expressing empathy, optimism, and reassurance when the clients talk about being "bad" or reveal personal weaknesses. Their image of the counselor becomes that of a warm, understanding, protective figure who will always accept whatever personal defects are revealed (see Goldstein, 1975; Truax & Carkhuff, 1967). This image is also reinforced if the counselor uses the clients' self-disclosures to provide fresh insights or cognitive restructuring that help them view their problems as solvable, regardless of how hopeless or "awful" they characterize themselves. For example, a counselor in a weight-reduction clinic can use a client's self-disclosures about overeating to help the client reappraise his or her difficulties and to develop a more facilitating set of cognitions that are incompatible with self-defeating thoughts. A client who says, "I'm such a pig about desserts" can be given insight into how this belief interferes with successful dieting—because eating any dessert confirms the belief, leads to self-blame, and contributes to demoralization. The client can be shown how to identify the situational context where desserts are most troublesome and change the cognition to one that is not demoralizing (e.g., "I'll have to avoid having any of those irresistible pastries around because those are the desserts that turn me on"). Many clients are quite capable of taking personal responsibility for their actions, but it requires some elementary insights, which a counselor can provide, about when, where, and how to do so. People are less likely to be demoralized when the causes of their misbehaviors are seen as situational and not as due to permanent personal dispositions (Janoff-Bulman, 1978; Rodin, 1978).

The theoretical analysis based on the conception of unconditional acceptance formulated by Rogers (1961) and elaborated by Bennis and his collaborators (1973) has some testable implications. One of the main predictions is that by encouraging a tolerable level of self-disclosure and by giving noncontingent acceptance in response to whatever disclosures are made by the clients, a counselor will elicit a relatively high degree of adherence in response to any feasible recommendations. The mediating psychological change is the clients' increased reliance upon the counselor for maintaining their self-esteem. This type of reliance will be much less likely to occur if self-exposure is followed by neutral, ambiguous, or negative feedback rather than explicit signs of acceptance conveyed verbally and non-verbally.

A client who has developed an image of the counselor during an initial session as someone who will provide unconditional acceptance may be especially vulnerable to disappointment later on, as soon as the counselor indicates that he or she expects the client to make a genuine effort to change, to live up to whatever norms are being endorsed. If the client's initial image of the counselor as a completely dependable enhancer of his or her self-esteem changes to that of an undependable enhancer, the counselor will lose motivating power. But, as will be seen shortly, an image that is intermediate between these two extremes may be most facilitating from the standpoint of achieving the goals of counseling.

Phase 2: Using Motivating Power in the Role of Norm-Sender

A major assumption in the foregoing discussion of the first phase is that a client will be much more receptive to the counselor's suggestions and recommendations if he or she is initially given noncontingent acceptance, which builds up an image of the counselor as a reliable source of self-esteem enhancement. The relationship is likely to be impaired, however, once the helper makes it clear that the client is expected to carry out a stressful course of action, such as staying on a diet, or to perform a difficult task, such as engaging in a thorough search for information before making a career decision. Any such demand creates a crisis in the newly formed relationship because of the threat that henceforth acceptance will be provided on a strictly conditional basis, which adversely affects the affiliative bond.

After receiving the first unambiguous recommendations or directives from the helper, the client expects thereafter to receive criticism and disapproval if he or she fails to do what is being urged. If the client concludes that henceforth approval will be contingent upon good behavior, any incipient hope for unconditional approval from the helper is likely to be shattered. After that the helper might no longer be seen as a dependable self-esteem enhancer. The client realizes that from now on acceptance will be contingent upon living up to the standards of the helper, who, like all other parental figures, will probably make more and more demands to the point where he or she will give few, if any, spontaneous signs of genuine positive regard. When this transformation of the image of the helper occurs, it is accompanied by disappointment, alienation, and withdrawal.

And yet, unless a counselor makes recommendations and elicits some degree of commitment to carry out a course of action, the clients are likely to remain relatively unaffected and will derive little benefit from the relationship as far as the common goals of counseling are concerned. If the practitioner makes no such demands, either explicitly or implicitly, the relationship of the client with the accepting counselor will continue in a warm, friendly way but will be ineffectual. Here is another of those human conditions where love is not enough.

When a counselor continues to express nothing but unconditional positive regard no matter what the persons says or does, the client is not likely to be motivated to do the work of careful search and appraisal necessary for sound decision making or to carry out a difficult course of action after the person has announced that he or she wants to do so. Such treatment given regularly over a long period of time might sometimes be successful in bringing about an increase in self-esteem and other types of personality change that are sought in client-centered psychotherapy. But in the more restricted short-term type of counseling relationship I have been discussing, if the counselor errs on the side of being too nondirective he or she may fail just as badly as by being too directive.

In order to facilitate adherence to a stressful decision it is essential for the counselor to use his or her social power to reinforce, in a nonthreatening way, the norms or behavioral standards that are implied by that decision (see Goldstein, 1975; Strong, 1968). For example, when clients want help in living up to the decision to stop overeating, the counselors in a weight-reduction clinic can invoke the norms of the medical profession concerning the proper rules of dieting. The counselors can express approval of those acts and intentions that are in line with the decision (e.g., resisting social pressure at a party to each rich desserts and other fattening foods) and can indicate that they do not approve of those acts and intentions that make for failure (e.g., overeating during a relaxed vacation weekend). Thus, in offering help to people who want to adhere to a stressful decision, counselors become norm-sending communicators. But in order to mitigate the crisis created by taking on this directive role, counselors may need to take certain additional steps, which I shall discuss shortly. Counselors can effectively convey behavioral norms and elicit commitment from their clients to live up to those norms without necessarily losing referent power and destroying the alliance created in the first phase of the helping relationship.

Eliciting from the clients a verbal commitment to strive to live up to the norms endorsed by the counselor increases their motivation to carry out the difficult course of action. The term *commitment,* which refers to "pledging or binding of the individual to behavioral acts" (Kiesler & Sakumura, 1966), is used in this context in the restricted sense of informing at least one other person (the helper) about one's intentions to perform a series of acts.

During the second critical phase, as the helper begins to use his or her motivating power by endorsing sound decision-making procedures or a specific course of action and eliciting commitment statements, the client focuses on a set of evaluative questions pertaining to the new demands that are implicitly or explicitly being made. The key questions, which the client tries to answer by processing the cues given by the norm-sender's verbal statements and expressive behavior, are: "What does the counselor really want me to do?" "Will the counselor find out whether I do it or not?" "Will the counselor be satisfied if I do the few things being asked of me or will there be more and more demands?"

There are obvious things a counselor can say to guide the clients' personal answers to these questions in the desired direction. The clients' answers to the third question, however, are much more difficult to influence than the other two. At this point is is necessary to introduce another major theoretical assumption: namely, that a *selective pattern of social reinforcement* can be used in a way that enables clients to regard the counselor as a basically dependable source of self-esteem enhancement who makes only a few demands. I postulate that when helpers are going to function as norm-senders, they are more likely to retain motivating power if they avoid both extremes by building a differentiated image through the judicious use of selective reinforcement. This can avoid the illusory overlay that enters into an image of the helper as someone who will always provide unconditional acceptance in all circumstances no matter what one does. It can also avoid the other extreme, an image of the counselor as a completely undependable source of self-esteem enhancement, which results in withdrawal from the relationship. Clients can come to realize that they will mostly receive spontaneous acceptance, including when they reveal personal weaknesses and shortcomings, *except* when they fail to make a sincere effort to live up to a *limited* set of norms. This modified expectation of partially contingent acceptance from the helper allows clients to look forward to receiving genuine acceptance and approval from the helper much of the time—and perhaps practically all the time, almost the same as when acceptance is invariably unconditional—provided that they make a sincere effort to follow just a few rules recommended by the helper pertaining to only a limited sphere of personal behavior.

The image of the helper as a *basically (but not perfectly) dependable enhancer of self-esteem* differs from that of an undependable enhancer who offers acceptance on a strictly conditional basis. Clients expect little or no approval from the latter type of helper except at times when they clearly earn it by conforming to all sorts of rules that will continue to be laid down by the helper to govern many different spheres of personal behavior, much like the seemingly endless rules imposed by strict parents who demand conformity with their extensive code of moral behavior and proper etiquette. Everyone knows that signs of acceptance from demanding authority figures are few and far between.

A major problem for the counselor during the second phase, then, is how to minimize the risk of provoking detachment or withdrawal from the relationship when it is necessary to make recommendations that specify behavioral norms, especially when he or she explicitly asks clients to commit themselves to those norms. The solution I have suggested—to use the pattern of selective verbal reinforcement—requires considerable sensitivity and artistry. The pattern consists of criticizing clients' counternorm actions or intentions in a nonthreatening way while expressing positive regard the rest of the time, including when clients talk about personal shortcomings that are irrelevant to the task at hand. In a dieting clinic, for example, the counselor would limit negative feedback to comments about the undesirability of counternorm behavior when a client admits having indulged in overeating or wanting to do so, which is incompatible with the agreed-upon norm of sticking to a low-calorie diet. This limited type of negative feedback can be effectively presented in a nonthreatening way by reminding the client of his or her goals, by calling attention to the negative consequences of the counternorm actions, and by praising the client's honesty in admitting counternorm tendencies. For all other admissions of personal weaknesses or defects that do not bear on adherence to the given decision, the helper can give explicit acceptance statements. And, of course, the helper can also give explicit praise for each instance mentioned by the client of successful adherence to the norm and for each spontaneous commitment statement concerning intentions to adhere to the norm in the future. In this way a counselor may succeed in conveying an image of himself or herself as someone whom the client can rely on most of the time as a self-esteem enhancer, someone who will often spontaneously give noncontingent acceptance responses with only occasional instances of conditional approval or disapproval that pertain to a very limited set of demands. This differentiated image of the counselor as supplying a nurturant diet of variable but basic acceptance, rather than either the meager bones of conditional acceptance or the rich but undigestible fare of unconditional acceptance, is assumed to be optimal for functioning effectively as a constructive helper.

A counselor always has the choice of trying to become a basically dependable enhancer of self-esteem in either of two ways—by starting to use selective reinforcement from the very beginning of the initial session or by introducing it in a tactful way after consistent use of noncontingent acceptance responses during the first phase of the relationship. A counselor who chooses the former approach (selective reinforcement from the beginning) runs the risk of failing to surmount the first crisis and thereby never acquiring any motivating power as a self-esteem enhancer. A counselor who adopts the latter approach (noncontingent acceptance at the beginning followed by the gradual introduction of selective reinforcement) runs the equally serious risk of accentuating the second crisis and thereby losing whatever motivating power as a self-esteem enhancer he or she has acquired. But the blow to the client of being confronted with the first contingent acceptance responses after an unbroken succession of noncontingent acceptance responses might be softened in various ways. One way is to attribute the norm being sponsored to a respected secondary group (e.g., by informing clients who come to a weight-reduction clinic that medical specialists regard the recommended diet as the safest and most dependable way to lose weight). Another way to soften the blow is for the counselor to explain frankly what he or she is going to do in advance and to engage in explicit negotiations with the client to arrive at an agreement about adopting the norm (e.g., by discussing with a client who seeks help in overcoming shyness whether he or she wants to be committed to the recommended homework involving assertive actions). After the client has explicitly agreed to carry out a difficult course of action, the helper's contingent approval and disapproval are more likely to be tolerated. Even so, however, the helper is unlikely to retain motivating power unless it is repeatedly made clear that contingent acceptance responses will be limited to the specific norm that the client has said he or she wants to live up to. It is especially important for the helper to convey that each failure to do so will elicit disapproval of the deviant act without changing the helper's basic attitude of positive regard for the client as a person.

Counselors may be able to retain their status as basically dependable enhancers indefinitely for most of their clients by continuing to make only a few demands, by abstaining from deliberate social pressure, and by giving positive feedback only when they genuinely believe what they are saying, so as to avoid inadvertently giving cues to deceit or simulation of feelings (see Rogers, 1961; Rubin, 1973). As long as clients ascribe this status to the helper, they will no longer be as pessimistic about achieving their goals as they had been before developing the relationship. With their newly found self-confidence, constantly bolstered by signs of basic acceptance from the helper, clients will see new vistas of self-improvement opening up, which may enable them to make successful use of their own dormant resources.

Phase 3: Retaining Motivating Power after Termination of Contact

A third major crisis arises when direct contact between the helper and the client is terminated, as is bound to happen when a counselor arranges for a fixed number of sessions to help a client arrive at a difficult decision or to get started carrying one out. When the sessions come to an end, even if prearranged by a formal contract, the client will want to continue the relationship insofar as he or she has become dependent upon the counselor for bolstering self-esteem. The client is likely to regard the counselor's refusal to comply with the demand to maintain contact as a sign of rejection or indifference. If this unfavorable change in the image of the counselor occurs, the client will no longer be motivated to live up to the norms advocated by the counselor and will show little or no tendency to internalize those norms after their contact has ended. Some clients' disappointment and anger may be so extreme that they will deliberately violate the counselor's norms, which wipes out all the progress they had so painfully achieved while the counseling sessions were going on.

The separation crisis, like the crisis provoked by the norm-setting demands in Phase 2, may be minimized if the counselor gives assurances of continuing positive regard. It may also be more tolerable if the counselor arranges for gradual rather than abrupt termination of contact.

Backsliding is much less likely to occur after contact is terminated if the client internalizes the practitioner's norms. Little is known about the determinants of the internalization process, but it seems plausible that it might be facilitated by the counselor in two ways. One way is to give reminders that foster a sense of personal responsibility for adhering to whatever decisions the client has arrived at. A second way is to give attributions bearing on self-control that build up the client's self-confidence about succeeding without the aid of the counselor. These two themes may be introduced by the helper in Phase 2, but in Phase 3 they require strong emphasis. Special effort is required to make clients feel fully confident that they are able to go forward on their own. In diet programs, for example, the health counselor can emphasize that the clients' initial weight loss and changes in eating habits demonstrate their capabilities for self-control. These attributions promote the clients' self-confidence about successfully losing weight and increase the likelihood of long-term maintenance (Rodin 1978; Rodin & Janis, 1979). If a client temporarily backslides, the failure usually can be attributed to situational factors such as overexposure to temptation during the holiday season, or to other changeable events in the environment rather than to the client's chronic personality weaknesses. Recovery from a temporary failure can be used to illustrate the client's basic strengths and capabilities for long-term success. When clients try to attribute their success to the counselor, it is important to point out that it was they themselves who were able to give up eating their favorite high-calorie foods and to make the necessary behavioral commitment that led to successful changes.

These and related themes that build up the client's self-confidence about being able to succeed without the helper's aid can be appropriately emphasized before it is time to say goodbye. The client can be encouraged to discuss frankly his or her feelings about termination of contact, as is a standard procedure in many forms of counseling and psychotherapy. In such a discussion the counselor has the opportunity to counteract explicitly a client's misinterpretations of termination as a sign of rejection, to point out the client's capabilities for self-control, and to talk about the future satisfactions to be expected from increased autonomy and mastery.

BECOMING A DEPENDABLE ENHANCER

The foregoing account of three critical phases contains several key theoretical assumptions that can be summarized as follows: The chances of counseling sessions being effective will increase if the client develops a differentiated attitude of reliance on, respect for, and emotional attachment to the counselor. This is a much more complex attitude than simple "liking" for a stranger as measured by standard scales of interpersonal attraction in current social psychological research (see Berscheid & Walster, 1978; Byrne, 1971). If clients reveal personal weaknesses to any type of practitioner—physician, nurse, lawyer, career counselor, psychotherapist, or whomever—noncontingent acceptance by the practitioner will result in improving their self-regard. This, in turn, will make for strong motivation to continue the relationship, with high reliance on the practitioner as a respected model. The clients will perceive the practitioner not merely as someone who sometimes dispenses positive reinforcements but also as a basically dependable enhancer of their self-esteem, worthy of deference, gratitude, and affection. From this point on, the helper becomes a significant reference person for the clients and has the potentiality of using his or her social power to influence their actions. This power can be used to encourage clients to go through the essential steps to arrive at a sound decision (see chap. 6) or to elicit commitment to a difficult course of action and to overcome temptations to backslide (see chap. 3). The most vital point is that all sorts of practitioners, including decision counselors, can acquire social power as significant reference persons if clients see them as dependable sources for enhancing self-esteem rather than as purely conditional accepters, who are undependable enhancers.

A vivid illustration of a client's response to a health-care practitioner who became a powerfully motivating norm-setter can be cited from the innovative work of Neal Miller and Barry Dworkin on biofeedback training. These investigators were pioneers in developing an instrumental conditioning technique with verbal rewards to help patients suffering from hypertension gain control over their blood pressure. A young woman who wrote down her impressions of an arduous 10-week training period, during which she temporarily succeeded in lowering her diastolic pressure from a dangerously high average of 97 to a satisfactory average of about 80, had this to say about her trainer.

> I always depend very heavily on Barry Dworkin's encouragement and on his personality. I think he could be an Olympic coach. He not only seems aware of my general condition but he is never satisfied with less than my best, and I cannot fool him. I feel we are friends and allies—it's really as though *we* were lowering my pressure. (Quoted by Jonas, 1972).

When the client regards the health-care practitioner as an Olympic coach, she conveys the idea that in some sense she thinks of the coach as treating her like an Olympic star. Not everyone who engages in professional work can expect to function like a successful Olympic coach with all clients. But perhaps a better understanding of the crucial ingredients of an effective helping relationship eventually will lead large numbers of practitioners to adopt improved means for building the type of relationship that is most effective. Physicians, lawyers, and other professionals who are in helping roles can probably improve their effectiveness if they take account of all the key variables in Table 2.1. The same can be said of psychiatrists, psychiatric social workers, and clinical psychologists who provide therapy, irrespective of whether they use a behavioral, cognitive, psychodynamic, or eclectic approach.

Unfortunately, there is much more to it than just becoming familiar with the crucial ingredients. For example, many physicians, nurses, and other health-care professionals who function as counselors are likely to resist changing their current ways of dealing with their patients in order to become more effective as change agents. One major deterrent is the extra effort needed to acquire the necessary interpersonal skills. Another, which is most salient of all, is the added time required, for which there appears to be little room in professional schedules that are already overfilled. Nevertheless, there is reason to expect that as more and more practitioners become aware of the demoralizing statistics on nonadherence to their recommendations, they will become *quality* oriented. That is, they will renounce quantity ambitions in order to expend extra time and effort with their patients or clients in accordance with the primary goal of improving the well-being of each of them as far as possible.

The key theoretical concepts introduced in the analysis of the three critical phases, including those pertaining to the image of the helper as a basically dependable source of self-esteem enhancement, provide a general framework that might account for what happens in a variety of other dyadic relationships—between a student and a teacher, a novice and a guru, a pair of work colleagues, friends, lovers, or marital partners—and also in relationships between group members and their leaders. In all these relationships, self-disclosure may initially occur inadvertently from overt acts even though the discloser has no intention at the time of saying anything about personal desires, hopes, fears, aspirations, frustrations, personal strengths, or weaknesses. For example, in encounters with a teacher or work colleague, self-disclosure of personal weaknesses may occur inadvertently when the person makes errors in his or her work or fails to carry out an assignment. If the teacher or colleague consistently reacts with acceptance and does other things specified by the theoretical framework, he or she will become a dependable source of self-esteem enhancement and will have the power to exert lasting social influence as a change agent. The point is that the three critical phases and their consequences, as specified by the theoretical analysis, are not limited to professional helping relationships. They may arise in all sorts of other potentially close relationships.

NEGLECTED VARIABLES IN CURRENT APPROACHES TO COUNSELING

The 12 variables highlighted in Table 2.1, as I have just indicated, are expected to be applicable to all forms of psychological treatment. The guidelines for effective counseling that follow directly from the list of key variables are undoubtedly being followed to some extent, either deliberately or without the helpers' quite realizing it, even by some behavior therapists and directive advisers who rely primarily on a theoretical framework that pays little or no attention to the counselor–client relationship. But it is unlikely that very many professional counselors at present take full account of all 12 of the variables in their daily practice.

Among the published guides for various forms of counseling by proponents of different counseling approaches—such as those based on behavior theories, cognitive theories, and psychodynamic theories—one finds considerable differences in the degree to which each of the three critical phases is taken into account or neglected. Let us briefly examine several of the prevalent approaches to therapy and counseling from this standpoint. I shall give a short summary of what the practitioner of each approach is expected to do and *not* to do in connection with the three critical phases. We shall see that some approaches neglect key variables in the first phase (building up motivating power), some neglect the second phase (using motivating power discriminately), and some neglect the third phase (retaining motivating power and promoting internalization after contact ends). In presenting descriptions of the different kinds of psychological treatments, I do not necessarily intend to endorse any of them. In fact, I am personally very skeptical about the alleged effectiveness of certain so-called therapeutic procedures although I think one or another component of each approach may prove to have something valuable to offer.

First to be considered is the *behavioral approach,* which is widely used in one form or another by large numbers of clinical psychologists. Manuals and monographs on behavior therapy, whether relying on Skinnerian or Pavlovian principles of learning or more recent work on psychophysiological principles of biofeedback, have a great deal to say about the five variables in Phase 2, which involve using the motivating power of the counselor (see, Blechman, Olson, & Hellman, 1976; Franks, 1969; Kanfer & Phillips, 1970; Schwartz, 1977; Wolpe, 1973). For example, they usually state exactly what kinds of directive statement and recommendation should be given to clients to help them set up and achieve their goals during the treatment sessions and in homework assignments (variable 4), how commitment can be elicited by means of drawing up a formal contract (variable 5), and how selective positive feedback should be given (variable 7). There are also comments that encourage practitioners to attribute their normative recommendations to scientific research experts in the behavioral sciences as a respected secondary group (variable 6). Some behavior-therapy manuals also prescribe devoting some time during the sessions to giving communications and training procedures that build up a sense of personal responsibility, mastery, and self-confidence (which involves to some limited extent variable 8 in Phase 2 and variables 11 and 12 in Phase 3). But the guides for behavior therapy are generally silent about the three variables in Phase 1 (building up motivating power) and about at least two of the variables, if not all four, in Phase 3 (retaining motivating power and promoting internalization after contact ends).

Similarly, the *neobehaviorist techniques* of participant modeling and guided performance—based on assumptions of a social-learning theory concerning vicarious learning from observing a model and the value of successful performance in feared situations—emphasize almost exclusively the variables in Phase 2 and the last two variables in Phase 3 (see Bandura, 1976). For example, when participant modeling is used, the client is told something like this:

> "This procedure has been used to help other people overcome fears or acquire new behaviors. There are three primary things we will do. First, you will see some people demonstrating ————. Next, you will practice this with my assistance in the interview. Then we'll arrange for you to do this outside the interview in situations likely to be successful for you. This type of practice will help you perform what now is difficult for you to do. Are you willing to try this now?" (Cormier & Cormier, 1979, p. 286)

Later on, as the final step in guided participation, the client is instructed to carry out prearranged tasks in real-life situations. For example, the transfer-of-training program for a client who is receiving assertiveness training is as follows:

> After the clients have perfected their social skills and overcome their timidity, they accompany the therapist on excursions into the field where they witness further demonstrations of how to handle situations calling for assertive action. The therapist then reduces the level of participation to background support and guidance as the clients try their skills in situations likely to produce favorable results. By means of careful selection of encounters of increasing difficulty, the assertion requirements can be adjusted to the clients' momentary capabilities to bolster their sense of confidence. As a final step in the program, the clients are assigned a series of assertive performance tasks to carry out on their own. (Bandura, 1976, pp. 262–63)

Note that the counselor makes very strong demands on the client to carry out difficult tasks that require a very high level of motivation. The theoretical framework presented in Table 2.1 leads us to expect that when counselors find any such technique to be successful with some of their clients, they are likely to have greater success with a higher percentage of their clients if they follow the guidelines corresponding to the key variables that they may be neglecting, most notably those in Phase 1 that could contribute to building up their motivating power and certain additional variables in Phase 3 that could contribute to retaining their motivating power after termination of the treatment.

In sharp contrast to behavior therapy and social-learning approaches, *client-centered counseling,* as developed by Carl Rogers (1951, 1967), places great emphasis on all three variables in Phase 1. It is, in fact, because of the pioneering work of Rogers that many contemporary forms of psychological treatment give great emphasis to conveying acceptance irrespective of what the clients reveal about themselves (variable 2) and to encouraging clients to make frank disclosures of their troubles, weaknesses, and aspirations (variable 1). The Rogerian mode of treatment also involves reflecting the emotional content of the client's statements for the purpose of conveying clarifications and insights, which sometimes result in cognitive restructuring (variable 3). A great deal of attention is also given in the writings for counselors by Rogers and other client-centered counselors to the variables in Phase 3, most especially to communicating, at the time of terminating the treatment, the basic theme that the counselor will continue to maintain an attitude of positive regard toward the client (variable 9). But the Rogerian nondirective approach deliberately *avoids* doing anything at all in line with the four variables in Phase 2 that are essential for effective use of the counselor's motivating power. Although such an approach may be effective with clients requiring therapy for certain personality disorders, it is likely to fail badly, according to the theoretical framework represented in Table 2.1, with the majority of clients who seek help in carrying out difficult courses of action (such as dieting or cutting down on smoking, alcohol, or hard drugs) and also with those facing decisional dilemmas (such as what to do about a serious physical disease, career dissatisfactions, academic failures, marital discord, wayward children, and other acute difficulties requiring the client to make vital choices).

Rational-emotive-therapy (RET), as expounded by Ellis (1977a) and Wessler and Wessler (1980), differs from the approaches just discussed in that it pays a great deal of attention to most of the key variables in Phases 1 and 2 but tends to neglect those in Phase 3. Like the behavior therapists, RET practitioners make very strong demands on their clients (Phase 2). Clients are often asked to carry out homework assignments and role-playing exercises intended to help them overcome inhibitions and attain mastery in distressing situation. "In RET," Wessler and Wessler (1980, p. 79) assert, "we often ask clients to do something that they do not want to do." This is especially so in counseling women who display what Ellis (1977b, p. 163) calls "pernicious" lack of assertiveness in "actively pursuing relationships with males they care for" or in continuing to "pretend they are sexually satisfied when they are not." Ellis advocates challenging the "irrational" beliefs of these women about the consequences of assertiveness, persuading them to adopt "more rational" beliefs, and assigning them tasks requiring assertive actions.

> RET has always been in the forefront of those therapies that promulgate assertion training. It especially does so by activity homework assignments. Thus, females in individual or group rational-emotive therapy are frequently given graduated series of assignments that finally enable them to pick up attractive males in public places (such as dances, singles gatherings, or bars); to phone their men friends instead of passively waiting for the men to call; to make sexual overtures when they wish to do so; to ask their partners to engage in sex-love practices that they particularly enjoy; to stop taking too much responsibility for their children; and to do many other "unfeminine" things that they truly would like to do. . . .
>
> If they have great difficulty in asserting themselves in these ways, they are frequently put through role-playing forms of behavior rehearsal in the course of their individual or group therapy sessions. Thus, a shy and meek woman may be rehearsed, in the course of a group session, to ask a man to dinner, to go to a party alone and break in on the conversation of three people who are talking together, or to

ask her lover to bring her to orgasm through oral-genital relations. (Ellis, 1977b, p. 163)

When dealing with any type of personal problem, such as phobias, depression, excessive hostility, or impulsive disorders, a typical session, as described by Wessler & Wessler (1980, p. 25), includes interventions that are likely to involve the variables of Phase 2: the counselor uses "discussion methods" to urge the client to change "irrational" beliefs that lead to anxiety or other distressing emotional reactions, checks on the last homework assignment, sets new goals, gets the client to commit himself or herself to working toward those goals, gives a new homework assignment, and asks the client to rehearse it during the session. The assignment almost invariably requires the client to risk undesired outcomes, "usually rejection or failure in some form" (Wessler & Wessler, 1980, p. 136).

Unlike behavior therapists, however, RET practitioners take some account of the variables in Phase 1 that are essential for building up the counselor's power to motivate the client to carry out the assigned tasks and to adhere to all the other demands made during the treatment, including persuasive efforts to induce the client to replace "irrational" beliefs with "realistic" beliefs that presumably will enable the client to avoid disruptive emotional reactions and to solve personal problems more successfully in a "rational" way. The RET counselor constantly urges the client to talk about emotional upsets and personal difficulties, which encourages self-disclosure (variable 1), and generally tries to use the disclosures to give the client fresh insights and cognitive restructuring (variable 3). The counselor also attempts to convey "nondamning acceptance rather than positive regard" (Wessler & Wessler, 1980, p. 245). The way this is handled, however, may not adequately represent variable 2, because when a client expresses self-derogatory ideas or any other global self-evaluations, the counselor argues with the client, challenging the client to justify and to give evidence for his or her self-evaluative conclusions. This is done to dissuade clients from constantly giving themselves "report cards" and to teach "the essence of self-acceptance," which is "that the individual fully and unconditionally accepts himself whether or not he behaves intelligently, correctly, or competently and whether or not other people approve, respect, or love him" (Ellis, 1977a, p. 101). But the counselor's unremitting persuasive efforts may sometimes be felt by clients as nonacceptance (if not outright disapproval) for expressing the wrong attitude, despite the counselor's disclaimers to the contrary.

When it comes to Phase 3, the RET practitioner is trained to try to build up the clients' sense of personal responsibility (variable 11) and their self-confidence (variable 12), but not to do very much about the other two key variables that may be essential for preventing subsequent retrogressive reactions to termination of contact with the helper. "Ideally," according to Wessler and Wessler (1980, p. 25), "the last session of therapy is devoted to helping the client review progress made to date and to identifying continuing or potential problems." Wessler and Wessler add that in general nothing special needs to be done to help the clients accept or "work through" the impending separation.

> Unlike some therapies, RET spends little time and energy on severing the therapeutic relationship. If, in fact, breaking the relationship does become a major issue, then the client is *not* ready to terminate, for this is an indication that the client relies on the therapist to fulfill some perceived need—perhaps approval, reassurance, or freedom from responsibility. If the client has indeed reduced irrational thinking—thinking that involves demandingness, awfulizing, and evaluation of self and others—and has acquired means of coping with such thoughts, dependency is not an issue. . . . The therapist may feel sad about no longer seeing this person but also, and more important, a sense of satisfaction that the client has progressed so far. The client is also likely to feel sad and perhaps a bit apprehensive about the future but, more important, a sense of confidence that life's problems can be dealt with in an autonomous way. RET terminations are primarily pleasant events. (Wessler & Wessler, 1980, p. 182)

It seems doubtful that very many clients could fulfill these high expectations even after very successful psychological treatment, although they might superficially comply with the attitude being expressed by the counselor and not fully express their "irrational" emotional reactions to termination. It may be that, despite what the RET textbooks say about termination, the most psychologically sensitive among RET practitioners intuitively take account of the problems of separation and spontaneously give the type of reassurances specified by variable 9 and leave open the prospects for future contact in line with variable 10. But those who follow the RET textbook accounts of how terminations (and acceptance by the counselor) should be handled may not be helping their clients to attain as many successful long-run outcomes as they could if they were to follow the guidelines for the variables they are neglecting.

A similar analysis could be made of the variables neglected by practitioners who use *cognitive-behavior modification* (Mahoney, 1972; Meichenbaum, 1977) and related cognitive verbal approaches that resemble rational-emotive therapy (e.g., Beck, 1976; Lazarus, 1976) and also those who rely mainly on evoking imagery of pleasant scenes or events to counteract anxiety or depression (e.g., Horan, 1973; Kazdin, 1976; Singer, 1974). In all such approaches, certain of the variables, especially in Phase 2, are well represented but others tend to be neglected. And again, as I have repeatedly stated, we could expect counselors who use each of those approaches to obtain better results with more of their clients if none of the 12 key variables was to be neglected. The same can be said about *transactional analysis* (Berne, 1961), the *gestalt approach* (Perls, 1969), and various *psychodynamic approaches* that are sometimes used by practitioners in short-term counseling as well as in long-term therapy (Erickson & Rossi, 1979; Malan, 1976; Winnicott, 1971).

TENTATIVE STATUS OF THE SUGGESTED GUIDELINES

Part of the art of counseling may reside in dealing with each of the three critical phases in a way that minimizes adverse effects. Perhaps only a small proportion of counselors have the interpersonal skills required to deal successfully with all three phases for the majority of their clients. Nevertheless, counselors with modest amounts of talent and skill in dealing with people in trouble may be able to improve their percentage of successful cases by taking account of the guidelines that follow from the analysis of the three stages. This is an assumption that must be carefully evaluated in the light of the available empirical evidence. The three chapters that follow present a great deal of supportive evidence concerning some of the key variables. Most of it is from systematic field studies of the effectiveness of certain types of counseling when one of the 12 variables is deliberately varied with all the others and everything else held constant. There is always the possibility, however, that for other kinds of counseling the results of such field experiments might be different. Furthermore, the clients who voluntarily come to our counseling clinics are self-selected; they may not be representative of the entire population to which we would like to be able to apply the generalizations about the ways a counselor can become more effective by establishing, using, and maintaining his or her motivating power as a helper.

The theoretical analysis of the three phases of an effective helping relationship is formulated in general terms as being applicable to every man, woman, and child, irrespective of personality differences. But the clinical observations on which it is based (and, as will be seen in the next chapters, most of the systematic research evidence that substantiates it) come mainly from counseling relationships with adults who have difficulty making or carrying out their personal decisions, particularly clients who come to clinics for help on controlling their overeating or smoking behavior. Future studies of the processes of social influence in dyadic relationships among persons who do *not* come to clinics might show that they are different in important respects. For example, adults who seek help with problems of self-control may be much more sensitive than others to empathic acceptance responses from helpers, perhaps partly as a result of having received insufficient or faulty empathic responsiveness from their primary caretakers during crucial developmental periods in childhood (see Kohut, 1977). It is quite conceivable, therefore, that whatever validity the suggested guidelines may have is limited to only one or a few categories of persons. Even so, those limited categories might turn out to include large numbers of clients who seek professional help.

3 Dealing Effectively with the Critical Phases

In this chapter and in the next two chapters I shall examine the findings from a series of more than 20 field experiments carried out in my counseling research program at Yale University. The purpose of these studies was to answer fundamental theoretical and practical questions about short-term counseling by testing prescriptive hypotheses derived from the theoretical framework of critical phases presented in the preceding chapter and summaried in Table 2.1 (p. 27). I shall feature the practical implications of the research evidence concerning what a counselor can do to improve his or her effectiveness.

In an extensive review of research on counseling, Krumboltz, Becker-Haven, and Burnett (1979) describe three major objectives that psychological counselors attempt to achieve. Counselors try to help their clients: (1) make satisfactory personal decisions, such as those affecting career choices and adjustments; (2) prevent problems in the future by providing anticipatory interventions; or (3) alter maladaptive behavior. The theoretical framework concerning the critical phases in counselor–client relationships is intended to be applicable to all three types of objectives. Our research studies, however, are limited mainly to the first two types of objectives. In fact, most of the studies involve short-term counseling on decisions pertaining to personal health, such as going on a diet or giving up smoking; they also involve attempts to prevent problems from arising in the future that would lead the client to backslide and fail to sustain the improved behavior. The studies indicate, as will soon be seen, that the effectiveness of this type of counseling can be increased if counselors take account of certain key variables in the theoretical framework. Obviously the findings are most directly applicable to the limited sphere of health counseling and to the prevention of health problems in the future. A few studies, however, involve different personal problems, such as decisions dealt with in career counseling. The findings from those studies, together with findings from research by other investigators, suggest that the main conclusions concerning key variables in the theoretical framework are more broadly applicable to other kinds of decision counseling and to other kinds of problem prevention.

Since the findings have not yet been extensively replicated by other investigators, all conclusions about how to improve counseling practice, even for the type of health decisions and anticipated problems most frequently investigated in our studies, must be regarded as tentative. Much more precarious are extrapolations (from the limited type of counseling research we have carried out so far) to the third main objective, helping clients change their maladaptive behavior. Our studies usually do involve changing certain specific types of maladaptive behavior, such as overeating and heavy smoking; but it remains for subsequent research to determine whether the same conclusions apply equally to treatment of phobias, anxiety attacks, depression, chronic shyness, sexual disturbances, and other behavioral disorders.

Although there are obvious limitations to the research evidence now at hand, it seems to me worthwhile to see what tentative inferences can be drawn to answer the central question of interest to practitioners: *What can counselors do to improve the effectiveness of whatever short-term counseling they do?* Putting the question in this way presupposes that short-term counseling is not a waste of time, that it can, in fact, be effective for at least some clients who seek help on personal decisions or problems. But is this assumption justified?

IS SHORT-TERM COUNSELING EFFECTIVE?

The first question to be answered before considering how effectiveness can be increased is a simple empirical one: Does short-term counseling of the type we investigate actually work? Although our studies were designed to be analytic experiments rather than descriptive evaluation research, many of the findings nevertheless can be used to answer this initial empirical question.

By and large, our field experiments show that short-term counseling is effective at least for a sizable minority of the clients and sometimes, when special procedures are used, for the majority. A fairly high percentage of the clients in our studies obtained short-term benefits from the two or three counseling sessions that each client typically was given. For a smaller, but nevertheless substantial percentage, some of the short-term counseling procedures we investigated proved to have highly significant long-term effects as well, extending over a period of many months and, in one instance, many years. It must be recognized that most of the evidence is from studies in antismoking and weight-reduction clinics whose clients voluntarily come for help because they are motivated to change their behavior.

Cogent evidence comes from a field experiment and follow-up study by Janis and Hoffman (1970, 1982), which provides clear-cut indications of the effectiveness of short-term counseling in helping people to get started on cutting down on cigarette smoking. After five weekly meetings with the counselor the majority of clients in all the treatment groups showed a marked decrease in number of cigarettes smoked. Control data from other studies in the same antismoking clinic, using clients who had been kept on a waiting list for about five weeks, indicate that in the absence of short-term contact with the counselor no change at all is to be expected over that time interval.

When we look at the long-term effects in the same study we see that the outcome depends on whether the counselor had used a special procedure of assigning his clients to partnerships, with instructions to phone each other every day for five weeks. The clients who had been given this supplementary procedure during the period when they came for weekly sessions with the counselor showed a highly significant sustained effect after one year and also after ten years. The control clients, who were not given the supplementary partnership treatment, showed no substantial decrease in smoking after one year or after ten years. Later on I shall give more details about this study and discuss the factors that are most likely to account for the success of the partnerships. For the present, it suffices to conclude from this field experiment that counselors in antismoking clinics who use educational films and other communications about the unhealthy consequences of smoking, together with interviews and discussions that encourage the clients to commit themselves to stop smoking, can help them succeed in getting started on a difficult new regimen of reducing cigarette consumption. But counselors apparently need to introduce special procedures during the few counseling sessions they conduct, such as setting up client partnerships, in order to increase their clients' long-term success.

In a comprehensive review of the relevant research on the effectiveness of antismoking clinics, Hunt and Bespalec (1974) reported that counseling is generally effective in helping people cut down on cigarette consumption for several weeks but the majority relapse within a few months. Nevertheless, according to these authors, a substantial minority show long-term success in abstaining, particularly those smokers who receive counseling treatments that provide educational information and social support. The findings from the Janis and Hoffman study are consistent with those conclusions.

Essentially the same conclusions can be applied to successful dieting, as was shown by an experiment conducted in the Yale Weight-Reduction Clinic by Nowell and Janis (1982). Again, the short-term counseling sessions were effective in helping clients in all treatment conditions to get started on a rigorous low-calorie diet (when assessed three weeks after the first session). By using the special device of setting up partnerships, the counselors were able to help their clients attain longer-term success in losing weight (when assessed after a period of two and one-quarter months). A second experiment reported by Nowell and Janis, however, indicates that under certain conditions—which seem to involve promising the clients too much—the effectiveness of short-term counseling is not increased by setting up partnerships (see p. 67).

Fourteen other studies were carried out in the Yale Weight-Reduction Clinic (Janis, 1982a). All of them reveal that even when counselors limit their contacts to only two or three sessions with each client and do not set up any client partnerships, they are generally effective in accomplishing the stated purpose of the counseling clinic, which is to get the clients started on a low-calorie diet. In one study after another we find significant decreases in weight, on the average, for each short-term counseling treatment when assessed after one or two months. And again the evidence from the clinic's waiting lists shows over and over again that when the clients receive no counseling treatment the average amount of weight loss over either a one- or two-month period is zero. Some counseling treatments, of course, were found to be much more effective than others, but even the least effective treatments generally resulted in a significant average amount of weight loss over a period of about two months.

Similar results on the effectiveness of short-term counseling come from our research project's studies in other settings. In these studies the counselor's recommendations deal with different types of clients making a variety of kinds of decisions: students deciding to donate blood during a Red Cross campaign (Mulligan, 1982), public school teachers deciding to adopt a new method of teaching arithmetic (Smith, 1982), young and middle-aged women deciding to attend an early morning exercise class (Hoyt & Janis, 1975), and hospitalized men and women being prepared to undergo elective surgery (Langer, Janis, & Wolfer, 1975). In each of these settings one or two sessions with a supportive counselor was found to make a significant difference in the degree of adherence to the decision when assessed from one to seven weeks later.

It must be emphasized that the favorable effects of counseling that we have observed in our field experiments pertain primarily to *short-term adherence* to the counselors' recommendations. When long-term adherence is assessed nine months or one year after the counseling contact has ended, we find mixed results. Some counseling treatments have detectable long-term effects and some do not. Other investigators who have studied the effectiveness of both short-term and long-term contact with physicians or health counselors have reported essentially the same mixed results, usually with the majority of clients showing backsliding about one or two months after having started to adhere to the physicians' or counselors' recommendations. (See the reviews of the literature by Hunt & Matarazzo [1973], Marston [1970], and Stone [1979].) There appears to be good reason, therefore, that many physicians, nurses, and other health counselors, like psychological counselors and social workers who give short-term counseling to help clients with other types of problems, are keenly interested in finding ways to improve their long-term effectiveness.

There is another issue that needs to be considered briefly prior to examining the variables specified by the theoretical framework in the preceding chapter. Ths issue pertains to a well-known factor that has repeatedly been suggested in the literature on counseling as a means for increasing the effectiveness of short-term counseling.

DOES INCREASING THE AMOUNT OF CONTACT WITH THE CLIENT INCREASE THE COUNSELOR'S EFFECTIVENESS?

Some clients in our weight-reduction clinic say that they want more contact with the counselor than our short-term counseling arrangement provides. A few openly ask for added sessions, a few others telephone the clinic from time to time to ask questions of their counselors. Occasionally, clients complain in the follow-up interview about the limited number of times they could talk with the counselor (Janis & Quinlan, 1982). The efforts of those clients to have more contact might be regarded as justifiable by quite a few practicing counselors; large numbers of practitioners deliberately arrange to have many more than just two or three sessions with each of their clients who seek help in cutting down on overeating or smoking.

Prior studies do not provide much support for this practice. A few positive findings have been reported suggesting that maintenance of weight loss (Brownell, Heckerman, & Westlake, 1976) and smoking cessation (Shewchuk, 1976) is increased if counselors stay in contact with clients, even if their contact is limited to brief telephone conversations. But there is much more impressive evidence from other studies, as will be seen shortly, that definitely goes against this conclusion and points to the potentially detrimental effects of additional contact. Nevertheless, some psychologists claim that the number of times the counselor is in contact with the client is more important in producing persistent change than what the counselor says or does. This claim is made by an American Psychological Association Task Force on Health Research in a survey article in *American Psychologist* (1976), but the only evidence cited is from an unpublished study on promoting toothbrushing. Other investigations do not support any such generalization. For example, a study by Best, Bass, and Owen (1977) in a clinic for heavy smokers shows that when telephoned by their counselors between sessions clients were more likely to relapse after the end of the treatment than when left entirely on their own. Leventhal and Cleary (1980, p. 382) cite additional research on smoking therapies indicating that "controlled studies of booster sessions show no advantage over standard treatments . . . for long-term follow-ups of 6 months." Romanczyk (1974) found that overweight clients who had been given "full" behavior-change treatments in a series of six weekly meetings with the counselor were not more successful in losing weight than overweight clients who were given only one session before and one session after a four-week interval. During the interval the latter clients were asked to carry out recommendations to change their eating habits without any contact at all with the counselor. Those clients lost significantly more weight than control subjects who were not given the recommendations, and after three months they were just as successful as the ones given three times as many sessions.

A more recent experiment by Carter, Rice, and DeJulio (1977) randomly assigned overweight clients to a group treatment program that had either ten weekly sessions or only four sessions over the ten-week period. Their data show that the clients given fewer sessions lost significantly more weight by the end of the treatment program and six months later. In direct contrast to the claim made by the APA Task Force, these investigators conclude their report by posing an embarrassing question for counselors and therapists: Are they perhaps doing a disservice to their clients by seeing them too often?

Is there any evidence from our studies of one-to-one counseling bearing on the claim that additional sessions are worthwhile? In order to answer this question we must look into studies that compare the effectiveness of different amounts of contact between counselor and client while holding constant all other relevant factors, such as the type of client being treated, the type of counseling procedure being used, and the type of problem being dealt with. Our studies provide some direct and some indirect evidence bearing on the issue. As far as our evidence goes, it does not indicate that the effectiveness of the type of counseling provided in a setting such as our weight-reduction clinic would be increased by increasing the amount of counselor–client contact.

Of the 16 investigations carried out in the Yale dieting clinic, the one in which the clients had the largest number of sessions with the counselor was the study by Nowell and Janis (1982). In this pair of field experiments, as in all our other studies, we adhered rigorously to a set of ethical and professional constraints that included the requirement that every client must be given genuine help by a trained counselor, even though he or she might be assigned on a random basis to a control group. In order to provide good clinical service to all clients who come to us for counseling, the control group is given standard counseling procedures based on prior research and clinical observations indicating that they are often helpful, while the experimental group is given the same standard procedures along with a new procedure for which there is no basis for suspecting potentially undesirable effects on even a small percentage of clients. (In the Nowell and Janis pair of experiments, the new procedure used with the experimental groups involved setting up partnerships in which pairs of female clients were asked to phone each other for ten minutes each day, as a feasible form of applying the buddy system.)

The standard counseling procedures used by Nowell and Janis with women randomly assigned to the experimental and control groups were essentially the same as those used in all the other field experiments conducted at the Yale Weight-Reduction Clinic. The counseling included the following eight components:

1. Conducting free-style discussions of the problems of dieting in which each client has the opportunity to talk about her own particular difficulties of self-control, special temptations, social pressures from her family, and the like, with the counselor responding in all instances by reflecting and clarifying the problems and encouraging the client to work out her own solutions, always expressing supportive attitudes of optimism and high confidence that the client can succeed in attaining her goal.
2. Providing information about a recommended well-balanced, low-calorie diet along with a set of sample menus, obtained from the Department of Dietetics of the Yale–New Haven Hospital.
3. Giving detailed explanations of all the main features of the recommended diet and providing opportunities for open-ended discussion devoted to answering the client's questions concerning the diet and clearing up any misconceptions about it.
4. Giving persuasive communications about the importance of mo-

tivation for successful dieting and about appropriate attitudes that help to sustain motivation to avoid overeating in the future.

5. Eliciting commitment by asking the client to sign a pledge card agreeing to begin immediately on the low-calorie diet, to make every effort to stick to it, and to attend all subsequent meetings.

6. Giving homework assignments that include self-monitoring of adherence to the diet by asking the client to fill out daily record sheets.

7. Arranging for counselor monitoring of the client's adherence to the diet by weighing the client at the beginning of each meeting and by asking the client to hand in her daily record sheets showing the degree of adherence to the diet.

8. Giving stress inoculation by means of preparatory information about the usual problems of dieting and suggestions about how to cope with them if they arise.

These procedures were used in the Nowell and Janis experiments in a series of three weekly or biweekly sessions; then, six weeks later there was a fourth, follow-up session. And yet the clients in the control groups given this relatively great amount of contact with the counselor did not lose significantly more weight than those given only one session and a follow-up interview in other studies carried out in the same weight-reduction clinic. For example, the clients given three weekly counseling sessions in the Nowell and Janis pair of experiments did not show a significantly greater amount of weight loss than the clients who received only one counseling session in the Riskind experiment (1982) when measures were obtained at a comparable interval (after about two months). From these observations we infer that the short-term counseling we provide in our clinics is not too short; there is no reason to expect that three times more of the same would produce better results.

Confirmatory findings indicating no consistent benefit from additional contact between counselor and client come from a study by Quinlan, Janis, and Bales (1982). In this field experiment systematic comparisons were made between clients randomly assigned to a condition in which they were given a series of four weekly telephone calls by the counselor during the month following the initial face-to-face interview and other clients randomly assigned to a control condition in which they had no additional contact after the initial face-to-face interview. Eight weeks later the clients who had been given the additional contact via phone calls from the counselor were not doing any better at losing weight than the controls. Additional findings from this study reveal that the effects of the extra contact varied depending upon the type of initial interview the clients had been given. The clients who had been asked to disclose a moderate amount of favorable personal information about their current assets and past achievements showed considerably *more* weight loss if they were given the added telephone contact. In contrast, the clients who had been asked to disclose a moderate amount of both favorable and unfavorable personal information showed *less* weight loss if they were given the added contact.

A replication of the latter finding, showing a negative effect from additional telephone contact, was obtained in a recently completed (unpublished) study conducted in the Yale Weight-Reduction Clinic by Blechman, Janis, and Bales. In this study clients were given a standard moderate disclosure interview, eliciting both favorable and unfavorable information about the self. On a random basis half the clients were asked to commit themselves to a contract and the other half not. Those given the high commitment treatment received a series of four phone calls from the counselor during the two weeks after the initial interview, whereas those given the control treatment received no phone calls. The results were that the clients in the high commitment treatment involving added telephone contact with the counselor were *less* successful in losing weight than the controls.

Follow-up interviews in the two studies of telephone contact suggest that one of the reasons the telephone calls from the counselor had unfavorable effects was that some clients thought the purpose was to keep them under surveillance, and they disliked being required to report to the counselor on their eating delinquencies. Whether or not this is a correct or complete explanation, the evidence indicates that more contact is not necessarily better and sometimes can be worse. Our evidence certainly does not support the conclusion that what a counselor does is less important than repeated contact with the client, as claimed by the American Psychological Association Task Force on Health Research (1976).

Obviously, further studies are needed in a variety of counseling settings in order to determine the conditions under which additional contact has beneficial effects and the conditions under which it has detrimental effects (such as mobilizing resistances and fostering buck-passing dependency rather than self-confidence). For the present, the only general conclusion we can draw with any certainty from our studies of adherence to dieting recommendations is essentially the same as the negative one that follows from Romanczyk's (1974) study of changing eating habits. We are led to conclude that by and large the treatments we used in our studies of short-term counseling in the Yale Weight-Reduction Clinic, which proved to be fairly effective with a sizable percentage of clients, would not yield better results if we were to offer the same kinds of treatment somewhat more intensively by giving the clients three or four times as many counseling sessions, either face-to-face or via telephone. Some evidence suggesting that this same conclusion is likely to apply to other kinds of counseling comes from studies of clients who seek help in making career decisions. In their extensive review of recent research on the effectiveness of career counseling, Holland, Magoon, and Spokane (1981, p. 286) state that "many brief treatments appear to be as effective as long-term treatments."

In line with expectations from the theoretical framework for effective helping relationships presented in chapter 2, the available evidence indicates that what a counselor does is far more important than the number of sessions per se. But, of course, if the counselor is doing the right things, giving social support in additional sessions could prove to be very helpful. It is also possible for a counselor to provide additional effective social support without increasing the number of his or her contacts with each client. This is the practical conclusion that emerges from our studies on the effectiveness of a variant of the buddy system.

PROVIDING SOCIAL SUPPORT
BY SETTING UP PARTNERSHIPS

In their review of advances in counseling research over the four-year period from 1974 to 1978, Krumboltz, Becker-Haven, and Burnett (1979) mention that only a little progress had been made in helping heavy smokers to quit. They point out that several different behavioral techniques, including stimulus control and aversive conditioning, have been found to produce short-term behavior changes but that few methods have been shown to have lasting effects six months or one year after treatment. One exception they cite is a report by Lando (1977) which showed good results after six months by providing social support after rapid smoking aversion therapy (requiring the smoker to smoke continuously for 25 minutes during the initial session and to engage in excessive smoking at home by consuming at least twice the usual number of cigarettes per day). But, according to other investigations cited by Krumboltz and his associates (1979, p. 570), this type of aversion therapy poses "numerous potential hazards to cardiovascular health." The auxiliary social support in Lando's study was provided as part of an elaborate broad-spectrum program that was very costly in terms of the counselor's time and effort. Seven additional formal sessions were held in which the counselor conducted group discussions that provided social support and encouraged exchanges about effective methods of maintenance; the special program also included inducing clients to make self-contracts and contracts with the counselor during the booster sessions with the clients. Lando (1977, p. 365) reports that "the groups became cohesive and the members were extremely supportive of one another.... A number of subjects spontaneously commented upon the importance of this group support to their success in remaining abstinent." Seventy-six percent of the clients who were given the social support program were found to have stopped smoking six months after the aversion therapy as compared with only 35 percent of the clients who were not given the additional social support.

Some of the research in our program provides similar successful results over a much longer follow-up period, obtained with a much less costly form of social support and without administering the potentially harmful aversion therapy. Impressive evidence of the effectiveness of the buddy system in combination with persuasive communications presented by a counselor in an antismoking clinic was reported by Janis and Hoffman (1970, 1982). The purpose of this field experiment was to investigate systematically the prior claims that had been made about the advantages of the buddy system. Proponents of Alcoholics Anonymous and Synanon have repeatedly asserted that the buddy system makes a major contribution to their members' success in "staying on the wagon" or "kicking the habit." My own earlier observations in Yale counseling clinics for clients who were trying to stay on a diet or to give up smoking were also suggestive. I noticed that the members who during our group discussion sessions spontaneously acquired a partner (with whom they were in telephone contact) reported more success than those who did not.

The Janis and Hoffman study, carried out with 30 adults who were heavy smokers (14 men and 16 women), was designed to find out whether our antismoking counseling would be more effective in the long run if the counselor arranged to have pairs of clients form partnerships and maintain daily telephone contact during the month or so when they were coming to the clinic, which could enable them to engage in mutual self-disclosures and to give each other social support. The main components of the counseling procedures we used (which are fully described by Janis & Hoffman, 1982) were as follows:

Every one of the 30 subjects attended five meetings of a three-person group, for which the same psychologist (D.H.) always functioned as the counselor. Sessions 1–4 were deliberately structured in such a way that the counselor functioned as a norm-sender during the first half of each meeting by giving standard recommendations and by presenting persuasive communications about cutting down on smoking. The other half of these sessions was devoted entirely to a spontaneous discussion between the two clients, which gave them an opportunity to discuss the messages they had just received in relation to their own lives. This was done partly to encourage the clients to develop a sense of personal responsibility for carrying out the decision to cut down on smoking. In order to minimize experimenter effects, the counselor presented all essential recommendations and information either by using a tape recording of his own voice or by reading aloud from a printed script. All the antismoking communications he presented were in the form of printed pamphlets, films, or tape-recorded lectures.

The counselor introduced the following specific procedures into the five meetings:

Session 1. The counselor presented to the two clients a brief lecture that he had tape-recorded on the nature of the smoking habit and how it could be broken. The tape recording included instructions about how to use the daily logbook to record smoking behavior. Then, after describing the clinic program in a standardized way, he gave somewhat different instructions to randomly assigned pairs of clients so as to create the three different experimental conditions: (a) for the high-contact condition, the standard instructions about the four subsequent meetings with the same partner were supplemented by an additional statement requesting the two clients to exchange their telephone numbers and to call each other every day in order to discuss their problems in connection with cutting down on smoking; the clients were also asked to make a notation in their daily smoking logbooks of each telephone call, indicating who initiated it, the content of the conversation, and how long it lasted; (b) for the low-contact condition, the same standard instructions about the four subsequent meetings were given, but the partners were asked *not* to telephone each other; (c) for the control (no stable partner) condition, the same standard instructions about the four subsequent meetings were given as in the other two conditions, except that the clients were told that they would be paired with a different fellow smoker at each meeting.

Session 2. The counselor played a tape-recorded lecture for the two clients summarizing numerous helpful hints offered in the psychological literature for people who wanted to stop smoking. The lecture also pointed out how relaxation and other gains from smoking can be obtained in other, more beneficial ways.

Session 3. The counselor played a tape recording of a documentary-like synthetic "case history," with an excerpt from a crucial session when the patient was told by his physician to stop smoking because his "smoker's cough" was due to a precancerous condition of his lungs (which was illustrated by a chest X ray). This was followed by an excerpt from a session two months later in which the patient was informed by the same physician that as a result of his having stopped smoking, the X rays now showed good recovery. The two clients were then given a pamphlet entitled *Your Health and Cigarettes* (distributed by the American Cancer Society), which was read aloud by the counselor while the clients underlined the main points in their own copies.

Session 4. The counselor presented the color film *One in 20,000* (distributed by the American Cancer Society), which tells the story of a young smoker who becomes a victim of lung cancer. One scene takes place in the operating room and shows the gory details of the surgical removal of the patient's cancerous lung. This film was used because it has been found to be effective in motivating smokers to stop smoking (Leventhal & Niles, 1964).

Session 5. The counselor reversed the usual sequence by asking the two clients to have their spontaneous discussion during the first half-hour. He then used the last half of this session to give a post-treatment interview and questionnaire. Each client was interviewed privately in an adjoining room while the other member of the pair filled out a questionnaire.

The results clearly show that the clients who were assigned to high-contact partnerships were more successful in cutting down on cigarette smoking than those who were assigned to low contact partnerships or to the control group. Long-term follow-up interviews conducted one year and ten years after the clinic treatment was terminated revealed that the clients who had been assigned to the high-contact partnerships were continuing over a very long period of time to be significantly more successful in abstaining from cigarette smoking. Ten years after the final meeting with the counselor, nine of the ten clients who had been assigned to high-contact partnerships reported that they were not smoking at all, compared with fewer than one-third of the clients in each of the other two groups.

These findings suggest that any counselor dealing with clients who want to change unhealthy habits like smoking may find it highly efficient to meet with two clients at a time, and perhaps even to meet with small groups of four to eight clients, assigning pairs to the same type of partnership set up in the Janis and Hoffman study. Obviously, however, the question of whether a counselor typically can save time and still be just as effective if he or she conducts sessions with two to four sets of partners simultaneously would have to be answered empirically by subsequent conceptual replication studies.

Additional evidence from the Janis and Hoffman study suggests that the prime conditions specified in chapter 2 for the development of effective helping relationships were met by the high-contact partnerships. The partners disclosed a fair amount of personal information to each other, as well as to the counselor, bearing mostly on temptations that made it difficult to cut down on smoking, withdrawal symptoms, and related problems. The partners' disclosures to each other generally were accompanied by mutual acceptance. Hence the conditions for the first phase of acquiring motivational power were met. At each of the weekly meetings, the counselor explicitly conveyed the expected norm by encouraging the partners to make genuine efforts to stop smoking. An analysis of tape recordings of the partners' conversations showed that they repeated this antismoking norm to each other. In their spontaneous conversations that were recorded during the clinic sessions, the clients in successful partnerships were much more likely than the other clients to praise each other for success in cutting down, to criticize acts of backsliding, and to be skeptical about excuses for not making any improvement. Hence the conditions were met for the second phase, which involved using the motivating power acquired during the first phase. The importance of the norm-sending requirement in the second phase was underlined by evidence from a supplementary study: When the same counselor in the same antismoking clinic set up high-contact partnerships *without* meeting with the clients to endorse the antismoking norm, the partnerships were not at all effective in helping to reduce the amount of cigarette smoking.

With regard to the third phase, the partners who had been meeting with the counselor could look forward to maintaining contact with each other when the time came to terminate the meetings of the three-person groups. This could reduce the disruptive effects of separation from the counselor. Evidence from follow-up interviews indicates that the partners did, in fact, remain in contact with each other for a month or so, on the average, after the final meeting with the counselor.

Because contact between the partners dropped off during the subsequent months, the extraordinarily high degree of success of the partnerships in reducing their cigarette smoking, found one year and ten years after the termination of the counseling sessions, cannot be attributed to the partners continuing to give each other direct social support. It appears most likely that the success of the high-contact partnerships is attributable to the increase in motivational power of the three-person clinic group headed by the counselor as group leader, which augmented the degree to which the clients internalized the norms set by the leader.

Confirmatory results from the study by Nowell and Janis (1982) on the effectiveness of high-contact partnerships in a dieting clinic can be interpreted in essentially the same way.

Phase 1: The partners made personal disclosures to each other as well as to the counselor, and they received positive feedback in the form of acceptance responses.

Phase 2: At each meeting of the three-person group in the clinic the counselor repeatedly conveyed the norm (to stay on the pre-scribed low-calorie diet in order to lose weight).

Phase 3: The partners responded to the loss of contact with the counselor by deciding to remain in contact with each other after the last session at the clinic. In follow-up interviews they reported having continued to maintain contact for an average of three weeks. Although many of the partners were no longer in contact with each other six weeks later, they were still markedly more successful in not overeating, as manifested by their weight loss, than the clients in the two groups that had not been asked by the counselor to form high-contact partnerships.

The success of the partnerships apparently depends upon how the counselor handles the partnership arrangements. We have seen, for example, that no advantages are to be expected when the coun-selor fails to function as a norm-sender. If the other essential con-ditions for the three critical phases are not met, according to my theoretical analysis (chap. 2), the partnerships cannot be expected to be successful.

Another condition for a successful outcome, indicated by a ser-endipitous finding in the Nowell and Janis study (1982), is that the counselor does *not* tell the partners that they are very similar and well matched on attitudes and background. Contrary to what might be expected from prior research on perceived similarity (e.g., Byrne & Griffitt, 1969), giving clients such information apparently gener-ates overoptimistic expectations that lead to disappointment. This adverse effect is avoided if the partners are told that an attempt was made to match them but that there are some divergences.

Undoubtedly, additional conditions essential for effective partner-ships will be discovered in subsequent research. From the evidence now at hand, however, it does not seem premature to conclude that *setting up high-contact partnerships can be an effective adjunct to counseling in antismoking and weight-reduction clinics—and perhaps in a variety of other clinical settings as well—provided that the counselor takes account of the essential requirements specified in the analysis of the three critical phases in effective helping relationships.*

Aside from setting up partnerships, what other things could a counselor do to increase his or her effectiveness in helping people carry out difficult decisions? A good psychological theory of helping relationships should supply promising answers to this question by pointing to key factors that determine the extent to which counselors will have a positive influence on their clients, not only during the period of the counseling sessions, but also long after contact has terminated. How good, in this respect, is the theoretical framework presented in chapter 2 (summarized in Table 2.1 on p. 27)?

EVALUATING THE GUIDELINES FOR
AN EFFECTIVE HELPING RELATIONSHIP

A key postulate of the theoretical framework is that when people have the intention of changing to a difficult course of action, such as dieting, the incentive value of gaining the approval of a counselor can help to get them started and to continue. A supportive counselor can build up and use potential motivating power, according to the theory, if he or she meets the main conditions specified for the three critical phases. The main guidelines that follow from this analysis include encouraging clients to reveal personal feelings, aspirations, troubles, or weaknesses; responding to self-disclosures with acceptance statements; and making only a few specific recommendations of very limited scope (for example, about sound decision-making procedures or about ways to avoid backsliding in order to maintain changes in behavior). When these and other conditions listed in Table 2.1 are met, the clients regard the counselor as someone they can count on for self-esteem enhancement as long as they keep on trying to live up to the small number of recommended norms.

The influence of the supportive norm-sending helper is threatened, however, by the client's disappointment and resentment about the termination of direct contact. After the contracted sessions with the helper have ended, clients will fail to internalize the norms the helper has been advocating if they interpret the termination of contact as a sign of rejection or indifference. These adverse reactions to separation may be minimized if the counselor offers assurances of continual positive regard, arranges for gradual rather than abrupt termination of contact, and gives reminders that continue to build up the clients' sense of personal responsibility for their own decisions. Internalization of the norms and adherence long after all contact has ended are also fostered if the helper builds up the clients' self-confidence about being able to succeed without the helper's aid, which might be done in the context of encouraging them to "work through" feelings about termination and to look forward to future satisfactions that can come from increased autonomy and mastery.

This preliminary framework was used as a basis for selecting variables to be investigated in our series of experiments on short-term counseling (Janis, 1982). Because the critical phases and the hypotheses related to them were inferred from clinical observations of clients who came for a series of up to 12 sessions with a professional counselor (the average being about 8 sessions), serious questions can be raised as to whether the guidelines derived from them are valid and whether those guidelines are applicable to briefer forms of counseling. Most of our field experiments on counselor–client relationships were designed to answer these questions. A number of them provide systematic evidence on the effects of the two main variables specified as crucial for Phase 1 (encouraging self-disclosure and responding with positive feedback), under conditions where the variables specified for Phases 2 and 3 are held constant. A few of our field experiments also bear on the effects of the variables specified for Phases 2 and 3. There are also some impressive findings in prior research by other investigators that bear directly on certain of these variables. However, not all of the 12 variables in Table 2.1 have as yet been systematically investigated.

In light of the empirical evidence now available, the theoretical framework appears to stand up quite well. That is to say, those key variables specified in the analysis of the three phases (Table 2.1) that were systematically investigated in the field experiments prove to have essentially the effects on attitudes and behavior that were predicted. But there are also a few unpredicted findings that point up the need to specify limiting conditions or to modify certain of the assumptions. The main modification will be discussed in the next chapter when we examine some evidence suggesting that under certain conditions an authoritative counselor (such as a highly directive physician, nurse, social worker, or behavior therapist) can effectively induce commitment and adherence to a stressful decision without forming the type of relationship with clients that involves becoming a dependable source of self-esteem enhancement. The unpredicted findings help us to delimit the type of counseling situations in which the guidelines derived from the framework for supportive helping relationships can be expected to apply.

As we look over the findings for each of the three critical phases, it will become increasingly apparent that the bulk of the research evidence supports the conclusion that the theoretical framework provides a useful set of guidelines, at least for the limited types of short-term counseling on personal decisions and problems that we have investigated. It remains for future research to determine whether the same guidelines are equally applicable to most other types of counseling, as the theoretical analysis leads us to expect.

The First Phase

The key variables in the first critical phase of the helper–client relationship specify the conditions under which counselors build up their motivating power. Three conditions are stipulated in Table 2.1:

1. Encouraging clients to engage in a moderate level of self-disclosure vs. not doing so.
2. Giving positive feedback (acceptance and understanding) in response to self-disclosures vs. giving neutral or negative feedback.
3. Using self-disclosures to give insight and cognitive restructuring vs. giving little insight or cognitive restructuring.

Unlike the first two, the third one is not an essential condition but nevertheless is expected to augment somewhat the motivating power of a counselor. The positive findings for a cognitive restructuring procedure, developed and investigated by Langer, Janis, and Wolfer

(1975), which will be discussed in chapter 7, can be interpreted as supporting this expectation.

The first two conditions, which are assumed to be essential for building up the counselors' motivating power, were investigated in a series of studies described in chapters 4 and 5. We shall see that by and large the findings support the conclusion that, as predicted, counselors will be most successful in inducing their clients to live up to specific recommendations, such as adhering to a low-calorie diet, if they start off by encouraging a moderate level of self-disclosure and respond by giving positive feedback in the form of explicit acceptance responses.

The Second Phase

For Phase 2 of the theoretical model (Table 2.1), the research done so far bears mainly on three of the following five variables:

4. Making directive statements or endorsing specific recommendations regarding actions the client should carry out vs. abstaining from any directive statements or endorsements.
5. Eliciting commitment to the recommended course of action vs. not eliciting commitment.
6. Attributing the norms being endorsed to a respected secondary group vs. not doing so.
7. Giving selective positive feedback after making recommendations vs. giving noncontingent acceptance or predominantly neutral or negative feedback.
8. Giving communications and training procedures that build up self-control attributions and a sense of personal responsibility vs. giving no such communications or training.

For variable 4, which involves making directive statements or endorsements, indirect evidence comes from the first study in which adherence to recommendations (assessed by reported number of cigarettes smoked per day) was found to increase when clients in an antismoking clinic were assigned to partnerships (Janis & Hoffman, 1970, 1982). As was indicated in our earlier discussion, the partners not only phoned each other every day to disclose mutual problems but also met once a week with a *norm-sending* counselor for five weeks. A supplementary study of 20 smokers (also reported by Janis & Hoffman, 1970) showed that in the absence of any contact with a directive counselor at the clinic (except for an initial phone call in which partners were assigned), the partnerships had a brief effect of decreasing cigarette consumption during the first month, but after that backsliding occurred in all cases. In contrast, when the same type of partners attended five weekly meetings with a directive counselor who explicitly endorsed the antismoking recommendations, they showed a marked and sustained reduction in cigarette consumption that was still observable ten years later.

Similar findings concerning the need for contact with a directive leader were found in an earlier study by Miller and Janis (1973). This study showed that student partnerships without any exposure to norm-sending communications had the opposite effect from what was intended. Instead of providing mutual support that would improve the students' morale and adjustment to college life, the partnerships had an adverse effect.

After obtaining this indirect evidence from two studies, I surmised that clients who come to a clinic for help with smoking, overeating, or any other such problem of self-control would not be likely to benefit from whatever treatments they were given if the counselors abstained from making any recommendations. Consequently, it seemed to me to be unethical to assign any such clients to the control treatment condition required to carry out an experiment designed to test variable 4 in Phase 2 of the theoretical analysis.

Variable 5 (eliciting commitment) can be investigated systematically without posing ethical issues concerning responsibility to offer genuine help to clients in clinical settings. Prior research on commitment suggests that it can have positive effects on adherence to difficult decisions, but the limiting conditions remain to be determined. (See the reviews of the research literature in Janis & Mann, 1977, chap. 11, and in Kiesler, 1971.)

A study by McFall and Hammen (1971) indicates that three very simple maneuvers by a counselor can be successful in helping heavy smokers to cut down: eliciting a statement of commitment, giving reminders of the commitment, and instructing clients to engage in self-monitoring, which frequently makes the commitment salient. This relatively simple combination was found to be just as effective as several more elaborate therapeutic procedures commonly used in antismoking clinics.

Findings on the positive effects of eliciting commitment have changed the conception of self-control in contemporary psychology. Earlier psychologists thought of self-control, as exemplified by adherence to a no-smoking or dieting regimen, almost exclusively in terms of predispositional attributes like ego strength and impulse control, just as many people in the lay public think that it is all a matter of having "will power." But as Kanfer and Karoly (1972) emphasize, the research evidence on determinants of self-control can best be conceptualized in terms of the joint action of situational and predispositional variables. Some of the main situational or environmental variables that influence persons who are capable of changing their behavior have to do with the degree of *explicitness* of commitment elicited by an interested party and the degree of *volition* or freedom of choice given to (and perceived by) the decision maker. Both of these variables have been found to be determinants of subsequent self-control in adhering to a difficult course of action such as stopping smoking or sticking to a prescribed diet.

In counseling practice, especially among proponents of behavior therapy, commitment is often elicited by means of a formal contract. Numerous clinical reports, based principally on case studies but also on a few field experiments, indicate that clients are more likely to change their behavior in line with their personal goals and to sustain the changes if they sign a contract with the counselor or with a friend or spouse (see Cormier & Cormier, 1979, pp. 506–12; De Risi & Butz, 1974; Ewart, 1978; Fish, 1973; Kanfer, Cox, Greiner, & Karoly, 1974; Rimm & Masters, 1974; Stuart & Davis, 1971; Vance, 1976). Stekel and Swain (1977), for example, found a marked increase in compliance with the prescribed medical regimen when hypertensive patients were given assistance in working out manageable steps to take for each component of the regimen (such as changing their diet) and then were asked to write it all down in the form of a contract. Other studies show that subsequent reminders that make the earlier commitment salient also influence adherence (see Kanfer, Cox, et al., 1974).

When helping clients to state their target behavior in a contract, many counselors encourage the clients to strive toward attaining "specific objectives rather than a single, omnibus outcome" (Bandura, 1969, p. 104). Some counselors introduce specific self-administered rewards into the contract (such as having a client agree to treat himself or herself to a good dinner at a restaurant after each week of successfully cutting down on cigarette smoking to a target number). Other counselors arrange for self-administering penalties (such as donating $10 to the Cancer Society—or as a worse punishment, to a political party the client dislikes—each week that the client fails). Usually the contract includes special provisions for self-monitoring by the client and for reporting the degree of success on a regular basis, such as once a week, to the counselor or to some other helper. These and other features are included in the list of six basic features of a good contract extracted from the clinical research literature by Cormier and Cormier (1977, p. 507):

1. The contract terms should be clear to all involved parties. The behavior to be achieved and an acceptable criterion level should be specified.
2. The contract should include a balance of rewards and sanctions appropriate to the desired behavior.
3. The contact should emphasize the positive and may include a bonus clause.
4. The contract should include a clause that involves the participation of another person. The person should have a positive rather than a negative role.
5. The contact should be written and include a place for signatures.
6. The contract should include a recording system (a progress log) that specifies the desired behavior to be observed, the amount (frequency or duration) of the behavior, and the rewards and sanctions administered. If possible, the recording system should be verified by one other person.

These authors (p. 507) give strong emphasis to the repeated observations that contracts are most likely to be effective "if at least one other person (the counselor or a client's significant other) participates" by monitoring the client (but not by administering any social punishments or other sanctions). They also give cautions about the timing as well as the contents of contracts: Counselors should first ascertain their clients' readiness for commitment and avoid making demands for which clients are not yet prepared, which might "scare

or discourage" them (p. 252). Taking account of the need to redefine
goals as counseling progresses, Cormier and Cormier add that "the
commitment contract can always be changed to reflect revised outcome goals and subgoals" (p. 189).

In several pilot studies in the Yale Weight-Reduction Clinic, my
colleagues and I compared the standard commitment procedure
used in all our studies (Janis, 1982a) with a contract procedure
intended to make commitment even more salient. The standard procedure involves asking each client at the end of a session to sign a
pledge card asserting that he or she is willing to try conscientiously
to stick to the recommended low calorie diet; the additional procedure involves asking each client to sign a much more detailed
contract asserting that the client will avoid eating certain favorite
fattening foods and will conscientiously stay on the diet for as long
as it takes to reach the target weight.

In these pilot studies we have found no evidence of any effect of
the additional commitment on adherence (as measured by weight
loss). These unpromising findings may be attributable to the use of
the standard commitment procedure as the control condition, which
may be so potent that it is already at the ceiling as far as commitment
effects are concerned. We have been reluctant to take the next step
in pursuing commitment effects in the weight-reduction clinic, which
would be to compare the standard commitment procedure with a
control condition in which no commitment at all is elicited. Again,
the reason is that ethical standards require that we do not use a
control condition that prior research indicates could run the risk of
undermining the effectiveness of the counseling sessions, which would
deprive the clients of genuine help. In future research some way
might be found to investigate commitment effects in field experiments without violating ethical standards, perhaps by carrying out
the research in a setting like that used by Mulligan (1982) in which
clients were encouraged to contribute blood to the Red Cross drive,
where the interviewers do not recruit subjects by offering a genuine
clinical service but can nevertheless make legitimate recommendations.

Little or no research has been carried out as yet on variables 6
and 7 in Table 2.1: attributing the norms being endorsed to a respected secondary group, and giving selective positive feedback after

the recommendations are presented. These variables are represented in the experiments conducted in clinical settings, such as the weight-reduction clinic, in that we arrange for the counselors to endorse recommendations that are truthfully attributed to appropriate medical authorities and to give contingent positive feedback after presenting the recommendations, so as to avoid reinforcing the clients' reluctance to comply. The only study in which a systematic variation was introduced was one by Quinlan and Janis (1982), in which the effects of noncontingent vs. contingent feedback throughout the initial interview were systematically compared. The findings on weight loss and other behavioral measures of adherence showed that it was equally effective to give contingent or noncontingent positive feeback throughout the initial interview. But this outcome might hold only in certain types of clinical settings, such as weight-reduction clinics, in which clients seldom express any intentions that go counter to the counselor's recommendations. In other settings, contingent reinforcement throughout the initial interview might prove to be more effective, as is suggested by the study by Mulligan (1982), discussed in chapter 4, in which the counselors' noncontingent positive feedback appears to have inadvertently reinforced the subjects' reluctance to comply with the recommendation to donate blood to the Red Cross.

The remaining variable specified for Phase 2—building up attributions of self-control and personal responsibility—was systematically investigated in a study of dieting women by Riskind and Janis (1982), which included a special procedure intended to promote long-term adherence by training clients to give themselves self-approval for successful adherence to dieting rules. Each client was asked to engage in two psychodramatic enactments in order to "look into the future." One of the role-playing scenarios stipulated failure to follow the diet and the other stipulated success. While acting out each scenario in turn, the client was required to say out loud what she would think of herself, particularly her thoughts and feelings concerning self-pride. Unexpectedly, the results came out in the opposite direction from what was predicted for clients who were given a standard type of intake interview that induced a moderate degree of self-disclosure. Those clients also expressed less confidence about their ability to diet successfully and more self-derogation than clients who were not given the self-approval training. Evidently the attempt to get the clients to focus on their own personal responsibility and to anticipate self-approval for successful dieting had a boomerang effect.

Perhaps enacting the failure scenario (which was always done first) had such a demoralizing effect that it could not be counteracted by enacting the success scenario. In any case the unfavorable outcome from the psychodramatic self-approval procedure has made us very wary about trying out any similar procedure because of the danger that it may do the clients more harm than good. Nevertheless, my colleagues and I are now trying other approaches that we think may prove to be more effective for building up self-control attributions and a sense of personal responsibility in a way that will facilitate long-term adherence.

What little evidence is available bearing on the facilitating conditions listed for Phase 2 seems to be consistent with the theoretical model (except for the last variable [8], since the one attempt to represent it in a field experiment yielded an outcome opposite from what was predicted).

The Third Phase

Ethical constraints again loom large when it comes to investigating the first of the four variables specified for handling termination (Phase 3 in Table 2.1), but not for the last three:

9. Giving reassurances that the counselor will continue to maintain an attitude of positive regard vs. giving no such reassurances.
10. Making arrangements for phone calls, exchange of letters, or other forms of communication that foster hope for future contact, real or symbolic, at the time of terminating face-to-face meetings vs. making no such arrangements.
11. Giving reminders that continue to foster self-control attributions and a sense of personal responsibility vs. giving no such reminders.
12. Building up the client's self-confidence about succeeding without the aid of the counselor vs. not doing so.

In all our studies carried out in clinical service settings, before saying good-bye the counselors always convey reassurance that they will continue to maintain a positive attitude toward each client, often by explicitly expressing their confidence that the client has what it takes to achieve and retain self-control over the problem behavior if he or she makes a genuine effort. Taking account of extensive clinical observations of clients' spontaneous fear of being rejected in response to the termination crisis, we have not tested the hypothesis that withholding this type of reassurance will have a demoralizing effect on many clients.

There is no reason to expect, however, that if such reassurances are given, demoralization or any other such adverse effect will result from withholding the other conditions specified for promoting a satisfactory outcome to the termination crisis. Accordingly, there appears to be no basis for ethical objections to investigating those three ameliorative variables.

Arrangements for future contact were systematically varied in two field experiments by Quinlan, Janis, and Bales (1982), in which half the clients had weekly telephone calls from the counselor after the initial session while the other half had no contact at all until the brief follow-up session one month later. The latter (low contact) condition corresponds to the standard amount of contact arranged in all other studies in the Yale Weight-Reduction Clinic. The arrangement to have the additional telephone contact had complicated effects on adherence, including both favorable and unfavorable outcomes, depending upon whether the clients had been induced to disclose positive or negative personal information and whether the level of self-disclosure was low or moderate. Nevertheless, it is noteworthy that under certain conditions (moderate level of disclosure in an interview that elicited only positive personal information), arranging for the additional telephone contact was found to result in much more weight loss than any other condition in this experiment or in any other of our field experiments on weight reduction (a mean weight loss of 10 pounds after eight weeks). Consequently it appears worthwhile to continue investigating this enigmatic variable to find out why it results in a marked increase in success under certain limited conditions but reduces success under other conditions.

Variable 11 in Phase 3, which involves reminders that foster personal responsibility, is very similar to variable 8 in Phase 2. Both variables were investigated in combination in the study by Riskind and Janis (1982) on weight reduction, which yielded results indicating that attempts to build up reliance on self-approval rather than on approval from others failed to increase adherence (as measured by subsequent weight loss) and appeared to have reduced the clients' self-confidence at the end of the initial interview. We cannot be at all optimistic about the kind of self-approval training used in that field experiment without making major changes. Nevertheless, we need not be pessimistic about finding some way to foster self-reliance that will increase rather than decrease self-confidence. One possibility, for example, would be to drastically modify the procedure used by Riskind and Janis by focusing only on expected successful outcomes in the future and leaving out possible failures.

A new approach to transforming other-directed to self-directed approval motivation is suggested by clinical observations in the Yale Weight-Reduction Clinic, particularly from process interviews such as the ones used in a study by Janis and Quinlan (1982). These observations fit in with a hypothesis suggested by Riskind and Janis (1982), which asserts that transitory dependency on the counselor helps the client get started on a stressful course of action but continued adherence requires that the client develop self-attributions of personal responsibility, with a corresponding decline in dependency upon the counselor. Our clinical observations seem to be in agreement with those of Davison and Valins (1969), who conclude from their research in a completely different setting that behavior change is more likely to be maintained when clients attribute the cause of the change to themselves instead of to an outside agent. A direct implication of this conclusion is that people who seek help in self-regulation will be more likely to adhere in the long run to a new course of action, such as dieting, if the counselor stresses the client's own role in whatever behavior change occurs (see Brehm, 1976, p. 168). But self-reliance obviously requires more than a sense of personal responsibility; it also requires self-confidence (variable 12).

I have noticed that some of our most successful clients go through a progression of steps in which other-directed approval motivation seems to be transformed into self-directed approval motivation, much as was postulated by Riskind and Janis (1982). Those clients start off feeling that with the counselor's help they will be able to stick to the diet. The second step comes during the first week or so of dieting, when they begin to feel that "I can do it on my own most of the time, as long as you are still available to give me some support and encouragement." The third step comes after they start losing some weight, when they see that, in fact, they have basically been doing it on their own for a while. They feel, "At first I needed your help, but now I can do it on my own with a little support from someone besides you." The last step comes when they realize that they are able to control their eating. Then they feel, "I can do it entirely on my own and I have already shown that I can do it." My impression is that the final attitude of self-reliance is predominant among those clients who are most successful at resisting temptations to backslide.

I suspect that this sequence of steps, moving from dependency to self-reliance, could be facilitated in many clients if counselors were to give them step-by-step guidance in self-talk about personal responsibility. In the initial session the counselors might make a frank statement about the problem of dependency and set up the ultimate goal of self-reliance after describing the successive steps. Then, at the appropriate times, they could encourage the clients to try to move on to the next step. For example, in a telephone conversation with a client who reports having lost weight for two successive weeks, a counselor might remind the client of the third step in the sequence and raise the question as to which one of the client's friends or relatives might be most suited to function as an additional helper. Later on, after the client has demonstrated weight loss in a follow-up interview, the counselor could encourage self-talk that embodies the final attitude of self-confidence, as specified by variable 12 in Phase 3. This type of procedure is currently being tried out in a pilot study to see if it looks sufficiently promising to warrant systematic testing in a field experiment.

Bandura's (1977) concept of self-efficacy is closely related to the type of self-confidence specified by variable 12 in Phase 3. He uses the term *self-efficacy* to refer to expectations that one can carry out successfully whatever actions are necessary in order to obtain a desired outcome. Perceived self-efficacy, according to Bandura, not only influences a person's decision about what courses of action to pursue but also affects the degree to which he or she will persist in trying to carry it out. He cites a number of studies that point to the crucial role of self-efficacy in changing undesirable behavior. For example, a field experiment by Bandura, Adams, and Beyer (1977) showed that a form of treatment for phobias that increases the client's sense of mastery in fear-evoking situations leads to generalized increases in expectations of personal efficacy and to a relatively high incidence of cures, compared with control treatments. The experiment was carried out with subjects whose lives were adversely affected by severe and chronic snake phobias. The effective treatment involved participant modeling with a live boa constrictor:

> To weaken the subjects' inhibitions, the therapist initially modeled the threatening activities before subjects attempted to perform them. . . . The therapist then introduced performance aids sequentially from a preestablished hierarchy to enable subjects to perform the feared activities successfully. Intimidating performances were broken down into easily mastered steps of increasing difficulty ranging from looking at, touching, and holding the snake; placing open hands in front of its head as it moved about; holding the snake in front of their faces; allowing the snake to crawl freely in their laps; to letting the snake loose in the room and retrieving it. Joint performance with the therapist was used to facilitate performances that the subjects could not execute on their own. . . .
>
> The inclusion of challenging tasks and progressive self-directed mastery was designed to ensure that subjects would ascribe their successes to enhanced personal efficacy rather than to external factors. The duration of treatment varied from 40 min. to 7 hours with the median time being 90 min. (Bandura, Adams, & Beyer, 1977, pp. 128–29).

Also related to clients' attitudes of self-confidence and self-efficacy are their beliefs about being able to *control* a stressful situation. There is now a sizable literature indicating that perceived personal control sometimes plays an important role in coping with stress. (See discussions of the research literature by Janis & Rodin, 1979, and by Seligman, 1975.) Perceived control refers to expectations of having the power to participate in making decisions with fairly confident expectations of obtaining desirable consequences (Baron & Rodin, 1978).

In our Yale clinics for people having trouble controlling their overeating, smoking, or other unhealthy behaviors, we often encounter clients who express little confidence about being able to succeed as they view the seemingly endless task of self-control ahead of them. Some clients explicitly express the attitude, "Sure, I can control my actions at present, but I can't expect to keep this up forever when I no longer have your help; sooner or later I'm bound to give in to temptation and go back to my old ways."

Recent research findings suggest that such adverse attitudes, which are likely to be self-fulfilling prophecies, can be counteracted to a significant degree by focusing the client's attention on immediate subgoals that can be mastered quite quickly rather than on the ultimate goal to be achieved in the remote future. The client's sense of mastery, control, and self-confidence about succeeding on a difficult course of action can sometimes be increased by structuring the long-term task as a series of short-term accomplishments, concentrating on those features that can most easily be mastered in the immediate future. A study of obese clients being treated by behavior modification techniques, reported by Bandura and Simon (1977), found that clients who were instructed to adopt short-term (daily) subgoals ate less and lost more weight than clients who were instructed to adopt a longer term subgoal in terms of weekly accomplishments.

Similar results were obtained in an experiment by Riskind (1982) (carried out independently before the Bandura and Simon experiment had been published), which was conducted with nonobese but overweight women in the Yale Weight-Reduction Clinic. He, too, found positive effects from encouraging dieters to focus on a short-term, day-by-day time perspective. The dieters were told to approach the low-calorie diet with the plan of living up to it for one day at a time. The counselor suggested that each day they successfully followed the diet could be seen as a separate accomplishment for which they justifiably could feel pride. This day-by-day perspective was compared with a long-term perspective that emphasized following the diet as long as necessary to lose the amount of weight each dieter wanted to lose. The clients given the day-by-day perspective were found to express more confidence about succeeding and a stronger sense of personal control than those given the long-term perspective. They also complied better with the request to send in weekly reports about their dieting behavior. Two months later, a subgroup of the women (those with a relatively high level of chronic self-esteem) showed considerable benefit from having been given the day-by-day perspective: They lost more weight than the corresponding subgroup of those given the long-term perspective. These research findings show that the day-by-day perspective was effective for those people who initially were fairly self-confident about achieving their goals but did not help those who were lacking in self-confidence. Riskind (1982) suggests that in the Bandura and Simon (1977) study the overweight clients who volunteered or were selected for the behavior modification treatment may have tended to be like the clients who scored above the median on chronic level of self-esteem in his study, which could account for the findings of a main effect of greater weight loss for those given the short-term time perspective. Persons with a relatively high chronic level of self-esteem may be responsive to counseling aids that increase their sense of personal control and their self-efficacy; clients with a relatively low chronic level of self-esteem may not benefit from a day-by-day approach or other such aids that encourage personal mastery because they are more externally oriented and require more reassurance and support from others.

The research findings reported by Bandura and Simon (1977) and by Riskind (1982) suggest that at least a small percentage of clients who seek help on a difficult task (such as avoiding overeating) might increase their sense of mastery, control, and self-confidence about succeeding on their own, long after the counseling relationship has ended, if the counselor structures the long-term behavioral change to be achieved as a series of short-term accomplishments and focuses on features that can be mastered rapidly. Clients can be instructed to approach the task step by step, just one day at a time, and then they can be encouraged to continue using this approach on their own as the key to ultimate success.

Further research on the effectiveness of the day-by-day perspective should provide essential information about whether it works only with clients who initially express a relatively high level of self-esteem, as Riskind (1982) found, and, if so, whether it can be modified or supplemented in some way so as to increase self-confidence about future success among clients who initially express a low level of self-esteem. (Personality differences in responsiveness to any such counseling procedure are to be expected; such differences in responsiveness to other counseling procedures are discussed at the end of chapter 7.)

As the preceding paragraph implies, more research investigations are needed on the effects of variable 12, as well as on the other key variables in Phase 3. All those variables must be regarded as part of an unfinished agenda on which research work is still in progress. Because the evidence currently at hand is fragmentary and indirect, we must regard the suggested guidelines for Phase 3, like most of the guidelines for Phase 2, as extremely tentative. In contrast, the evidence in support of the guidelines for Phase 1, to be examined in the next two chapters, is quite substantial.

4 Conveying Acceptance and Other Forms of Positive Feedback

This chapter continues to explore ways in which the effectiveness of counselors can be increased. It focuses on guidelines for using one of the most important variables in building up the counselor's motivating power. As we view the evidence on the effects of giving clients positive feedback, we shall see that the findings not only tend to confirm a key theoretical assumption but also help to answer a specific practical question that confronts all counselors: What is the most effective way to conduct the initial session? This is an especially important issue in short-term counseling, when the initial session comprises most, if not all, of the counseling that is provided.

The theoretical model with which we started (chap. 2) assumes that a counselor's motivating power can be built up if he or she does certain things to take on the role of a basically dependable source of self-esteem enhancement for each client. According to this model, at the beginning of a supportive relationship there are two principal variables that determine the motivating power of the counselor, both of which involve specific kinds of verbal behavior on the part of the counselor in his or her interactions with the clients: first, encouraging or eliciting a moderate degree of *self-disclosure,* and second, responding to self-disclosures with *positive feedback,* especially acceptance statements. We shall review first the evidence on the effects of positive feedback, which is much less complicated than the evidence on the effects of eliciting different amounts of self-disclosure.

EVIDENCE OF POSITIVE EFFECTS OF ACCEPTANCE

Relevant findings come from our field experiments carried out in the Yale Weight-Reduction Clinic. In each of these studies, the clients were randomly assigned to two groups, one given neutral feedback and the other given positive feedback, with all the other features of the counseling sessions held constant. Neutral feedback consists of responding in a noncommittal way, essentially by saying nothing except, where necessary, acknowledging having heard the client's answer to the interview question and giving a transition to the next question (for example, "OK, now this next question involves a different kind of problem . . ."). In contrast, positive feedback involves conveying explicit acceptance by giving supportive, empathic comments (for example, "It's quite understandable why you feel that way") and positive statements about the client's cooperation during the interview (for example, "You're being very frank; it's good that you are aware of that problem"), together with frequent restatements of the client's answer to show that the counselor understands and is not critical of what the client is saying. The restatements are intended to indicate that the counselor has a strong positive interest in what the client has to say and is listening intently and empathically. They include paraphrases of the essential content of the client's statements reflecting the feelings that the client is expressing. Sometimes the paraphrases are accompanied by requests for clarification of what was just said (e.g., "Are you saying that . . . ?") (see Cormier & Cormier, 1979, pp. 62–69).

The counselors in all our studies are trained to give positive comments in a friendly, conversational tone of voice that conveys positive regard and empathy. The training also includes adopting a set to respect each client as a person, to empathize with each client's feelings, and to regard each client as having the potential to change (which, in the weight-reduction clinic, means a positive attitude about each client's prospects for succeeding in adhering to the diet and maintaining reduced weight). The counselors are also instructed to *avoid* the following types of conversational topics or tactics that Cormier and Cormier (1979, p. 50) mention as likely to interfere with the goals of counseling:

1. Expressing criticism or blame.
2. Engaging in "cocktail party chitchat."
3. Trying to give psychological interpretations or "analysis" of the clients' motives, conflicts, or defenses.
4. Engaging in extensive or intimate self-disclosures of the counselors' personal problems.

5. Giving ad hoc advice that is not included in the standard set of recommendations for all clients.

A field experiment by Dowds, Janis, and Conolley (1982) and a replication of it by Conolley, Janis, and Dowds (1982) show the same outcome. Both of these experiments, conducted in the Yale Weight-Reduction Clinic, clearly indicate that consistently positive feedback from the counselor has favorable effects when given during an interview that induces a moderate amount of self-disclosure. In both experiments consistently positive feedback was compared with consistently neutral feedback and with predominantly positive feedback marred by a single instance of very mild negative feedback. Of the three forms of feedback treatment it was the consistently positive that was found to result in the most favorable attitudes toward the counselor and also in the greatest adherence to the counselor's recommendations, as manifested by weight loss two months later. (Unexpected findings from these experiments indicating that under certain conditions neutral feedback can also be highly effective will be discussed later in this chapter.)

In the first of the two experiments, which was carried out with 64 women, Dowds, Janis, and Conolley found that the clients who were given consistently positive feedback lost an average of about three pounds over a two-month period whereas those who were given the same type of session but with neutral feedback in response to the client's answers to the counselor's questions did not lose any weight and, in fact, showed a slight gain in weight, on the average, over the same time period. A third group of clients, who were given positive feedback in response to their answers throughout the interview but were given one instance of negative criticism (being told that they could have performed better on a motivation test, which involved holding up a five-pound weight with an outstretched arm) came out essentially the same as those given neutral feedback. They showed a slight gain in weight, on the average, over the two-month period. In the second experiment Conolley, Janis, and Dowds obtained similar results, with consistently positive feedback again proving to be significantly more effective than neutral feedback.

Several important features of both of these experiments are emphasized by Dowds, Janis, and Conolley (1982):

We introduced a major constraint into the counseling setting in order to eliminate the possibility that the effects of the counselor's acceptance statements might be influenced by the counselor's facial expressions, gestures, or other visual cues that could be confounding variables. The constraint was that the client could not see the counselor (as in counseling by telephone). More specifically, we used a counseling setting with a remote audio system whereby the client, who was alone in an interviewing room, heard the counselor's voice at normal speech level from a high-fidelity speaker and responded by talking into a microphone. This setup made the interview similar to talking with a counselor over the telephone, which is becoming a popular way of conducting counseling not only at suicide centers but also in organizations like Rescue, Inc. for the elderly and in other crisis intervention centers that have hotline services for troubled people who want help on problems concerning marriage, sex and pregnancy, family disputes, employment, or health (see Lester & Brockopp, 1973). In addition to resembling telephone counseling, the audio setup we used might become a common way of conducting intake interviews in clinics that adopt on-line computer diagnostic systems to treat large numbers of clients (see Cochran, Hoffman, Strand, & Warren, 1977; Harris, 1974). [p. 113]

• • •

One problem that arises in testing any hypothesis about the effects of explicit acceptance statements is that if the counselor expresses approval when clients admit that they have done or are planning to do something undesirable (e.g., to ignore the counselor's recommendations), he or she will be reinforcing the wrong actions. An additional problem is that, as Jourard (1968) points out, acceptance statements given in a mechanical, nonempathic manner by someone who is playing a contrived role may have little effect, unlike acceptance statements given by someone who is authentically expressing goodwill and empathy. These problems can be avoided, as they were in the present study (and in the subsequent studies [carried out in the Yale Weight-Reduction Clinic (Janis, 1982)] . . .) by limiting positive feedback to genuine praise of the client's honesty at times when he or she makes self-disclosures about undesirable actions. That is, the counselor expresses empathy and acceptance through the use of reflecting or restating responses only with those disclosures that do not refer to attitudes, intentions, or activities that would interfere with adherence to the recommended course of action. In this way we attempt to evoke what Deutsch and Solomon (1959) refer to as a "positivity effect" (the tendency to respond favorably to someone who gives positive evaluations), without saying anything that could be construed by the clients as approval of acts or intentions that run counter to the counselor's recommendations. [pp. 110–11]

As an illustration of the way positive feedback is modified to avoid reinforcing the "wrong" intentions or actions, when an overweight client seeking help in dieting says that he or she feels strong doubts about being able to follow the standard recommendation to avoid eating desserts with whipped cream or other favorite fattening foods, the counselor's modified form of positive feedback might be, "It's quite understandable that you would feel that way about it right now, but of course you will have to overcome those feelings because eating that kind of food will keep you from losing weight." Such comments, which are used by counselors to give *selective* positive feedback (one of the variables listed in Phase 2 of an effective helping relationship in Table 2.1, p. 27), might be perceived by a sensitive patient as a criticism; consequently the counselor should word all such comments carefully, to avoid implying lack of acceptance of the client as a person. This can usually be done by talking specifically about the expected undesirable consequences of detrimental intentions or actions and by conveying an optimistic attitude about the client's ability to overcome the obstacles.

In a third field experiment, consistently positive feedback (which included occasional selective acceptance responses to take account of detrimental intentions expressed by some of the clients) was again found to be more effective than neutral feedback. This study was a doctoral dissertation by Chang (1977), designed under the supervision of Edward Conolley and carried out in a weight-reduction clinic at the University of Southern California, modeled after the one at Yale. It differed from the first two studies at Yale, however, in one important respect, which reflects favorably on the validity of the findings for standard counseling settings: The counselor interviewed each client in a typical *face-to-face* counseling session. Chang compared consistently positive feedback with an ambiguous type of neutral feedback (no response at all from the counselor except for impassive or skeptical facial expressions). He found significantly more weight loss after a period of about three weeks among the clients who had been given positive feedback during their initial interview, irrespective of whether the interview questions induced only positive or only negative disclosures about the self.

EFFECTS OF NONVERBAL CUES

Further evidence that consistently positive feedback fosters adherence to the counselor's recommendations comes from another study in the Yale Weight-Reduction Clinic by Greene (1982), which introduced a variation in physical proximity that had not been investigated in the earlier studies. Greene found that when the seating arrangement for the face-to-face interview placed the client at a normal distance of about two feet from the counselor, positive verbal feedback had the expected favorable effect, as shown by significantly greater weight loss five weeks after the interview. But when the seating arrangement placed clients at a relatively far distance from the counselor (5 feet away), which they apparently interpreted as a nonverbal sign of withdrawal or detachment, the favorable effect of positive verbal feedback was lost. These results point to the same conclusion suggested by subsidiary findings from the earlier experiments in the Yale clinic: In order for positive feedback to be effective, the counselor must use it *consistently* throughout the interview, abstaining from saying or doing anything that could be construed by the clients as withdrawing from them or criticizing them.

In Greene's study, adherence to the counselor's dieting recommendations was clearly influenced by the degree of consistency between verbal and nonverbal components of the counselor's communications during the face-to-face interview. The counselor's nonverbal cue conveyed by his seating arrangement apparently had the effect of increasing or decreasing the psychological impact of his positive verbal feedback, depending on whether he sat near or far from the client. Other nonverbal cues given by the counselor, whether deliberately or inadvertently, can be expected to have similar effects in modifying the impact of positive verbal feedback. In their review of clinical and experimental studies on the effects of nonverbal communications, Cormier and Cormier (1979, pp. 29–46) single out the following nonverbal cues as the main ones that can convey positive regard:

- Total body facing toward the other person vs. body orientation at an angle;

- Leaning forward toward the other person vs. bending away from the other person or slouching in chair;
- Maintaining direct eye-contact during much of the interview vs. having little sustained eye contact, making darting glances, lowering the eyes, or staring fixedly at the other person;
- Smiling vs. pursing lips tightly together, biting the lips, or opening the mouth, as when suppressing yawns;
- Nodding head up and down while the other person speaks vs. shaking head or hanging head down;
- Keeping arms unfolded and using hands for gesturing during conversation vs. keeping arms folded across chest, holding arms in a stiff position, clenching fists, or fidgeting with one's hands;
- Speaking in a clear, audible voice with few hesitations vs. speaking in a barely audible voice, hesitating, or remaining silent for long periods when the other person has stopped talking.

It seems likely that most or all of these nonverbal cues and probably a number of others involving tone of voice, facial expressions, hand gestures, and body movements can augment the impact of one's positive verbal statements (see Knapp, 1972). But very little systematic research has been carried out so far in *counseling* situations to see if this is so. Probably the safest assumption for counselors to make is that their nonverbal communications will reinforce their verbal expressions of positive regard and will thereby contribute to building up and maintaining effective working relationships with clients if they have *genuinely* positive attitudes toward those who come to them for help. As Cormier and Cormier (1979) point out. "Genuineness means being oneself without being phony or playing a role. . . . Genuineness also implies that the counselor is congruent, that the counselor's actions and words match her or his feelings" (p. 20).

What does it take to be genuine? This is an elusive problem, so rarely investigated by psychologists or psychiatrists that one must rely solely on clinical lore to guess at the answer. Part of the answer probably involves having a fairly strong belief in the efficacy of feeling as well as honestly expressing positive regard toward the people one is trying to help. (Some of the evidence I have just reviewed, especially on nonverbal cues, might contribute to such a belief.) Reinforcement of this belief by professional norms probably helps counselors to resist the temptation to think badly of those clients who seem to be behaving badly, especially when they are insulting or are apparently sabotaging one's best efforts to help them. Another part of the answer probably has to do with the personality of the counselor. D. W. Winnicott (1971) mentions several important personality characteristics, which, on the basis of his 30 years of clinical experience as a child therapist, he regarded as essential for selecting psychiatrists, social workers, and psychologists for training in the brief form of therapeutic consultation he developed for working with certain types of disturbed children. I suspect that the same characteristics may be essential for therapists and counselors in general if they wish their professional actions to be consistent with their belief in the value of maintaining a genuine attitude of positive regard toward clients. The three main factors Winnicott singles out are "a capacity to identify with the [clients] . . . without loss of personal identity"; "a capacity to wait for [the] resolutions" [of each client's difficulties and conflicts] instead of "anxiously looking around for a cure"; and "an absence of the tendency to retaliate under provocation" (Winnicott, 1971, p. 2).

EXCERPTS FROM CASE STUDIES OF SUCCESSFUL DIETERS

In one of our studies in the Yale Weight-Reduction Clinic we used the method of comparative case studies to obtain some indications of how a single session in which each counselor gave consistently positive feedback affected the attitudes and expectations of the clients who were most successful in losing weight during the month after the session. It was a small-scale experiment by Janis and Quinlan (1982) on the effects of eliciting a high versus a moderate level of self-disclosure during the initial interview (a topic which will be discussed in the next chapter). We arranged for each of the 18 clients in the study to have a one-hour process interview immediately after the first hour, which was devoted to the self-disclosure interview. The process interview included 25 questions asking each client to describe her feelings during the preceding interview, her expectations with regard to succeeding on the diet, and her current mood. Throughout each process interview, the counselor continued to give consistent acceptance, just as was done throughout the preceding interview. Thus, each client was given about two hours of consistently positive feedback from the counselor. About one month later the clients returned for a follow-up interview during which they were again asked some of the questions from the process interview and were weighed in order to determine how much weight they had lost.

When we examined the recordings of the process interviews and follow-up interviews of the clients who were successful (and compared them with those who had lost little or no weight), we obtained some clues suggesting that consistently positive feedback contributed to the motivating power of the counselor and was a crucial factor in successful adherence to the diet during the month following the two-hour session. The following extracts from brief case studies reported by Janis and Quinlan (1982) highlight the main clues obtained from the 12 women who were most successful in losing weight among the 18 included in the study. (Cases labeled with the letter *H* were given an initial one-hour interview containing questions that elicited a *high* level of self-disclosure; those labeled with the letter *M* were given an initial one-hour interview that elicited a *moderate* level of self-disclosure). During the month following the two-hour session, without any additional contact with the counselor except for their mailing in weekly reports, all 12 of these women succeeded in attaining the goal suggested by the counselor: losing an average of one pound (or slightly more) per week by staying on the recommended low-caloric diet.

Case H-5. This 49-year-old married woman, who worked full time as a teacher, wanted to lose 25 pounds. At the beginning of the process interview she complained that the session had not got her "all fired up" as she had hoped. She said very little about her image of the counselor, just enough to imply that she thought she was regarded as just another routine case: "I assume you think that I am someone who wants to lose some weight ... and I fill the bill as far as being a candidate, I guess."

About midway through the process interview, after describing her negative reactions to the preceding interview, she began to express a more hopeful outlook: "I can't say that I am disappointed because, who knows, I may go home and find this works fine." At the end of the process interview she acknowledged that "maybe *getting some-*

one else involved in it would help." After having said good-bye, she delayed leaving to state that she probably had felt discouraged because she had obtained the recommended diet from a friend about a week earlier but had not been able to stick to it. She added, *"I probably shouldn't have tried it without talking to you first."* What she seemed to be saying just before leaving was that, in contrast to the way she had felt at the beginning of the process interview, she now regarded the session as having some potential value and she was ready to make a conscientious effort to succeed.

In any case she did in fact succeed in losing 6 pounds during the next four weeks. She reported at the follow-up session that she had gone off the diet temporarily several times but *resumed dieting because she had agreed to send weekly reports to the counselor; otherwise, "I might not have gotten back on."* She recalled that during the initial session she had been disappointed and pessimistic because "I had expected to get more support and more psyching up." Yet, when she got home she was surprised to find herself refusing to eat rich food that was not on the recommended diet. Thereafter, on most days she followed almost all the rules of the diet recommended by the counselor. When she gave in to temptation every few days, according to her account, *she promptly got back on the diet by thinking about her obligation to return her progress report each week to the counselor.*

Case H-6. This 60-year-old woman, who works full time in a professional role, wanted to lose 20 pounds.

At the outset of the process interview *she described the counselor as understanding, sympathetic, and the kind of person with whom she was able to achieve close rapport.* She said that she had disclosed much personal information that she would not have revealed to anyone else under other circumstances and that the interview made her feel that she would try to control her appetite. But she added, "I'm not absolutely convinced of being able to do it" because *"I feel like I need a big crutch."* She elaborated on her qualms and weaknesses, indicating that the interview had generated self-derogatory thoughts, that she was far from being confident about succeeding, and that *the counselor was not offering enough support in the form of regular contact.* As the process interview went on, this client continued to complain about insufficient contact with the counselor, for example, "I'm not dissatisfied with you in any way ... [but] I would perhaps say I might be disappointed with the clinic [because] *I would like it much better if I were able to have some contact in this period of a month and perhaps subsequent to that* ... I'm just reaching out for any help that I can get." At the end of the process interview, however, she asserted that she would have to "face up" to her own problems and that success would depend "really and truly [on] my motivation." She said that *the counselor had "given me support which I felt that I needed and I am even more reinforced in my motivation* ... I have gotten a prod and *I feel also that you would like me to do it and so I would like to do it partly to oblige you as well as me."* In this case there is a remarkable transformation from pleading for more contact with the counselor to a sense of inner resolution to control her own behavior, partly to please the counselor and partly to satisfy her own needs.

At the four-week follow-up interview, after expressing gratification about her success in having lost the expected amount of four pounds in four weeks, she asked if she could continue sending in her weekly reports for another month or so, because doing so had been very helpful. She made it clear that *she still felt dependent upon the counselor* but was willing to accept the termination of their direct contact without complaint and to rely on her own resources for continuing on the diet. *"Seeing you today,"* she said, *"will give me a new lease,* which I need to get off this plateau. ... It's hard [to diet] but not *that* hard; it's all mental." She added that the initial session had been helpful because she had to "dredge up things I hadn't ever specifically thought of before ... about how I felt toward myself, about being fat but also my good points which I sometimes forgot. *I have to think well of myself to succeed and ... [you] helped me to achieve that balance."*

Case H-7. This 28-year-old woman with one child was a full-time student in a community college.

In the process interview this woman asserted that she was surprised by many questions that she had never thought about before. Although they were "basically all logical questions," she was perturbed about some of her answers because she found out that "I'm weaker than I thought I was." She said she had been proud of herself but now she wonders "if I'm so strong, then how come I can't keep to a diet which I logically want?" She said that she would try to diet but was not sure about succeeding: "I wouldn't bet money on me, but I have been known to come up from behind in a pinch."

Although she said many positive things about the counselor, she nevertheless made a large number of minor complaints: the counselor gave poor directions for finding the building, she could have made a better recording of her voice on the taped instructions, she ought to learn shorthand to take interview notes more rapidly, the interview room was stark, and "I don't care for your interior decorator at all." She said she noticed that the counselor was following a standard interview procedure of being accepting, "as taught in psychology classes," but it "was done well." When asked what she thought the counselor's opinion of her was, she became evasive after first making a joke of it, as she had done in making most of her minor criticisms: "*I think I'm fantastic, therefore you must think I am fantastic.* But I logically know you have your own mind . . . that's your business, it doesn't affect me." Toward the end of the interview her surface manner of detached objectivity and mild bantering changed momentarily to much more serious bantering, implying an unsatisfied wish for a closer or more reciprocal relationship. Here is what she said when asked whether she felt in anyway dissatisfied with the interview: "*I don't feel we know enough about each other.* . . . I don't know a *thing* about you."

In her weekly written reports she mentioned that her husband was exerting a bad influence on her dieting and that she wished the counselor had given her a diet "that works magic overnight." But she also wrote that "no one can do this for me."

Upon returning for the follow-up interview she was pleased to see that she had lost more than 6 pounds according to the clinic scale. She reported that the *weekly reports [to the counselor] were helpful.* She said at first that she could not remember the initial interview a month earlier but then added, "I don't think I was that honest in my answers." She explained that she cared more about being overweight than she had acknowledged and that she was *concerned about the first impression she was creating.* She claimed that she always had the latter concern, but "after that I have confidence that I have enough personality to *make friends."* She also asserted that many features of the prior session had been helpful, including the counselor's statement that "the diet was not magical," which she reported having thought about during her daily periods of silent thought. Overall, in the follow-up interview she was less evasive and less detached than she had been earlier.

In this case the high self-disclosure interview during the initial session seems to have evoked considerable resistance, which took the form of evasiveness, frequent presentation of her social mask to the counselor rather than her "real self," and efforts to maintain a mildly critical, detached stance toward the counselor despite longing for a warmer, affectionate relationship. Perhaps her realization that she was being excessively defensive during the process interview, as the counselor consistently accepted one provocative complaint after another, led her to adopt an autonomous attitude ("No one can do this for me"), which seems to have contributed to her success in dieting.

Case H 8. This 40-year-old, upper middle-class housewife was a college graduate and had been trained as a nurse. She wanted to lose 45 pounds.

In the process interview the client said that the interview had been more or less what she had expected from doing case histories herself when she had worked as a nurse. She added that it made her a little more aware of what she already knew. *What will be helpful,* she said, is *"knowing that I'll be checked,"* which she referred to as *"an extra crutch."* At the end of the process interview she admitted for the first time to feeling a bit dissatisfied with herself for not having gone on a diet sooner. She also expressed, for the first time, strongly positive feelings toward the counselor, in contrast to her earlier coolly polite statements to the effect that in her opinion the counselor was simply carrying out her role adequately. She said that her husband did not care at all whether she was fat or thin, but *from this session she now knew "really that somebody cares."* Her dieting resulted in a very substantial amount of weight loss (seven pounds) at the time of the four-week follow-up interview.

The client reported that she had *thought about the initial interview while carrying out the diet* during the intervening weeks and that *the weekly reports to the counselor were helpful.* She was *very enthusiastic about having had the opportunity to talk over her problems with the counselor: "That helped more than anything else."* She came away from the first session, she said, *feeling that the counselor was offering her genuine help but that dieting was something she would have to do for herself.*

In this case there is a paradoxical contrast between the client's evasive answers during most of the initial attempted high disclosure interview and her subsequent glowing account of how much she learned about herself from that interview. There is no way of knowing to what extent, if any, the client's success in dieting was attributable to that apparently constricted interview or to the subsequent process interview during which she opened up much more and revealed a sense of loneliness and a wish for an emotional attachment to the counselor. In any case it is impressive to note that here again we have a successful case who reports that among her sustaining thoughts while adhering to the diet were the notions that she was able to cope better with the demands of the diet *because of the relationship with the counselor along with the realization that coping was nevertheless her own responsibility.*

Case H-9. This 56-year-old housewife, who had less than an eighth grade education, was working part-time in a routine clerical job. She wanted to lose 25 pounds.

In the process interview this client continued to deny having any unpleasant feelings and gave conventionally polite answers to all questions about her reactions to the high self-disclosure interview and to the counselor. She thought the counselor would "like to see me lose weight because your job here is to encourage and it would be good for your program here." This implicit assertion that the counselor was not interested in her personally was the closest she ever got to expressing any complaint. At the end of the interview she said she felt encouraged and was going "to give it a good try." She then repeated a current theme that she had emphasized throughout the process interview, namely, that she was going to adopt a day-by-day approach rather than allow herself to think about the entire month ahead.

According to the client's weekly reports, she stuck to the diet almost every day and steadily lost weight throughout the month (for a total of six pounds). On the last report she wrote that she had *thought about the coming appointment with the counselor, and that when she cheated on the diet she was "mad at myself for doing so."* This low-level concern about external surveillance by the counselor, combined with a strong sense of internal personal standards that should not be violated, was again manifested in the follow-up interview when she spoke about being *"mad" at herself* for temporarily breaking the diet by eating sweets.

Cases M-4, M-5, M-6, and M-7. These four clients were middle-aged housewives, ranging in age from 42 to 57. All four responded to the moderate self-disclosure interview by revealing a moderate amount of personal material about their eating problems and related aspects of their lives. One of them, for example, said that at times she had an uncontrollable urge to eat, like an addict. During the process interview all four described themselves as highly motivated and confident about dieting. And they all said that the session with the counselor was definitely beneficial. There were hardly any signs of conflict or ambivalence toward the counselor to undercut their *favorable comments about the counselor's interest and about the value of "knowing that someone will be checking on me,"* as one of the women put it.

All four lost the expected amount of weight, an average of approximately one pound a week for the four weeks. In the follow-up interview these four clients were confident that they would be able to continue dieting successfully and *expressed gratitude to the counselor.* Each one said that *sending the weekly monitoring reports to the counselor had been helpful* but each also showed signs of having *internalized* the norms, rather than being primarily dependent on the counselor's approval or disapproval. "I can't stand to cheat on the diet," one of them asserted, "because I don't want to do it in front of my kids."

Case M-8. This 38-year-old housewife was a college graduate who wanted to lose 25 pounds.

At the outset of the process interview she said she felt relieved that she had not been put under pressure to admit to having all sorts of personal problems, because she had heard this was required of participants at the meetings of a popular national organization that offered help for overweight people. She felt disappointed that the recommended diet was not very different from the diets she had been on before and that the only new gimmick was the recommended daily period of meditation about dieting. Nevertheless, she thought the interview was "well handled," felt confident about succeeding, and wanted to "hurry up and do it." She felt *pleased that now she would be able to "report to somebody."* She made it clear, however, that her view of the counselor was as a strictly detached professional person, not as a friend or a parental type of helper.

In the weekly reports this client wrote extensive notes indicating that she felt an *inner compulsion* to stick to the diet and to get back on it any time she deviated. In the four-week follow-up interview she reported that her feelings of self-confidence helped her to keep going on the diet. And yet, despite these apparent signs of internalization of the dieting norms and despite the strong reinforcement of her self-confidence from her great success in losing approximately eight pounds during the four-week interval, she said that *she was afraid of losing her momentum unless she could continue to be checked by the counselor.* (She did, in fact, phone the counselor a few weeks later to report having lost an additional two pounds and to *request another follow-up session.*) In this case the client manifested a fairly high degree of inner control but apparently needed reinforcement in the form of external social support from the counselor as a dependable authority figure.

Case M-9. This 72-year-old unmarried woman had retired from a lifelong career as an administrative assistant. She wanted to lose about 25 pounds.

In the process interview the client characterized the counselor as firm, quiet, and dependable. *She felt gratified that the counselor was willing to devote time and interest to her without "bawling her out."* She was glad that *the counselor was not trying to push her but was letting her make her own decision.* She felt *"inspired" by the counselor* she said *because the counselor's confidence in her gave her confidence in herself.* She also said that *she would be ashamed to face the counselor if she were to fail.* Her remarks indicate that *her image of the counselor,* which appears to be similar to that of most of the other clients in the moderate disclosure group, *was of a benign, dependable authority figure.*

According to the client's weekly reports, she was highly successful in adhering to the diet during the first week and thereafter was slightly less rigorous but continued to lose weight. In the follow-up session she was pleased that the scale showed she had lost a total of 9½ pounds during the one-month interval.

One of the main things that kept her going, she reported, was remembering that the counselor had said, "It won't be easy" and she had thought, *"I'll show her!"* She reported that she had gotten her brother and sister interested in following her dieting progress. She also said that she wanted to continue filling out the weekly reports "for myself" because she intended to lose more weight. Here again, as in some of the other successful cases, the client seems to have displayed a fairly high degree of autonomous inner control but nevertheless manifested a continuing need for external surveillance, which this elderly lady arranged for herself by getting both her brother and sister involved.

> From what the clients said in the process interview . . . it is apparent that one of the principal functions of giving acceptance responses is to build an image of the counselor as a benign helper who is "on your side." But expressing a great deal of warmth and empathy seems also to sow seeds of discontent among some of the clients because they expressed vague fears of becoming too dependent or of somehow being hurt [and these clients were *not* as likely to be successful in losing weight].
>
> We get the impression that most of the successful cases saw the counselor as a detached, *nonevaluating* professional person who was *genuinely interested in giving them the limited amount of help offered* but could not be expected to do anything more than that. It is this type of image of the counselor that seems to go along with the client's readiness to continue the task of dieting with a minimum of external social support (although routine surveillance by someone seems to be strongly desired by most of the successful clients).
>
> An effective working relationship with the counselor apparently requires the client to come to terms with unrequited longings for a close relationship with the counselor. There are some faint indications here and there of fantasy images of what the desired relationship might be

like. For some clients what seems to be involved is primarily a wish for unconditional acceptance by an all-loving maternal helper. For others it may be a wish to be guarded from temptations and helped to overcome other weaknesses by a powerful authority who will somehow provide magical protection. Neither of these fantasy images seems to facilitate success in adhering to the task of dieting. (Janis & Quinlan, 1982, pp. 243–44. Italics added)

EVIDENCE FROM OTHER FIELD EXPERIMENTS

Supporting evidence concerning the effectiveness of giving consistently positive feedback in response to self-disclosures induced by an interviewer's questions has been obtained in a pair of field experiments conducted by Mulligan (1982) in a setting entirely different from the Yale Weight-Reduction Clinic. Mulligan conducted his research during a Red Cross campaign to elicit blood donations from male college students.

Each subject in every condition was seen by two male psychologists in order to separate two different roles: the "proselytizing investigator" presented information, which was persuasive and stress inducing, on behalf of the Red Cross campaign, whereas the "interviewer" asked questions in the manner of a relatively nondirective counselor. . . .

The proselytizing investigator truthfully informed each subject that (a) one of the main reasons for organizing the research project around the American Red Cross Blood Program was his personal feeling that the ... program served an important social function and needed all the volunteer support it could get, (b) the subject's decision would be regarded as a sincere commitment, and (c) if he signed a pledge card, that card would be forwarded to the Red Cross and a follow-up inquiry would be made to determine whether the pledge was honored. The subject was asked to postpone giving his decision until requested to do so later on, near the end of the interview.

This series of procedures was designed to parallel those that occur in a medical clinic when the relative of a patient with kidney disease is asked to donate a kidney to save the patient's life. The relative is reminded of the strong social and moral arguments for making the donation but at the same time is given realistic information about the suffering and deprivations he will have to undergo and ... [then] is asked to think it over before committing himself (Fellner & Marshall, 1970; Simmons, Klein, & Simmons, 1977).

Immediately after the initial session with the proselytizing investigator, the subject was taken to a separate room and introduced to the interviewer. The interviewer's opening comments were intended to put the subject at ease and to emphasize the differences between his and the investigator's roles in the study. The subject was told, for example, "Unlike Mr.——(the proselytizing investigator), I am *not* primarily interested in whether or not you decide to donate.... Although I personally think donating blood is a good thing to do, I am *primarily* interested in talking with you about a variety of experiences you have had and decisions you have made." In all conditions the interviewer gave this brief endorsement of the blood donation decision. Later, near the end of the session, he asked the subject whether he had decided to respond to the Red Cross appeal for blood donors. Each subject was reassured about the voluntary nature of the interview and the confidentiality of his statements (Mulligan, 1982, pp. 267–68).

One variable that Mulligan investigated involved eliciting a moderate level of self-disclosure during the interview on recent personal decisions versus eliciting a much lower level. (The results for this variable are discussed in the next chapter.) Another variable investigated in the same pair of experiments was positive versus neutral feedback.

Positive feedback included positive social reinforcement and reflective comments. When giving positive social reinforcement, the interviewer praised the subject for having given appropriate answers and for having done "good work" during the interview (e.g., "Very good, those are exactly the kinds of decisions I was looking for; I appreciate your trying as hard as you have to answer my questions"). Reflective comments attempted to concentrate on the essential content of the subject's answers in the manner described by Rogers (1961) (e.g., "So your parents wanted you to continue to attend church, but you felt religion was becoming less relevant each day").

In the *neutral feedback* condition the interviewer tried to maintain a very businesslike exterior. He was silent a much greater percentage of the time than in the positive feedback condition, and his comments were limited to simple acknowledgment that the subject had spoken and had completed an answer to a question (e.g., "Uh-huh; O.K., the next question is . . ."). It should be emphasized, however, that in this condition the interviewer's role was defined as requiring that he withhold explicit positive feedback rather than give negative feedback. Nonverbally the counselor displayed a friendly interest in everything the subject was saying. This type of feedback might have been perceived by the subject as mildly positive rather than neutral (Mulligan, 1982).

Mulligan found that consistently positive feedback from the interviewer, compared with neutral feedback, increased the amount of adherence to the interviewer's recommendation to donate blood to the Red Cross. This was the outcome when the interview elicited self-disclosures that were not directly relevant to the current decisional conflict. But the opposite outcome was obtained when the interview included the additional issue of whether or not to donate blood, which gave the clients the opportunity to express their reluctance to do so. These findings imply that although positive feedback may generally be more effective than neutral feedback in response to a person's self-disclosures, it can be less effective if it reinforces the "wrong" decision from the recommender's standpoint. Even though counselors deliberately attempt to avoid reinforcing "bad intentions," they may inadvertently do so by expressing understanding and empathy during interviews in which clients talk about not wanting to carry out a recommended healthful or socially desirable course of action.

In all the studies just cited, positive feedback took the form of making acceptance statements in response to whatever the clients disclosed about themselves. For example, if a woman who comes for help in the weight-reducing clinic comments favorably about herself as being a prudent and conscientious person, the counselor would respond with a reinforcing comment such as "It's clear that you do have a lot going for you." If the client says something unfavorable about herself by reporting an incident to illustrate her lack of self-control, the counselor would respond with an empathic comment that conveys understanding and continued acceptance, such as "It's quite understandable that you would not approve of such actions and would want to change." Additional ways of presenting positive feedback can be used when clients are being monitored after they have started carrying out a difficult task like dieting. The counselor can make favorable comments about the progress that the clients are making and express his or her belief that they have whatever it takes to succeed at the task.

This form of self-esteem enhancement was used in a field experiment by Smith (1982) studying 40 schoolteachers who were being instructed in a difficult new method of teaching arithmetic to improve their classroom competency. On a random basis, half the teachers were privately given this form of positive feedback by a counselor, focusing on their professional capabilities, during the period when they were attempting to learn and practice the new procedures. The counseling treatment consisted of making encouraging comments about the teacher's progress and their potentialities for mastering the new instructional methods despite whatever problems they were having.

> The setting for the ... study was a workshop for inner-city elementary schoolteachers, who generally lack opportunities for positive feedback in their daily environment. All subjects engaged in self-disclosure of their learning skills and their feelings, specifically about their professional roles and competence. But unlike the earlier experiments involving self-disclosure ..., where positive feedback was given immediately after each of the subject's answers during self-disclosure interviews, positive feedback (self-esteem enhancement) ... was applied to the teachers' performances and spontaneous comments in the workshop. (Smith, 1982, p. 284).

In both experimental and control conditions the instructor provided the training expertise and made all recommendations and suggestions about possible applications of workshop materials in a classroom setting. The author, acting as a tutor and counselor, circulated in the workshop classroom and provided assistance on an individual basis. In the control condition he functioned exclusively as a *tutor,* making comments appropriate to the work task at hand ("Are you ready for the next step?" "If you need help raise your hand." "If there is something you don't understand, please ask about it." "Help each other as much as you can."). In the experimental group the author functioned in the same way as a tutor but he also took on the role of *counselor.* He made the same types of comments about the work tasks as in the control group, but in addition he discussed briefly the problems each teacher was having. His comments consisted of *positive reinforcement statements on each teacher's skills, designed to function as self-esteem enhancement feedback* (e.g., "You're making excellent progress." "No one understands this the first time." "You're doing exceptionally well."

"You have a real talent for this." "I really like what you're doing.")
(Smith, 1982, p. 287. Italics added)

Unobtrusive observations made two weeks later revealed that those
teachers were using the recommended new procedures in their own
classrooms to a much greater extent than were the teachers in the
control group, who had received the same instruction and the same
amount of practice but without the self-esteem enhancement feedback from the counselor. Smith also found that the teachers who
where most responsive to the self-esteem enhancement counseling,
as manifested by their subsequent adherence to the workshop recommendations in their own classrooms, were those who initially
obtained *low* self-esteem scores on the California Personality Inven-
tory. (For the control group, which received a tutoring treatment
that did not involve giving positive feedback that might enhance self-
esteem, no relationship was found between initial level of self-esteem and subsequent adherence to the recommendations.) Smith
points out that the initial low self-esteem scores of those who responded best to the counseling treatment do not necessarily imply
a chronically low level of self-esteem. All of them were working at
inner-city schools under adverse conditions that make for disillu-
sionment and lowering of self-esteem. Their low self-esteem scores
could reflect, therefore, a situationally induced state caused by the
stresses of their work, which might make them especially responsive
to a brief counseling treatment that involves self-esteem enhancement.

Riskind (1982) investigated a different type of self-esteem enhancement in the Yale Weight-Reduction Clinic but it did *not* have
the intended effect of increasing adherence to the counselor's recommendations. He used a "positive disclosure" interview about the
client's assets, capabilities, aspirations, and past achievements, some
of which involved activities having nothing to do with dieting. In
response to the positive self-disclosures the counselor made explicitly positive comments. One form of self-esteem enhancement treatment consisted of pointing out personal strengths and resources that
were applicable to dieting successfully. Another consisted of em-
phasizing the clients' assets that would help them to be generally
successful in life despite any lack of immediate success in dieting.

On a random basis one group of clients was given the first form of treatment, a second group was given the second form, a third group was given both, and a fourth group was given neither.

Riskind's results indicate that both forms of self-esteem enhancement made clients feel much better about themselves (as indicated by their responses on a posttreatment questionnaire), but both failed to have the anticipated effect on adherence to the low-calorie diet. Contrary to expectations, clients given the self-esteem enhancement treatments showed less weight loss after eight weeks than those not given either treatment.

Riskind's self-esteem enhancement treatments may have failed to help the clients adhere to the diet for two reasons. In some clients unearned praise from the counselor may create doubts about the counselor's sincerity; in other clients it may foster complacency, which would reduce their motivation to diet rigorously.

A modified version of the same type of self-esteem enhancement procedure was used with some success in a field experiment by Quinlan, Janis, and Bales (1982). This time the positive disclosure interview was confined to questions relevant to the overweight problem, and the counselor's comments encouraged the clients' expectations of success at dieting without using "hard sell" statements about the clients' hitherto unrecognized assets. And this time the positive disclosure interview proved to be effective both in increasing self-confidence about carrying out the tasks of dieting (as indicated by immediate posttreatment questionnaire responses) and in increasing adherence to the diet (as indicated by subsequent weight loss two months later), provided that the interview was followed during the first month by weekly telephone calls from the counselor. In the absence of such telephone calls, however, the positive disclosure interview was relatively ineffective. These findings lead us to surmise that among many of the clients given the self-confidence enhancement interview there were still some residual doubts about the counselor's sincerity, which did not clear up until the counselor demonstrated genuine interest by making the phone calls.

Whether or not this explanation accounts for the negative findings on adherence in Riskind's study, the crucial point is that in six of the seven pertinent studies consistently positive feedback from the counselor (compared with inconsistently positive and/or neutral feedback) had the effect of significantly increasing adherence to the counselor's recommendations. The tentative conclusion that seems warranted from the series of studies is an affirmative answer to the key question: *Does positive feedback result in more adherence to the counselor's recommendations?* Although the answer from the evidence now at hand is *yes,* some important provisos must be added.

WHAT ARE THE PROVISOS?

One obvious proviso, suggested by Mulligan's (1982) pair of experiments discussed above, is that the counselor must *avoid ambiguity* when expressing understanding and empathy in response to client's disclosures about not wanting to carry out the course of action recommended by the counselor. Ambiguity can inadvertently reinforce the "wrong" decision. The counselor can avoid this error by making favorable comments about the client's honesty (for admitting reluctance to do what is recommended) and then explicity labeling the client's resistance to the recommended course of action as a problem to be overcome in order for the client to achieve his or her goals.

A second major proviso is that the positive feedback from the counselor must be given *consistently,* with no deviating comments and no nonverbal cues that could be construed by clients as indicating criticism, insincerity, and rejection, or exploitative intent. In three of the confirmatory studies carried out in the Yale Weight-Reduction Clinic (which showed that consistently positive feedback from the counselor resulted in a significant increase in subsequent adherence to the counselor's dieting recommendations) we obtained the following surprising, additional results.

1. The study by Dowds, Janis, and Conolley (1982) showed that positive feedback from the counselor throughout a moderate disclosure interview resulted in more subsequent adherence to dietary recommendations (as manifested by weight loss) only if the counselor also gave a positive evaluation to each client's performance when he imposed a minor task (a motivation test). If the counselor told the client that she did not perform as well as expected on the minor task, neutral feedback from the counselor throughout the

interview resulted in more subsequent adherence than did positive feedback.

2. The study by Conolley, Janis, and Dowds (1982) showed that positive feedback thoughout a moderate disclosure interview resulted in more subsequent adherence to dietary recommendations (as manifested by weight loss) only if the minor task (a motivation test) imposed by the counselor was relatively easy. If the minor task was very difficult (making the clients feel that they failed), neutral feedback throughout the interview resulted in more subsequent adherence than did positive feedback.

3. The study by Greene (1982) showed that positive feedback throughout a moderate disclosure interview in a face-to-face session resulted in more subsequent adherence to the dietary recommendations (as manifested by weight loss) only if the counselor seated himself at a normal distance from the client (about two feet away). If the counselor seated himself at a relatively remote distance (about five feet away), neutral feedback throughout the interview resulted in more subsequent adherence than did positive feedback.

To these unpredicted findings I must add that the study by Riskind (1982) not only failed to obtain the expected increase in adherence but obtained a decrease in adherence (as manifested by amount of weight loss) when the counselor gave a supplementary interview in which he responded with consistently positive feedback to whatever answers the clients gave to a series of questions designed to elicit self-disclosures only about the clients' personal assets and past successes. The counselor's acceptance of these positive self-disclosures may have induced in some clients a sense of complacency or self-satisfaction which could lower their motivation to make the effort to adhere to the recommended dietary restrictions. Also, because the counselor gave unearned praise, sometimes accompanied by favorable comments about personal strengths that the clients had not mentioned, some clients may have been skeptical about the counselor's sincerity.

All these unexpected findings, from four different studies of weight loss, indicate that under certain limited conditions we can expect that counselors will *not* increase their effectiveness if they respond with positive feedback during an interview that elicits a moderate level of self-disclosure. Counselors can be expected to fail if they give a great deal of unearned praise or if they are somewhat inconsistent about giving positive feedback in response to the self-disclosures elicited from their clients. The inconsistency may take the form of making just one slight criticism of a client's behavior, demanding that the client carry out a difficult task not directly pertinent to the problem for which the client is seeking help, or presenting nonverbal cues that can be construed as signs of detachment or withdrawal, as when the counselor sits at a relatively remote distance from the client. It must be emphasized that in the studies to which I am referring, each one of these disturbing events was presented in such a mild form that the investigators had not expected it to have any adverse effect at all. Nevertheless, each proved to have a profoundly disturbing and long-lasting effect which was revealed by significantly less weight loss at the time of the follow-up interview five to eight weeks later. The findings suggest that if counselors for any reason find it necessary to expose clients to a disturbing event, such as giving clients an unfavorable rating on a test, they will be better off (from the standpoint of motivating the clients to adhere to their recommendations) if they give neutral feedback, rather than positive accepting feedback, throughout the entire intake interview.

Most surprising is the evidence that the disturbing events, as I have been calling them, actually had a favorable effect on clients who were given neutral feedback. The first study showed that the amount of adherence of the clients who received neutral feedback, when assessed by weight loss eight weeks later, proved to be significantly higher if they had been given an unfavorable rather than a favorable rating on the extraneous motivation test. The second study (in which the disturbing event consisted of a high demand made during the motivation test) and the third study (in which the disturbing event consisted of a remote seating arrangement) showed the same trend, again implying that among clients who are given neutral feedback, subsequent adherence might be increased by inserting one or another of these disturbing events into the intake interview.

The paradoxical findings just reviewed suggest that building up an image of the counselor as a firm, demanding authority figure by withholding positive feedback throughout the entire initial session, and by occasionally expressing mild disapproval or withdrawal, can sometimes have considerable motivating power. Nevertheless, in each of the three experiments, when counselors gave neutral feedback along with one or another disturbing event (unfavorable rating, high demand, or remote seating), they were *not* so successful in inducing subsequent adherence as when they gave consistently positive feedback (with no disturbing event). The difference is statistically significant, however, only in the third study. If this trend continues and proves to be statistically significant in subsequent conceptual replications of these field experiments with clients who meet with a counselor individually or in groups, it will carry the implication that *when counselors are seen by their clients as nurturant supportive helpers they tend to be more successful in inducing adherence than when they are seen as businesslike authority figures who are critical, withdrawn, or excessively demanding.*

By a nurturant supportive helper I mean a person who is seen by the clients as *someone who can be counted on to enhance their self-esteem, provided only that they make a conscientious effort to do what the counselor recommends.* The evidence I have reviewed indicates that counselors can build up this kind of image and thereby elicit increased adherence if, as specified in Phase 1 of the theoretical model for acquiring motivating power, they induce a moderate degree of self-disclosure and give positive feedback, with due regard to the provisos inferred from the unpredicted findings. But the evidence bearing on the provisos suggests that in the first stage, when counselors are starting to build up their motivating power in this way, such power is rather fragile. Clients evidently are extremely sensitive to cues that might show that the counselor has a low opinion of them or will be too hard to please. Any little comment or gesture by the counselor could be misconstrued as a sign of rejection and greatly reduce the counselor's motivating power. Clinical observations from longer term counseling, however, suggest that if the counselor continues to express positive regard most of the time during subsequent sessions, clients can tolerate quite well an occasional criticism of their behavior and an occasional stringent demand that might have had an adverse effect if presented during the first session. That is to say, the motivating power of the counselor might be expected to increase and to become much more robust if the counselor continues to meet the conditions for Phase 1 during the second, third, and fourth sessions. The fragility we noted in our studies might, therefore, prove to be characteristic only of short-term counseling that is limited to just one initial session before the client is expected to adhere to a diet or to carry out some other recommended course of action, as in ten of the eleven studies summarized in this chapter.

What I am saying here may at first seem like a contradiction of what I said earlier in chapter 3 about the effects of increasing the number of sessions. The main conclusion from the available evidence on frequency of contact was that the number of sessions per se is less important as a determinant of adherence than what the counselor does during each session. That conclusion does not preclude the plausible suggestion that, if the counselor continues to do the appropriate things specified for Phase 1 to build up his or her motivating power, each additional session will strengthen the positive effect, contribute to building up a more robust relationship, and lead to more adherence.

The absolute amount of positive feedback that is required during Phase 1 and 2 for a counselor to acquire and maintain motivating power as a dependable enhancer of self-esteem will probably vary from one client to another depending upon the client's chronic level of self-esteem, social competence, and a number of other background characteristics. Among the crucial determinants of individual differences in this respect would be those social background factors that affect the client's *comparison level* (see Thibaut & Kelley, 1959). At one extreme would be an alcoholic ex-executive unable to get a job and long ago kicked out of his own home who is now generally treated as a worthless nobody. Just a few words of genuine noncontingent acceptance by an employment counselor might make a deep impression on someone in such a lowly state, even though the person might at first react in an indifferent or a hostile way on the surface in an effort to protect himself from further humiliation or disappointment. Such a person's comparison level is so low (expecting practically no acceptance at all from an authority figure) that an empathic comment gleams like a campfire in a bleak wilderness. The donor can very quickly become highly prized as the only potentially dependable source of self-esteem enhancement in the client's entire social world.

For a client who is a successful executive, constantly surrounded by admirers, even a long series of noncontingent acceptance comments by a counselor may fail to make much of an impression because they do not reach or exceed the expected level of homage that the client is accustomed to receiving. Furthermore, superstars are supersensitive to signs of ingratiation and may be supersuspicious of genuine noncontingent acceptance as being nothing more than a phony smoke screen to cover manipulative intentions. Counselors may never succeed in becoming sufficiently valued persons to have any effect at all on the level of self-esteem of such clients unless they first prove their value in an extraordinary way, such as by giving uniquely illuminating insights. Consultants to high-level executives sometimes discover that they remain nonentities until they start offering some such rare gems, after which their approval and acceptance are sought.

The *content* of the empathic, appreciative, and approving comments that a counselor offers as noncontingent acceptance responses is probably another important determinant of success in building his or her motivating power with clients who are constantly alert to signs of ingratiation and are concerned about being exploited. Even ordinary citizens have learned to be wary of encounters with manipulative pseudo-admirers, especially of the opposite sex (see Jones, 1964). Most people have had painful experiences of being elated by others who sound as if they mean it when they say, "I'm thrilled to meet you," and "I think you are a wonderful person," but who soon switch to contingent acceptance that is intended to evoke compliance with sexual, financial, or other demands ("I know you are such a wonderful and generous person that you will do this favor for me"). Thus, even though a counselor carefully avoids saying anything that sounds like an obviously ingratiating compliment, he or she nevertheless may arouse wariness by making positive statements that the client finds difficult to regard as credible or that might cue the client to manipulative intent. Probably the best policy in this regard, as well as for ethical purposes, is for the counselor to be completely honest in his or her acceptance statements, avoiding exaggerations or broad generalizations that might be unwarranted when making favorable comments that are likely to be construed as compliments. In order to formulate his or her acceptance statements in an appropriate way the counselor will no doubt have to use a great deal of tact as well as tacit knowledge about each client. This is another of the many aspects of counseling that will continue to require a high degree of artistry even if subsequent research proves to be highly successful in transforming counseling into something more of a science.

After a counselor has acquired a great deal of motivating power as a dependable enhancer of self-esteem by giving consistently positive feedback, as indicated in the discussion of the second and third critical phases of a helping relationship (chaps. 2 and 3), he or she must still exercise considerable skill to maintain motivating power and to use it effectively. There is something fragile about any helping relationship, especially when contact is limited to only a few sessions. The counselor will no longer be perceived as a basically dependable enhancer of self-esteem if his or her demands exceed the bounds of what the client regards as legitimate and reasonable. This is one of the principal reasons that counselors may find it advantageous to *restrict their recommendations to only one specific sphere* when trying to help clients adhere to a stressful course of action, such as abstaining from alcohol or hard drugs, giving up smoking, staying on a diet, or undergoing painful medical treatments.

As long as a counselor continues to give positive feedback, he or she is likely to continue to be regarded as a dependable source of self-esteem enhancement. If the counselor does not make too many demands, his or her endorsements of a given course of action introduce powerful new incentives. The here-and-now reward value in signs of acceptance from a respected helper, which enhance the client's self-esteem, can tip the balance in favor of good intentions at times when the client is tempted to avoid the here-and-now costs and suffering. The new social incentive arising from self-esteem enhancement—built up when the counselor gives positive feedback in response to the client's self-disclosures—seems to compensate for the relative weakness of anticipated long-term gains when the client is reluctant to be committed wholeheartedly to a new course of action requiring short-term deprivations.

The bulk of the evidence presented in this chapter supports the following conclusion: *When a moderate amount of self-disclosure is induced in short-term counseling sessions, the degree to which the clients subsequently adhere to the counselor's recommendations will be increased if the counselor responds to the self-disclosures during the sessions by giving positive feedback, provided that it is given consistently and within the obvious limits of plausibility and credibility.*

5 Eliciting a Moderate Level of Self-disclosure

The theoretical analysis of helping relationships in terms of self-esteem enhancement (chap. 2) asserts that there are two main conditions which, in combination, build up the motivational power of the counselor. One condition involves giving positive feedback, discussed in the preceding chapter. The other is the main topic of this chapter: eliciting self-disclosure. Although the theoretical analysis is vague about the upper limit of self-disclosure that might be optimal, it implies the following general hypothesis: *Counselors will be more effective in inducing adherence to their recommendations if they first elicit a moderate degree*—rather than a very low degree—*of self-disclosure in the initial session with a client* (provided that they give positive feedback in the form of acceptance responses and display no signs of indifference, rejection, or hostility). After describing various ways in which counselors elicit self-disclosures from their clients, I shall summarize the evidence concerning the validity of this hypothesis. I shall then examine studies showing the detrimental effects of eliciting a very high level of self-disclosure. Then, in the final section of the chapter, I shall call attention to ways in which these detrimental effects can be avoided or mitigated when a counselor considers it necessary to induce clients to reveal personal information that they would ordinarily be inclined to withhold even from their intimate friends.

HOW DO COUNSELORS ELICIT SELF-DISCLOSURE?

Sociolinguists point out that no matter how trivial the topic of conversation may be, every verbal interchange entails some self-disclosure (see Labov & Fanshel, 1977). When clients seek help from a professional counselor, they are usually prepared to reveal much more about themselves than when they engage in everyday conversations with acquaintances. The amount they actually do reveal depends to a large extent on where and how the counselor conducts the session.

Physical features of the counselor's office may contribute to a sense of intimacy that makes it easy for clients to speak openly about themselves. These environmental features include cushioned chairs, soft lighting, rugs, and pictures on the wall rather than wooden furniture, fluorescent lighting, bare floors, and bare walls (Chaiken, Derlega, & Miller, 1976). Certificates on the wall showing that the counselor is an authorized professional undoubtedly contribute to an environmental atmosphere conducive to self-disclosure. Arranging the chairs so that there is a normal seating distance of about two feet between counselor and client also encourages self-disclosure during the initial interview (Stone & Morden, 1976).

Once the client starts to tell about his or her troubles, the counselor's response has a profound effect on the client's willingness to reveal additional personal information. The various ways in which counselors give positive feedback—discussed in detail in the preceding chapter—not only affect client's perceptions of the counselor as being warm and empathic but also increase their tendency to disclose private thoughts and even carefully guarded secrets (Krumboltz, Becker-Haven, & Burnett, 1979).

In addition to giving positive feedback, there are other things counselors do that elicit personal information from clients. Sometimes a counselor "primes the pump" by modeling self-disclosure. For example, when a client hints at feeling qualms about becoming too attached to certain friends, the counselor might respond with a similar but somewhat more explicit self-disclosure, such as, "There are times when I, too, have felt a bit scared of my deep feelings for one or another of my friends." Jourard (1971) claims that this kind of modeling is a useful and desirable way to elicit self-disclosure from clients. But other clinical observers strongly disagree on the grounds that it is unprofessional and often impedes rather than facilitates the counseling or therapeutic treatments (see, for example, Polansky, 1967).

Aside from those objections, it is a separate empirical question whether a counselor's modeling of self-disclosure does or does not increase the amount of self-disclosure by clients. Although numerous studies have been carried out, no clear-cut answer can be given to this question, because the results of the various studies do not agree. In reviewing pertinent research, Cormier and Cormier (1980, pp. 95–98) point out that some studies report positive effects while others indicate negative effects and still others suggest that a moderate level of self-disclosure by the counselor may have more positive effects than either a low or a high level. If a counselor discloses a great deal about his or her own feelings and personal life, the clients may become wary about relying on the counselor's discretion and professional skills because the counselor is perceived as untrustworthy, self-preoccupied, or mentally ill (Cozby, 1973; Levin & Gergen, 1969). Taking account of the available evidence, Cormier and Cormier (1980) recommend that counselors engage in self-disclosure to their clients with considerable discretion, making sure that any such disclosures are obviously linked to the client's statements by being similar in content and mood.

Evidence from a systemic study suggests that instructing clients to speak openly is sufficient for eliciting self-disclosure (Stone & Gotlib, 1975). In this study the investigators found that such instructions alone elicited as much self-disclosure as when the instructions were combined with the counselor's modeling of self-disclosure.

Even without giving any explicit instructions, a counselor can induce clients to engage in self-disclosure—and to some extent can control the degree or level of their self-disclosure—by asking appropriate questions during interviews. Particularly during the initial session, the amount of self-disclosure has been found to vary tremendously, depending largely on the questions asked by the interviewer. (The correlation between types of questions asked and amount of self-disclosure elicited is expected to be high when the interviewer is a respected professional counselor, but lower when the interviewer is seen as someone interested only in collecting information in a public opinion poll or, worse yet, a nosy stranger prying into the interviewees' personal life for illegitimate or exploitative purposes.)

In a number of our studies we have investigated the effects of different levels of self-disclosure by varying the content of the counselor's questions while holding constant the personality of the counselor, the length of the interview, the recommendations being made, and everything else we could think of that might affect the outcome

(Janis, 1982a). In these studies, systematic content analysis of the clients' answers to the counselor's questions consistently indicates very large and significant differences in the amount of self-disclosure and degree of intimacy of the disclosures actually induced by interviews designed to elicit a moderate versus a low level of disclosure and also between those designed to elicit a high versus a moderate level. According to the interviewer's notes, the self-disclosures elicited from the clients generally were given in a spontaneous manner, with tone of voice and facial expressions conveying feelings congruent with the intimate information being revealed.

From my own observations of a wide range of levels of self-disclosure elicited in interviews by professional counselors in many different clinical settings, I rate the routine intake interviews conducted in the Yale Weight-Reduction Clinic as eliciting a relatively low level of self-disclosure. These routine interviews are limited to questions about food preferences, eating habits, and related events of daily life. At the opposite extreme are high disclosure interviews, which contain intimate questions about current or past joys and sorrows, body image, sex life, guilt feelings about misbehavior, secret longings, and other such personal information that is sometimes elicited by probing clinicians but is likely to be withheld from most, if not all, members of one's family and close friends. The moderate type of self-disclosure interview, which we have used to supplement the routine interview in the Yale Weight-Reduction Clinic, includes questions about personal strengths and weaknesses, sources of worry, aspirations, and the like, all of which are likely to be discussed openly with good friends and sympathetic relatives but seldom with strangers, unless they are being consulted as professional counselors.

WHEN CLIENTS ARE GIVEN CONSISTENTLY POSITIVE FEEDBACK, DOES INDUCING SELF-DISCLOSURE INCREASE THE COUNSELOR'S EFFECTIVENESS?

Several experiments in our research project were designed to investigate the self-disclosure hypothesis stated at the beginning of this chapter. The first such experiment, which was conducted with 80 women in the Yale Weight-Reduction Clinic by Colten and Janis (1982), can be interpreted as tending to confirm the hypothesis. In this experiment, the *moderate* self-disclosure interview included questions that elicited personal information concerning each client's overweight problem, such as her feelings in connection with overeating and in what ways being overweight affects her family life, relationships with friends, and self-appraisals. The *low* self-disclosure interview asked about eating habits and related factual material about the client's daily life, which involved little or no affect-laden or confidential personal disclosures. Under conditions where the counselor consistently gave positive feedback in response to whatever the clients said, those who were given only the low disclosure interview showed less adherence to the counselor's recommendations (including less weight loss) than those who were given the moderate disclosure interview combined with a balance-sheet procedure. The latter procedure elicited additional self-disclosures concerning the favorable and unfavorable consequences they would expect to experience personally if they adopted the alternative courses of action they were considering for dealing with their overweight problem.

Two similar experiments conducted in the Yale Weight-Reduction Clinic by Quinlan, Janis, and Bales (1982) yield partially confirmatory evidence in support of the self-disclosure hypothesis, together with some indications of limiting conditions. One of these experiments showed that there was a significantly favorable effect on subsequent adherence when the counselors elicited a moderate degree as against a low degree of self-disclosure from the clients. This outcome (more weight loss after eight weeks resulting from the moderate disclosure interview) was found, however, only under certain conditions that were also present in the Colten and Janis (1982) study: namely, when (1) a standard type of intake interview was given containing questions about both positive and negative aspects of the self and (2) no contact occurred between the counselor and the clients during the interval between the initial session and the first follow-up interview. When those conditions were changed (by giving interviews that elicited only positive self-disclosures or by having weekly telephone conversations during the four weeks following the initial session), the outcome was not the same.

Some suggestive evidence from self-reports appears to be consistent with the theoretical assumptions from which the self-disclosure hypothesis was derived. In this pair of experiments there are indications that (1) eliciting self-disclosures about personal short-comings had a favorable effect with regard to subsequent weight loss when it mobilized a self-confrontation in the clients that generated shame and guilt about continuing to be overweight and (2) eliciting self-disclosures about personal assets had a favorable effect insofar as it built up the clients' self-confidence about achieving future success in changing their undesirable behavior. This combination is consistent with the theoretically derived expectation (from the assumptions presented in chap. 2) that as a result of being perceived as an enhancer of the client's self-esteem, a counselor's motivating power will increase if he or she consistently gives acceptance and encouragement while conducting a moderate (rather than low) self-disclosure interview.

A more direct test of the crucial combination of variables is provided by Mulligan's research (1982) with male college students in the setting of a Red Cross blood donation campaign. Mulligan confirmed the positive effects on compliance of eliciting a moderate degree of self-disclosure compared with eliciting a low degree of disclosure. He assessed compliance with the interviewer's recommendation by a behavioral measure: the students' signing of pledge cards to donate blood, which was found to be highly correlated with actually making the donation of blood. As I mentioned earlier (chap. 4), Mulligan also found that positive feedback resulted in more compliance than neutral feedback did, provided that the clients were not given the opportunity to discuss their disinclinations to donate blood by being asked to talk about their current decisional conflict. The most effective set of conditions, then, was just what was expected on the basis of the theoretical analysis of supportive helping relationships (chap. 2): when the interviewer (1) gave a *moderate self-disclosure* (rather than low disclosure) interview and (2) gave consistently *positive feedback* (rather than neutral feedback) in response to the disclosures but (3) *avoided expressing acceptance of the client's reluctance to comply* (by not asking any questions about willingness to comply).

The confirmatory results from Mulligan's research help to preclude the possibility that the theoretical analysis of the first critical phase in the development of motivating power on the part of a counselor or interviewer, with its emphasis on moderate self-disclosure and positive feedback, holds only for people who are especially defective in self-control. All the other supporting evidence, except for Smith's (1982) study of the effects of positive feedback on women teachers who were seeking help in improving their teaching skills (summarized in chap. 4), comes from studies of women who could be regarded as chronically lacking in self-control because they could not control their overeating without external help. Mulligan's findings indicate that inducing a moderate level of self-disclosure and giving positive feedback have essentially the same positive effects on healthy young males (who are not seeking help of any kind) as those we have repeatedly observed among overweight female clients in the weight-reduction clinics.

SHOULD COUNSELORS AVOID ELICITING A HIGH LEVEL OF SELF-DISCLOSURE?

A serious question arises as to whether encouraging as much self-disclosure as possible in the initial interview is effective. On the one hand, high disclosure may increase self-esteem enhancement if a counselor responds to the disclosures with positive feedback. On the other hand, after revealing all sorts of personal weaknesses, the client may feel discouraged or develop negativistic reactions that could impair the counselor–client relationship (see Cozby, 1973; Kaplan, Firestone, Degnore, & Moore, 1974).

The available evidence from our studies does not support the notion that the more disclosure the better. Two weight-reduction studies—one by Quinlan and Janis (1982) and the other by Riskind and Janis (1982)—show that eliciting a relatively high level of self-disclosure, as defined earlier in this chapter, results in less behavioral adherence to the counselor's recommendations than eliciting a moderate level of disclosure. The high self-disclosure interviews used in these studies elicited a great deal of confidential material about the client's weaknesses and shortcomings that seldom, if ever, is disclosed even to intimate friends. They are similar to the probing intake interviews used by some depth psychologists who treat people seeking help to control their eating, smoking, or drinking habits. The findings suggest that, in the absence of additional sessions devoted to psychotherapeutic treatments, such intake interviews are likely to be far less effective in helping the clients change their behavior than those that elicit only a moderate amount of personal information.

Of course, individual differences among clients are to be expected with regard to the upper limit of tolerable self-disclosure beyond which unfavorable effects are likely to be evoked. In their review of cogent research on counseling, Krumboltz, Becker-Haven, and Burnett (1979, p. 572) report that they could find no evidence to support the view that eliciting highly intimate self-disclosure generally leads to more successful outcomes and that a number of studies indicate that "what may be appropriate self-disclosure for one person in a particular situation may not be seen as appropriate for another." Some data, they add, show that "cultural differences exist in what is judged to be appropriate self-disclosure."

In view of the available evidence, counselors would be well advised to avoid trying to induce clients to reveal a great deal of intimate personal information in the initial interview and to be especially alert to signs of embarrassment or discomfort so as not to push any client beyond his or her upper limit of tolerable self-disclosure. Perhaps it is best to err on the side of excessive caution by limiting probing questions to a few general ones, such as "Can you tell me more about that?" and not asking specific probing questions on topics that are likely to be sensitive for the client. Nevertheless, a counselor can end the initial session—as was done in the moderate self-disclosure interviews used in most of our studies in the Yale Weight-Reduction Clinic (Janis, 1982a)—with a general question about whether there are "any personal matters that you think I should know about," which allows the clients to disclose as much or as little about their personal problems as they wish.

WHY DOES ELICITING A HIGH LEVEL OF SELF-DISCLOSURE HAVE DETRIMENTAL EFFECTS?

No definitive answer can be given to this question, but our studies provide suggestive leads to what appears to be going on in the minds of the clients when they are induced to reveal a great deal of personal information. Attitude questionnaire findings in our field experiments that compared the effects of a high versus a moderate self-disclosure interview suggest two likely sources of detrimental effects. Both were also discerned, even more clearly, in a small sample study by Janis and Quinlan (1982) that used more sensitive indicators from intensive process interviews (which provided the series of case studies presented in chap. 4). In this study, 18 clients who came to the weight-reduction clinic were given the intensive process interview immediately after the initial high disclosure or moderate disclosure interview. Two main types of detrimental effects were observed. First, numerous signs indicate that participating in a high self-disclosure interview makes the clients somewhat demoralized. Despite all the acceptance statements made by the counselor in response to disclosures of personal weaknesses, some clients feel dissatisfied with themselves, as well as with the counseling session, and their self-confidence is shaken. When this occurs, the clients feel less certain than ever that they can succeed in carrying out difficult tasks, such as adhering to a low-calorie diet. An initial counseling session that elicits high disclosure from the clients apparently runs the risk of lowering rather than enhancing self-esteem, even when the counselor gives consistently positive feedback.

The second type of detrimental effect, suggested by more indirect and subtle indicators, is a relative increase in conflict about entering into a dependent relationship with the counselor. Many of the clients given a high disclosure interview express vague uneasiness and dissatisfaction about the counseling session. When an effort is made to pin down what is bothering them, some clients admit being concerned about having lost the respect of the counselor or about the threat of somehow being hurt as a result of becoming too trusting, too affectionate, or too dependent upon the counselor. A few explicitly express a sense of vulnerability from having revealed so much. Other clients seem to manifest overinvolvement in the emerging dependent relationship by saying that they really want the counselor to give them more time and more directive advice, not just about the problem at hand (such as being overweight), but also about other problems that were discussed in the high disclosure interview (such as marital difficulties).

Both types of detrimental reactions are well illustrated in the following case material from the Janis and Quinlan study (1982):

Case H-1. This married woman was in her early fifties and had not graduated from high school. She wanted to lose 25 pounds, but during the four weeks after the initial session she reported that she did not adhere to the diet at all and she failed to lose any weight.

At the outset of the initial interview she said, "You people do a lot of good." She added that she had a lot of respect for the clinic because five years earlier she had come to the clinic at Yale for heavy smokers [actually as part of one of our earlier research studies], which helped her to cut down permanently from three packs of cigarettes a day to none at all. In the initial high self-disclosure interview she spoke freely about how unattractive she was and about her concern that her sex life would deteriorate because she would not be able to keep a man interested in her. She revealed that her marriage was breaking up. She had been angry with her husband ever since they quarreled about her having an abortion. Every day, she said, he humiliated her and he constantly got at her through their children. She would leave him if it were not for the children. She also revealed that she now had a boyfriend with whom she would like to run away. The counselor responded to each of these disclosures in a warm, accepting manner, in accordance with the standard procedure of consistently expressing positive regard, which was conscientiously followed by the counselors in all interviews in this study.

On the postinterview questionnaire this woman gave consistently favorable answers. According to her check marks, the interview made her feel better, less discouraged, more willing to diet, more able to control her eating behavior, and more confident that she would succeed in losing weight; she liked and respected the counselor and wanted very much to talk to her again in a month; she believed that the counselor liked her, respected her, really wanted her to succeed, and really cared about what happens to her.

Quite a different picture emerges, however, from the process interview carried out immediately after this woman completed the questionnaire. She started off many of her answers with conventionally polite compliments to the counselor (in agreement with her very positive answers to the questionnaire), but then she went on to describe in much more vivid language the unfavorable feelings engendered by the interview. Here are several examples:

"[The interview] makes you step back and take a closer look at yourself and I think that can be helpful ... *but* I'm unmerciful [to myself] at times.

I feel more confident right now than when I came in ... [*but*] I don't know if I'm motivated enough to really get into this as I should.

I feel a lot happier right at the moment than I was [before the interview]. ... I know it's all up to me *but* maybe I can do it [stick to the diet] if I really want to. It seems that it gets harder all the time; old age has a way of creeping up. ...

[During the interview my mood was] apprehension and depression because I felt, 'Rats, I won't succeed. Do I really want to do this?' ... I'm not sure and that's the truth."

In addition to expressing great conflict about undertaking a rigorous diet and strong doubts about having what it takes to succeed at it, she asserted that the interview generated other self-derogatory thoughts as well. This was most apparent in her response to the following question about feelings of discouragement: "A few women who have been here told me that they felt a bit discouraged or felt dissatisfied with themselves after the interview. Do you have any feelings like that?" Her answer was: "Yes, when I look back over this past year especially, I am much disappointed ... with myself. ... That came out very strongly at one point; I guess that's why I was close to tears."

Along with clear-cut signs of self-derogation and acute decisional conflict about the diet, there were numerous subtle manifestations of conflict about entering into an affectionate relationship with the counselor. Both the positive and negative components of her ambivalence appeared to be related to what she had revealed about herself during the high self-disclosure interview. On the positive side, she said at the beginning of the process interview: "I felt easy with you, which is good. Maybe that's why it all came out." Later on in the interview she added a comment about the counselor's consistent acceptance of her disclosures of personal weaknesses: "Well, you haven't stomped on me or hassled me at all. I like that! You've got a soft sell, I like that! ... You're not trying to cram it down my throat and in the end everybody has got to decide for themselves."

But on the negative side, she also displayed feelings of dissatisfaction because she wanted more directive guidance from the counselor than she was getting, to help her with all her personal problems in addition to the problem of losing weight.

> "I would have wished that you would have told me better how to cope with what's happening to me in all aspects that I mentioned. I would like it if you gave your impressions of . . . my problems. Well, I mean, what you would do in similar circumstances, or something. I don't know what I mean. . . . I wish you'd be more responsive in that area, whatever I brought up. . . . I guess you always hope someone else can help you cope."

The client went on to ask explicitly for more directive advice about how to deal with her marriage and her extramarital affairs. These requests were accompanied by implicit assertions of considerable uneasiness about the possibility of being badly hurt by becoming too affectionate and too dependent upon the counselor. She spoke about having had "few close women friends in my life," then added:

> "I'm more upset than I thought. It just kind of popped out, I'm really quite astonished about that. Sometimes people are too kind and that hurts more. You can bear it more if they are unkind, you can cut them yourself. But if they are maybe too pleasant and kind when you are vulnerable, then, oh I don't know. It's easier to let things out and be hurt, I mean, or feel the hurt, I guess, I don't know. Am I making any sense at all? . . . Maybe you're as vulnerable as me, deep down."

The client's implicit reference to being "cut" by the counselor was not the only danger to which she alluded. Elsewhere during the process interview she asserted that although she was "prepared to bare my soul" to the counselor, she worried that doing so was making the counselor "uncomfortable" and she wondered if the counselor "can understand anything like that." Then she went on to say: "I don't know how to put it; I hoped you didn't have a big mouth anyway." After being reassured that everything she said was confidential and was kept within the clinic, the client responded:

> "Yes, but people are only human . . . and sometimes I've been hurt by people I have trusted, quite often. I'm very gullible . . . I tend to always feel that people are better than they are or that they will do their best because that's what I do. But not everybody else does. You find out the hard way. . . . [During the interview] I had the fleeting thought, 'Oh

fooey, here I am letting my soul hang out and what's she going to do with it? Maybe I made a mistake?' "

While talking about her sense of vulnerability from having re-vealed so much about herself, she asked with some urgency, "How *do* you feel about me?" "But how are you judging me?" After being reassured that the counselor felt that she understood her and thought that her problems could be solved, the client came out with the statement about being disappointed in herself, which brought her close to tears.

One of the outstanding features, then, of this client's process in-terview is the repeated manifestations of ambivalence toward the counselor to whom she had "bared her soul," with some indications that she feared being hurt from allowing herself to become too affectionate and too trusting. Another key feature is her explicit expression of doubts about being able to succeed at the task of dieting, along with feelings of depression and self-derogation.

In the weekly reports she mailed in and again in the follow-up interview the client reported that she had started off dieting for a few days but soon went back to her usual eating habits. When she stepped on the scale at the four-week follow-up session it became apparent that she had not lost even one pound. She claimed that she failed primarily because she had to be out of town, visiting at her father's home, where her stepmother "sabotaged" her diet. What she said about the sabotage, however, sounded very much like an excuse or a rationalization because it would account for only a few hidden calories—her stepmother secretly sprinkled a little sugar on the grapefruit before breakfast and denied doing so.

Signs of ambivalence toward the counselor were again present during the four-week follow-up interview. On the positive side the client answered the question about what she remembered of the interview that took place a month earlier by stating that she really liked the counselor and then giving a glowing account of how won-derfully sympathetic, empathic, and receptive the counselor was. Throughout the follow-up interview the client seemed to be trying to reinstate that type of warm, accepting relationship by wandering off the subject, talking about a number of personal troubles, which required the counselor to bring her back to the specific issues of dieting. The client reported, however, that during the month since the initial session she never even once thought about the counselor or anything the counselor had said. Only vague, dim memories remained of the earlier session with the counselor: "It seems like I saw you six months ago instead of just a few weeks ago."

The client's attitudes and behavior in the follow-up interview consistently suggest that she had adopted a coping pattern of defensive avoidance: not thinking about the counselor or any of the counselor's specific recommendations about dieting. One gets the impression that she overreacted to her fear of being hurt from becoming too affectionately involved with the counselor, which was repeatedly expressed in the process interview at the end of the initial session, by suppressing memories and thoughts about the initial counseling session.

The ambivalence and emotional turmoil that characterized this client's relationship to the counselor were manifested in the intensive process interviews of most other clients who had been given the *high* self-disclosure interview. We noted similar manifestations, including feelings of shame, humiliation, and fears of becoming too deeply attached to the counselor, in a few of the clients who responded to the *moderate* self-disclosure interview by spontaneously revealing a relatively large amount of personal information (although not quite as much as that elicited in most of the high-disclosure interviews). We also observed that among the clients given the *moderate* self-disclosure interview, just as among those given the *high* self-disclosure interview, *the ones who spontaneously disclosed the most tended to be least successful in adhering to the low-calorie diet recommended by the counselor, as manifested by their failure to lose weight.*

Evidently the typical client experiences shame and lowered self-esteem from having come to a weight-reducing clinic, where she has to present herself not only as "fat" but as a weak and perhaps despicable person, lacking in self-control because she cannot stop overeating even though she desperately wants to. Whether the interview induces moderate or high self-disclosure, the client typically expresses much chagrin along with repeated concern about what the counselor "must think of me." A major problem for short-term counseling is to prevent shame or social anxiety from interfering with the helping relationship and, if possible, to transform it into an asset.

One of the main findings from the comparative case studies is that fewer signs of self-derogation and demoralization occur among the clients given the moderate self-disclosure interview than among those given the high self-disclosure interview. It seems as though the occasional revelations about relatively common personal weaknesses evoked by the moderate disclosure interview are about as much disclosure as these clients can bear in the initial session. If the counselor adds to their burdens by asking for fuller disclosure of personal weaknesses in the initial interview—as the pressure of a high caseload might lead psychiatrists, psychologists, or social workers to do in a typical community setting requiring rapid diagnostic workups—the clients' emotional disturbances may seriously impair their relationship with the would-be helpers. . . .

We had not realized until we examined the process interviews that eliciting high self-disclosure was perceived by the clients as making a rigorous *demand* on them during the initial session. We had thought that the clients would realize that they could evade answering if they wanted to because the counselors did not exert any direct pressure and consistently expressed acceptance of whatever they said. But it is apparent that the clients did feel under pressure to answer the personal questions and some said that they had disclosed more than they had wanted to. Perhaps the clients were right about this because of the general demand characteristics of the interview situation. . . .

The negative effects of an initial high disclosure interview on the clients' self-confidence and attitude toward the counselor may be the result of their being induced to disclose too much too soon. In smaller doses, spread over a longer time period, in a less transient relationship with the counselor, a client might be able to speak more freely about his or her personal shortcomings and to come to terms with them without feeling humiliated or ashamed and without developing ambivalent feelings toward the person to whom the disclosures are made. There are even some indications in the present case material that the additional hour or so of interaction in the intensive process interview (which involved eliciting a fairly high degree of disclosure about current weaknesses, fears, conflicts, and aspirations) was sometimes successful in overcoming the detrimental effects of the initial high disclosure interview that had preceded it. (Janis & Quinlan, 1982, pp. 240–41).

In general, clients given a moderate or low self-disclosure interview seem less likely to regard the counselor as someone who could become an indulgent parental figure or as a savior who will solve their problems by telling them exactly what to do. At the end of the initial session they appear to accept with more emotional equanimity a friendly relationship with the counselor and do not feel deprived because of the limited amount of help offered them. They regard the counselor as warm, genuinely helpful, and doing a good job but seem less likely to be hoping to bask in the warmth of intimacy with an invariably affectionate, indulgent parent figure.

CAN THE POTENTIALLY UNFAVORABLE EFFECTS OF HIGH DISCLOSURE INTERVIEWS BE MITIGATED?

Although there is clear-cut evidence from a number of our studies showing that high self-disclosure interviews run the risk of being less effective in inducing clients to adhere to the counselor's recommendations than moderate disclosure interviews, many counselors can be expected to continue to ask personal questions that elicit high disclosure in their intake interviews. Even if they become familiar with the evidence and believe it to be correct, there are two major reasons that they are likely to do so. First, a counselor may be convinced that he or she cannot properly evaluate a client's problem or apply an appropriate counseling strategy without learning about how the problem is related to other important aspects of the person's life, which requires obtaining a great deal of personal information during the intake interview. Counselors who are aware of the potential drawbacks of eliciting intimate disclosures may feel that it is still worthwhile to obtain the intimate material they regard as essential for adequate diagnosis and treatment, relying on their clinical skills to counteract whatever drawbacks may become apparent. Second, many clients who come to a counselor for help are in a perturbed state, thoroughly prepared to talk about what is bothering them. They want to reveal their most pressing difficulties. If the counselor were to try to discourage men and women who are primed to tell their personal story, especially the ones who believe that they should "let it all hang out," those clients would be disappointed and perhaps become less responsive than if they were permitted to unburden themselves despite the drawbacks. (In our studies we regularly encounter a small minority of clients who spontaneously start revealing all sorts of intimate information that is not asked for during the low or moderate self-disclosure interviews.) For these two reasons, despite whatever evidence accumulates on the detrimental effects, I expect that at least for a minority of clients, if not for the majority, intake interviews that elicit high self-disclosure are here to stay.

A few leads concerning ways of mitigating the potentially unfavorable effects of eliciting a high level of self-disclosure have emerged from the research carried out in the Yale Weight-Reduction Clinic and in other settings. One hypothesis suggested by the intensive process interviews I have just discussed is that the decrease in self-confidence and other unfavorable effects resulting from an initial high self-disclosure interview might be counteracted if a retrospective interview were conducted immediately afterward. A *retrospective* interview is one in which the counselor asks the clients to discuss their reactions to the earlier high disclosure interview, allowing them to ventilate whatever misgivings and self-derogatory feelings might have been generated. This type of supplementary interview would, of course, require positive feedback from the counselor to reassure each client that he or she is not despised or thought to be a hopeless case. A crucial component for counteracting the demoralizing effects of high disclosure would be clear-cut signs that the counselor continues to regard the client as worthy of respect and to have high hopes of success on the task at hand, despite all the personal weaknesses and past failures revealed by the client in the intake session.

No systematic study has been done as yet on the effects of a supplementary retrospective interview following high disclosure. But we do have some evidence that a role-playing procedure conveying signs of positive regard on the part of the counselor after a high disclosure interview can have the expected counteracting effect. Riskind and Janis (1982) tried out in the weight-reduction clinic a new procedure designed to build up expectations of social approval by inducing clients to participate in a psychodrama. The scenario focused on the approval they could expect to receive from the counselor if they succeeded in adhering to the recommended diet. In the absence of any such approval training, the clients given a high disclosure interview were relatively unsuccessful in losing weight compared with those given a moderate disclosure interview. But when the social approval training was given right after the interview, the high disclosure interview proved to be relatively more effective than the moderate disclosure interview. The findings indicate that the relatively adverse effects of inducing high disclosure can be modified by the approval training, as manifested by amount of weight loss five weeks later.

These findings can be plausibly interpreted in the following way: Clients who were not given the social approval training felt that they had created an unfavorable impression on the counselor as a result of the derogatory information they had revealed about themselves during the high self-disclosure interview. They had little hope, therefore, of changing the counselor's basically negative attitude toward them even if they were to do all the things recommended. In contrast, when clients were given the approval training after the interview, their hopes in this regard were at least partially restored, so that they left the session in a "steamed up" state similar to those who had received the moderate self-disclosing interview without approval training. Consequently, during the weeks following the interview the expected approval of the counselor may have functioned as an incentive for adhering to the diet only among those high self-disclosure clients who had received the approval training. The important point is that the evidence from the Riskind and Janis study (1982) supports the assumption that the potentially adverse effects of eliciting a high degree of self-disclosure can be reduced and perhaps overcome by using special procedures to restore the motivating power of the counselor.

It should, therefore, be worthwhile to keep an eye on new research on the problem of determining the conditions under which people can tolerate a relatively high degree of self-disclosure. Such research could increase our understanding of the psychology of intimacy and point to additional practical ways of counteracting the potentially unfavorable consequences of inducing clients to disclose personal information.

6 General Guidelines for Decision Counseling

In the preceding chapters we have seen that a counselor's relationship-building interventions can markedly affect the client's motivation to follow his or her recommendations. It is quite clear what recommendations the counselor will make when a client comes for support in carrying out a difficult course of action, such as cutting down on smoking or sticking to a diet. But what recommendations should the counselor make when a client is seeking an answer to a dilemma such as "What is the next step I should take in my life?" Assuming that the counselor can succeed in building up his or her motivational power, what should it be used for? This chapter answers the question by presenting a broad theoretical framework which provides a set of general guidelines for professional counselors when they are dealing with people who ask for help in making vital decisions: for example, choosing a career, entering or quitting college, changing to a different job, getting married or divorced, or undergoing elective surgery.

OBJECTIVES OF DECISION COUNSELING

"Here I am," says the proverbial middle-aged man, "stuck with a miserable career chosen for me by an uninformed 19-year-old boy." Why do so many young people make choices they live to regret? Why do so many middle-aged men and women fail to correct their erroneous decisions of the past and continue to make poor choices? Similar questions can be raised about all sorts of ill-conceived decisions by people of all ages and in all walks of life. In recent years research investigators in social psychology, cognitive processes, and various other areas of psychology have been trying to answer such questions, to explain why people so often make decisions in public

This chapter is based on Janis and Mann (1977, 1982) and Wheeler and Janis (1980).

or private life that give rise to fiascoes. Some of the theoretical concepts and findings that have emerged point to ways of preventing gross miscalculations and improving the quality of decision making, which are the primary objectives of decision counseling.

By asking certain types of questions, supplying information, and introducing specific intervention techniques, a counselor can help clients go through a recommended series of decision-making stages in order to arrive at a sound choice that takes full account of their personal values and goals. The interventions are designed to aid clients in selecting effective courses of action that they will not regret. Many counselors abstain from making the choice for the client; they avoid recommending any particular course of action as the best one. Rather, these counselors limit their interventions to making recommendations about decision-making *procedures* that could improve the quality of the clients' search and appraisal activities in order to help them use their own resources to make choices they can live with. These decision counselors do not refrain from using their expert, legitimate, and referent power to convey norms, but the norms they talk about pertain to avoiding making a choice on an impulsive or a defensive basis. What they advocate is that their clients spend the necessary time and effort seeking clarification of the issues involved, striving to be open-minded while carrying out the essential procedures for effective decision making. This approach to decision counseling appears to be well warranted on the basis of psychological research (see Janis & Mann, 1977).

What decision-making procedures should a counselor recommend? On the basis of the relevant research literature, the following seven problem-solving procedures have been extracted as the basic ones for arriving at a sound decision (Janis & Mann, 1977): The decision maker (1) thoroughly canvasses a wide range of alternative courses of action; (2) takes account of the full range of objectives to be fulfilled and the values implicated by the choice; (3) carefully weighs whatever he or she knows about the costs or drawbacks and the uncertain risks of negative consequences, as well as the positive consequences, that could flow from each alternative; (4) intensively searches for new information relevant to further evaluation of the alternatives; (5) conscientiously takes account of any new information or expert judgment to which he or she is exposed, even when the information or judgment does not support the course or action he or she initially prefers; (6) reexamines the positive and negative consequences of all known alternatives, including those originally regarded as unacceptable, before making a final choice; and (7) makes detailed provisions for implementing or executing the chosen course of action, with special attention to contingency plans that might be required if various known risks were to materialize.

Failure to meet any of these seven criteria is assumed to be a defect in the decision-making process. Decisions that suffer from most or all of these defects generally have much less chance of success than those that do not. The more of such defects that are present before the decision maker becomes committed, the greater are the chances that he or she will undergo unanticipated setbacks and postdecisional regret, which make for reversal of the decision. Although systematic data are not yet available on this point, it seems plausible that "high quality" decisions—in the sense of satisfying these procedural criteria—have a better chance than others of attaining the decision maker's objectives and of being adhered to in the long run.

CRUCIAL STAGES IN MAKING A DECISION

Five main stages in arriving at a *stable* decision and the major concerns associated with each are summarized in Table 6.1. The stages were inferred mainly from observations of people who made decisions that they subsequently carried out *successfully,* compared with people who committed themselves to the same types of decisions but subsequently *regretted* having done so and *failed* to adhere to them. If decision makers omit any of the stages prior to committing themselves, or carry any of them out in a perfunctory manner, they will not meet one or another of the criteria for sound decision making. When that happens, as I have already indicated, the decision makers are likely to overreact with postdecisional regret and reverse the decision soon after the first difficulties arise. This assumption appears to be plausible for for a wide variety of personal decisions (see Janis & Mann, 1977, chap. 7).

Stage 1: Appraising the Challenge

Decision making begins when a person is confronted with a challenge to his or her current course of action. The challenge can be

Table 6.1. Stages in arriving at a stable decision (Based on Janis and Mann, 1977)

Stage	Key questions
1. Appraising the challenge	Are the risks serious if I don't change?
2. Surveying alternatives	Is this (salient) alternative an acceptable means of dealing with the challenge?
	Have I sufficiently surveyed the available alternatives?
3. Weighing alternatives	Which alternative is best?
	Could the best alternative meet all essential requirements?
	If the best alternative is unsatisfactory, could one of the existing alternatives be modified to meet all essential requirements?
4. Deliberating about commitment	Shall I implement the best alternative and allow others to know?
	If the best alternative is satisfactory, what are the drawbacks or obstacles to implementing it and allowing others to know my choice?
5. Adhering despite negative feedback	Are the risks serious if I *don't* change?
	Are the risks serious if I *do* change?

either events or communications that convey threats or opportunities. The central question facing a decision maker during this stage is whether the threat or opportunity is important enough to warrant the effort of making an active decision about it. Ignoring or rejecting the challenge leads to complacent pursuit of the original course of action without any change, simply continuing business as usual. Once the decision maker gives a positive response to the first key question, he or she accepts the challenge and decides to decide. This promptly leads to the next stage of active decision making.

Stage 2: Surveying Alternatives

After their confidence in the desirability of the old course of action has been shaken by the information contained in the challenge, vigilant decision makers begin searching for alternatives (Stage 2). They consider their goals or values relevant to the decision and search carefully for available courses of action that have some promise of achieving the goals. They become more attentive to recommendations from experts or acquaintances for dealing with the challenge, even though the advice may be inconsistent with their present commitments. Most decision makers are inclined, of course, to cling to the policy to which they are currently committed, if possible. But after a powerful challenge they are hungry for fresh information about better alternatives.

Stage 3: Weighing Alternatives

During Stage 3 the advantages and disadvantages of each alternative are carefully considered. This stage usually involves substantial effort in searching for dependable information relevant to the expected utilities of the outcomes and the likelihood that each of the possible outcomes will occur. Vigilant decision makers seek facts and forecasts from a wide variety of sources about all the various consequences of the alternatives they are considering. They carefully weigh new evidence that may go against their initial preference. At the end of Stage 3 the cautious decision maker usually reaches a tentative decision based on all the information he or she has gathered.

Stage 4: Deliberating about Commitment

After having tacitly decided to adopt a new plan of action, the decision maker enters Stage 4, in which he or she considers implementing the plan and conveying the intention to do so to others. Whether he or she is about to stop smoking, get married, change to a new job, or start a lawsuit, the decision maker realizes that sooner or later people in his or her social network who are not directly implicated (family, friends, business associates, and casual acquaintances) will find out about it. As a vigilant decision maker the person becomes concerned about their possible disapproval, which he or she may not have thought about earlier. These fresh concerns deter the person from taking immediate action without first paving the way by giving intimates an inkling of the direction in which he or she is moving. Before letting others know about the chosen course of action—particularly if it is a controversial one, such as seeking a divorce—the person will be inclined to think up ways of avoiding disapproval from family, friends, and other reference groups. This often leads to working out social tactics and auxiliary contingency plans for ensuring the success of a new decision (e.g., preparing strong arguments to give those who might object). During this stage, decision makers also reexamine the information they have gathered on practical difficulties in implementing the decision, figure out how to overcome them, and make contingency plans for losses that are likely to materialize.

Stage 5: Adhering Despite Negative Feedback

Many decisions go through a honeymoon period in which the decision maker is quite happy about the choice and implements it without any qualms. All too often, however, this idyllic postdecisional state is rudely interrupted, sooner or later, by setbacks or temptations that create regret. In Stage 5, decision makers are inclined to discount any minor challenges in the form of new threats or opportunities. They tend to give a negative response to the initial key question for this stage (Are the risks serious if I *don't* change?). When major setbacks or losses occur, however, they may give a positive response to this key question, in which case Stage 5 becomes equivalent to Stage 1 of a new decision. Nevertheless, Stage 5 is different from Stage 1 when the person has carefully gone through all the preceding stages in arriving at a stable decision: Even though the challenge may be a strong one, the decision maker tends to be only temporarily shaken and to end up deciding not to give up implementing the decision.

A person will remain in Stage 5 indefinitely, until he or she encounters a challenge that is so powerful as to provoke intense dissatisfaction with the chosen course of action. Then the decision maker embarks once again on a painful tour through the successive stages, this time seeking a different and better alternative. Obviously, the stability of a decision depends to a substantial degree upon the amount and intensity of negative feedback the person encounters when carrying out the chosen course. But stability also depends upon the person's *capacity to tolerate negative feedback,* which, in turn, depends partly on how completely and accurately he or she has worked on the essential tasks during the preceding stages of arriving at the decision.

The specific stage reached by a client cannot always be sharply differentiated by the counselor because earlier key questions keep cropping up if they have not been resolved. In presenting a schematic description of the stages of decision making, I do not intend to imply that a vigilant decision maker always proceeds in a completely orderly way. Some decisions appear to move along in linear fashion from Stage 1 to Stage 5, but many involve a great deal of fluctuation back and forth. Reverting to Stage 2 from Stage 3 or 4 is especially likely if the decision involves changing social affiliations, as when a person is contemplating divorce, converting to another religion, or switching membership from one organization to another.

CLIENTS' PROBLEMS: EXCESSIVE DELAY AND PREMATURE CLOSURE

The seven procedural criteria and the five stages of vigilant decision making can be regarded as *prescriptive norms*. They specify what a person should strive to do in order to avoid making regrettable errors in selecting a course of action. But they certainly do not furnish an adequate description of the way most men and women make their decisions most of the time. When we look into accounts of how people actually do make decisions, we soon discover that they often deviate from these prescriptive norms.

One common problem among clients who seek help on vital decisions involves *excessive delay in arriving at closure*. This may be a result of vacillation, which greatly prolongs the early stages of decision making, or procrastination, which postpones carrying out the essential tasks of search, appraisal, and choice. At the opposite extreme are clients who are all too ready to indulge in *premature closure*. They are inclined to commit themselves impulsively without going through the earlier stages that are requisite for arriving at a sound choice. Some clients at either extreme may benefit considerably from a few sessions with a decision counselor who guides them through the essential stages.

There is undoubtedly much room for improvement in the information-seeking and appraisal activities of most people. This has been a neglected social problem for which new solutions, in the form of special counseling services and innovative educational programs, are now being developed to aid people facing fundamental life decisions. A new type of counseling service might also help persons in low-income families to become aware of the hidden consequences of the limited alternatives available to them and to work out personal or collective strategies for opening up more choices.

Decision makers who are threatened by a loss of self-esteem in the face of a decision dilemma that is extremely difficult to resolve can be helped by a counselor who builds up their confidence about being able to arrive at a sound decision and to adhere to it. But a few sessions of decision counseling obviously cannot be expected to overcome deep-seated neurotic disorders that give rise to chronic procrastination, chronic evasion of responsibility, or chronic denial of unfavorable outcomes. Probably some persons are predisposed to display time and again the same defective coping pattern, irrespective of the issues at stake or the situational opportunities and constraints that uniquely characterize each decision. If so, they require intensive psychotherapy or other psychological treatments far beyond the scope of decision counseling.

Nevertheless, even with clients who appear to be chronically inhibited, evasive, or impulsive when making vital decisions, it may be worthwhile to try a bit of decision counseling. All too often counselors encounter clients who regard themselves as hopeless failures as a result of their past mistakes. Some of them are in utter despair and believe it is too late to change their lives, like the central character in Saul Bellow's *Seize the Day:*

> [F]or three months Wilhelm delayed his trip to California. He wanted to start out with the blessings of his family, but they were never given. He quarreled with his parents and his sister. And then, when he was best aware of the risks and knew a hundred reasons against going and had made himself sick with fear, he left home. This was typical of Wilhelm. After much thought and hesitation and debate he invariably took the course he had rejected innumerable times. Ten such decisions made up the history of his life. He had decided that it would be a bad mistake to go to Hollywood, and then he went. He had made up his mind not to marry his wife, but ran off and got married. He had resolved not to invest money with Tamkin, and then had given him a check.

Despite a history of ten poor decisions, which could imply a chronic neurosis or a deep-seated character disorder, such a person might still learn something in a few sessions with a decision counselor that would enable him to do much better on the eleventh decision and perhaps even to correct some of his past mistakes. But, of course, the prospects for successful decision counseling are much better with people who do *not* have a history of chronically poor decision making. For such clients who seek help at times when they are having unusual difficulty with a particular decision, a session or two with a skilled counselor has a good chance of bringing about a marked improvement in the quality of their decision-making procedures.

EFFECTS OF PSYCHOLOGICAL STRESS ON RATIONALITY

During the past three decades, models of rational choice, based on "game theory" and "subjective expected utility" theory, have been dominant in the psychological research literature on decision making. These models assume that decision makers deliberately choose their courses of action on a rational basis by taking account of the values and the probabilities of the consequences that would follow from selecting each of the available alternatives. (See, for example, Edwards 1954; Miller & Star, 1967; Raiffa, 1968.) They have led to new developments of formal methods for decision analysis, which provide some useful normative rules that specify how people should make sound decisions when they have to take risky actions (see Wheeler & Janis, 1980). One central idea is that it is essential to make the best estimates of the probability that each of the expected consequences will occur; another is that the relative importance of each of the anticipated favorable and unfavorable consequences should be taken into account—their expected utility value from the decision maker's own standpoint.

Although valuable for prescriptive purposes, rational models run into considerable difficulties when they are proposed as *descriptive* theories that explain how people actually do make decisions. (See, for example, Broadhurst, 1976; Kahneman & Tversky, 1979; Nisbett & Ross, 1980.) One major reason that people deviate from a rational model pertains to the cognitive limitations of the human mind (see Simon, 1976). People simply cannot understand and keep in mind all the relevant information needed for optimal solutions to the decision-making problems they face. Furthermore they do not have at their command all the necessary knowledge about cause-and-effect relationships and all the data essential for making accurate probability estimates of alternative outcomes. Other sources of error involve misinformation, prejudice, and reliance on faulty rules-of-thumb (heuristics) or misleading analogies. Still another major reason that people do not consistently follow rational procedures has to do with the effects of emotions on the cognitive processes involved in decision making. This is where psychological stress enters the picture.

Stress can arise from the decision makers' awareness of their own limited knowledge and problem-solving capabilities in the face of a consequential dilemma. Major sources of stress include fear of suffering from the known losses that will be entailed by whichever alternative is chosen, worry about unknown things that could go wrong when vital consequences are at stake, and concern about making a fool of oneself in the eyes of others or losing self-esteem if the decision works out badly. Vital decisions often involve conflicting values, which cause the decision maker to realize that any choice he or she makes will require sacrificing ideals. As a result the decision maker's anticipatory anxiety, shame, or guilt is increased, which adds to the level of stress.

When the level of stress is very high, the decision maker is likely to display *premature closure*—terminating the decisional dilemma without generating all the alternatives and without seeking or appraising the available information about the outcomes to be expected for the limited set of alternatives under consideration. A high level of stress reduces the decision maker's problem-solving capabilities, especially when he or she is dealing with the complicated cognitive tasks posed by decisions that are difficult because of numerous competing values. The person's attention and perceptions are somewhat impaired and there are various manifestations of cognitive rigidity. These cognitive deficiencies result in narrowing the range of perceived alternatives, overlooking long-term consequences, an inefficient information search, an erroneous assessment of expected outcomes, and the use of oversimplified decision rules that fail to take account of the full range of values implicated by the choice. There are various cognitive crutches that many people rely on when beset by uncertainties and threats that generate stress. A common example is to decide on the basis of what friends or relatives seem to want one to do without considering the main outcomes to be expected. Another is to rely on a general formula based on popular proverbs, religious principles, or an analogy to a past decision as the primary guide to action, without examining in detail the specific issues at hand.

Stress encroaches most profoundly on decision-making processes when a person is in a dilemma about what to do about imminent dangers that could undermine his or her career, love life, or physical well-being. Threats of physical suffering, bodily injury, or death are especially likely to lead to gross deviations from the decision-making behavior predicted by descriptive rational models for many crucial decisions, such as those made by people who need medical treatments or surgery. For example, the vast majority of patients with acute myocardial infarctions, according to Hackett and Cassem (1975), realize that they may be having a heart attack but delay calling a physician for four or five hours. "The decision making process," these researchers assert, "gets jammed by the patient's inability to admit that he is mortally sick" (p.27). Similarly, maladaptive delays of weeks or months, which significantly increase the chances of dying, have been observed among patients suffering from symptoms of cancer (e.g., Blackwell, 1963; Kasl & Cobb, 1966). Few of the patients who postpone having a medical examination are unaware of the danger. The majority have been found to be familiar with the danger signs of cancer, more so than patients who decide to seek medical aid promptly (Goldsen, Gerhardt, & Handy, 1957; Kutner, Makover, & Oppenheim, 1958). The most plausible explanation for the delay seems to be that the patients fail to make a decision on a rational basis because they are trying to ward off anxiety by avoiding exposure to threat cues, such as distressing information from a physician.

Clients who seek a counselor's help because they do not know what to do about an acute dilemma—whether it involves their health, career, finances, social life, marriage, or family problems—are likely to cope with the stresses of the decisional conflict by short-circuiting the essential stages of search and appraisal. Decision makers are often inclined to deceive themselves into thinking they have conducted a complete information search after brief contact with a so-called expert and perhaps a few informal discussions with friends and acquaintances. This sometimes happens even when the decision is a crucial one that could entail serious, lifelong consequences. In such instances, a decision counselor can serve a number of valuable functions. Even highly experienced decision makers might benefit from professional guidance designed to help them to carry out a more effective information search, correct some of their biased judgments, and become more aware of the consequences of inadequate courses of action that they might be tempted to choose.

THE CONFLICT-THEORY MODEL

Stress does not always have detrimental or maladaptive effects. On the contrary, anticipatory fears of undergoing undesirable losses sometimes prevent premature closure. Such concerns can serve as incentives to carry out the adaptive "work of worrying," which leads to careful information search and appraisal (see Janis, 1958, 1971; Janis & Mann, 1977). This brings us to another major problem that requires theoretical analysis and empirical research: Under what conditions does stress have favorable versus unfavorable effects on the quality of decision making? In other words, when is stress healthy and when not?

A conflict-theory analysis formulated by Janis and Mann (1977) attempts to answer this question as well as the broader question I alluded to earlier concerning the conditions under which people will use sound decision-making procedures to arrive at a rational choice. It focuses on the different ways in which people deal with stress when they are making vital decisions, contrasting those coping patterns that result in defective forms of problem solving with a vigilant coping pattern that generally meets the standards of sound decision making.

An initial assumption is that stress engendered by decision conflict frequently is a major determinant of failure to achieve high quality decision making. *Decisional conflict* refers to opposing tendencies within the individual to accept and at the same time to reject a given course of action. The most prominent symptoms of such conflicts are hesitation, vacillation, feelings of uncertainty, and signs of acute psychological stress (anxiety, shame, guilt, or other unpleasant affect) whenever the decision comes to the focus of attention.

Psychological stress arising from decisional conflict stems from at least two sources. First, the decision maker is concerned about the material and social losses he or she might suffer from whichever course of action is chosen—including the costs of failing to live up to prior commitments. Second, the person recognizes that his or her reputation and self-esteem as a competent decision maker are at stake. The more severe the anticipated losses, the greater the stress. In assuming that the stress itself is frequently a major cause of errors in decision making, we do not ignore the influence of other common causes, such as information overload and the limitations of human information processing, group pressures, blinding prejudice, ignorance, organizational constraints, and bureaucratic politics. We maintain, however, that a major reason for many ill-conceived and poorly implemented decisions is the motivational consequences of decisional conflict, particularly attempts to ward off the stresses generated by agonizingly difficult choices.

In line with our initial assumption, we postulate that there are five basic patterns of coping with the stresses generated by any realistic challenge that confronts a person with a vital choice (Janis & Mann, 1977, chap. 3). Each pattern is associated with a specific set of antecedent conditions and a characteristic level of stress. These patterns were derived from an analysis of the research literature on psychological stress bearing on how people react to warnings that urge protective action to avert health hazards or other serious threats.

The five coping patterns are:

1. *Unconflicted adherence.* The decision maker complacently decides to continue whatever he or she has been doing, ignoring information about the risk of losses.
2. *Unconflicted change to a new course of action.* The decision maker uncritically adopts whichever new course of action is most salient or most strongly recommended.
3. *Defensive avoidance.* The decision maker escapes the conflict at least temporarily by procrastinating, shifting responsibility to someone else, or constructing wishful rationalizations to bolster

the least objectionable alternative, remaining selectively inattentive to corrective information.

4. *Hypervigilance.* The decision maker searches frantically for a way out of the dilemma and impulsively seizes upon a hastily contrived solution that seems to promise immediate relief, overlooking the full range of consequences of his or her choice as a result of emotional excitement, perseveration, and cognitive constriction (manifested by reduction in immediate memory span and simplistic thinking). In its most extreme form, hypervigilance is referred to as "panic."

5. *Vigilance.* The decision maker searches painstakingly for relevant information, assimilates information in an unbiased manner, and appraises alternatives carefully before making a choice.

Although the first two patterns are occasionally adaptive in saving time, effort, and emotional wear and tear, especially for routine or minor decisions, they often lead to defective decisions if the person must make a choice that has serious consequences for himself, for his family, or for the organization he or she represents. Similarly, defensive avoidance and hypervigilance may occasionally be adaptive but generally reduce the decision maker's chances of averting serious losses. Consequently, all four are regarded as defective patterns of decision making when serious consequences are at stake. The fifth pattern, vigilance, although occasionally maladaptive if danger is imminent and a split-second response is required, generally leads to decisions that meet the main criteria for rational or sound decision making (see Table 6.2).

According to the conflict-theory model, people will weigh the benefits of a recommended course of action against the perceived costs or barriers to taking that action, as is assumed by rational-choice models, *only when their coping pattern is vigilance.* When any of the four defective coping patterns is dominant, the decision maker will fail to carry out adequately the cognitive tasks that are essential for arriving at stable decisions. Then, when they experience undesirable consequences, such as the usual unpleasant side-effects of a standard medical treatment or unexpected demands for overtime work shortly after starting on a new job, they are likely to overreact to the minor challenge. They suffer not just from the dis-

Table 6.2. Predecisional behavior characteristic of the five basic patterns of decision making

	Criteria for high-quality decision making							
	(1)	(2)	(3) Careful evaluation of consequences		(4)	(5)	(6)	(7)
Pattern of coping with challenge	Thorough canvassing of alternatives	Thorough canvassing of objectives	a. Current policy	b. New policies	Thorough search for information	Unbiased assimilation of new information	Careful reevaluation of consequences	Thorough planning for implementation and contingencies
Unconflicted adherence	−	−	−	−	−	+	−	−
Unconflicted change	−	−	+	−	−	+	−	−
Defensive avoidance	−	−	−	−	−	−	−	−
Hypervigilance	−	−	±	±	±	−	−	−
Vigilance	+	+	+	+	+	+	+	+

Source. Janis & Mann, 1977.

All evaluative terms such as *thorough* and *unbiased* are to be understood as intrapersonal comparative assessments, relative to the person's highest possible level of cognitive performance.

Notes. +, the decision maker meets the criterion to the best of his ability; −, the decision maker fails to meet the criterion; ±, the decision maker's performance fluctuates, sometimes meeting the criterion to the best of his ability and sometimes not.

tressing setback itself but also from strong feelings of postdecisional regret, which may interfere with their ability to curtail the losses or to make a sound new decision that will enable them to recover rapidly from the setback. Postdecisional regret often entails intense emotional arousal, such as anxiety and rage, which makes for a high level of stress and could give rise to psychosomatic disorders.

What are the conditions that make for vigilance and how do they differ from those that make for each of the four defective coping patterns? The answer to this question is presented in Figure 6.1, which is a schematic summary of the conflict theory of decision making. This conflict model specifies the psychological conditions responsible for the five coping patterns and the level of stress that accompanies them.

The coping patterns are determined by the presence or absence of three psychological conditions: (1) awareness of serious risks for whichever alternative is chosen (i.e., arousal of conflict), (2) hope of finding a better alternative, and (3) belief that there is adequate time in which to search and deliberate before a decision is required. Although there may be marked individual differences in preference for one or another of the coping patterns, all five patterns are assumed to be in the repertoire of every person when he or she functions as a decision maker. In different circumstances the same person will use different coping patterns depending on which of the three crucial conditions are present or absent.

The theoretical analysis of vigilant versus defective patterns of coping with decisional conflict has some direct implications for counseling designed to help people improve the quality of their decision making. Some of the main implications will be discussed shortly; other implications will be examined in the next chapter, where the results of field experiments on the balance-sheet procedure, outcome psychodrama, and several other new types of intervention are described. With appropriate changes, the general guidelines and proposed interventions probably can also be used by a consultant who is asked for advice by a chief executive or group seeking help in arriving at major decisions affecting the welfare of their organization.

At present the majority of counselors and consultants use a completely improvised approach, relying on their personal sensitivity,

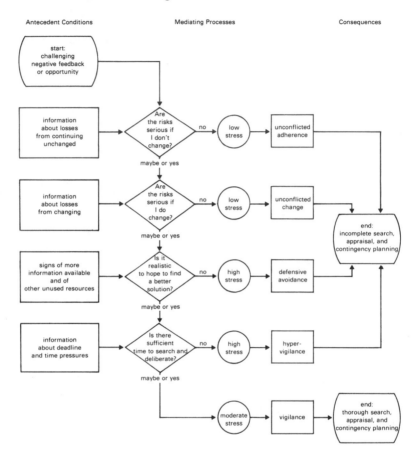

Figure 6.1.   Conflict-theory model of coping patterns (based on Janis & Mann, 1979).

intuition, and clinical experience to determine what they say to their clients. In contrast, the proposed guidelines based on the conflict-theory model provide a more structured approach, including a set of standard diagnostic procedures and corresponding interventions that take account of what is now known about the psychology of decisional conflict. Although highly structured, the proposed coun-

seling procedures still leave plenty of room for flexibility, improv-
isation, and artistry.

COUNTERACTING DEFECTIVE COPING PATTERNS

In only one or two hours of counseling, the strategies and interventions suggested by the conflict-theory model may prove to be effective for many clients. The decision-counseling guidelines are intended
primarily for people who occasionally display the common varieties
of defective coping patterns.

At the beginning of the first session the decision counselor asks
the client to discuss the important issues involved in the decision
and to talk about the steps he or she is planning to take before
making a final choice. During the interview, the counselor can use
his or her clinical skills to help the client speak frankly and not
cover up emotionally sensitive topics by resorting to conventional
evasions. This, of course, involves eliciting self-disclosures, which
can be kept to a moderate level; the counselor can respond to the
client's self-disclosures by expressing acceptance and giving other
forms of positive feedback (see chaps. 4 and 5).

Decision counseling, although different from psychotherapy, can
make use of some of the strategies used by many well-trained psychotherapists (see Corsini, 1968; Garfield & Bergin, 1978). For example, when clients want to be told which course of action they
should follow, the counselor can avoid taking on the role of an
authority figure who tells them what to do, consistently conveying
the notion that all decisions are being left up to them as their own
responsibility. Nevertheless, the decision counselor can strongly recommend careful appraisal of alternatives and effectively use other
interventions that are directive in guiding the client through the
essential stages of decision making.

From a free-style diagnostic interview, using the items in part A
of Table 6.3 as guidelines, the counselor should be able to diagnose
the client's current coping pattern on the basis of answers to the
four key questions from the conflict model. Once this diagnosis is
made, the conflict model suggests what the counselor can do to help
counteract whichever defective coping pattern the client may be

Table 6.3. Diagnostic questions (based on the conflict-theory model) to be answered by the decision counselor in order to determine the most appropriate interventions.

A. *Reactions to the challenging threat or opportunity*
1. Does the client believe that the risks are serious if his or her present course of action is *not* changed?
2. Does the client believe that the risks are serious if his or her present course of action *is* changed?
3. Does the client believe that it is realistic to *hope* to find a satisfactory alternative?
4. Does the client believe that there is sufficient *time* to search for and evaluate a satisfactory alternative?

B. *The client's decisional balance sheet*
   For each of the alternatives he or she is contemplating, how completely and accurately has the client taken account of the full set of consequences pertaining to:
1. Utilitarian gains and losses for self?
2. Utilitarian gains and losses for significant others?
3. Self-approval or self-disapproval?
4. Social approval or disapproval from significant others?

Source. Janis & Mann, 1977.

displaying. The following prescriptive hypotheses specify general counseling procedures for promoting vigilant search and appraisal.

1. Suppose that the client is ignoring a challenging threat and appears to be showing *unconflicted adherence* to whatever course of action or inaction he or she has been pursuing. What the counselor can do is raise questions that induce the client to consider the possible unfavorable consequences of ignoring the threat and encourage the client to obtain objective information and expert opinion about the costs and risks of not changing.

2. Suppose that the counselor has a client who is not ignoring a challenging threat but sees no serious risks in adopting a protective course of action and appears to be on the verge of *unconflicted change*. What the counselor can do is encourage the client to obtain objective information and expert opinion about the risks of making the intended change and to consider carefully the un-

favorable outcomes that might otherwise be overlooked, including potential losses from failing to live up to prior commitments.

3. Suppose that the counselor has a client who expresses little hope about resolving an acute decisional conflict and appears to be displaying one of the three forms of *defensive avoidance*—procrastinating, shifting responsibility to someone else, or bolstering the least objectionable alternative with rationalizations. What the counselor can do is try to build up a more optimistic outlook. One of the main ways of doing so is to encourage the client to discuss the dilemma with respected individuals in his or her personal network of relatives, friends, and advisers. They might supply new perspectives, which could raise the client's hope of finding a satisfactory solution. The counselor might also recommend appropriate experts who could be consulted. Above all, the decision counselor can convey a sense of optimism about the client's chances of finding a good solution to the problem. This can be done most effectively when the counselor has already built up a good working relationship with the client so that he or she is regarded as a dependable source of self-esteem enhancement, as described in chapter 2.

4. Suppose that the counselor has a client in a state of acute conflict who believes there is insufficient time to find a good solution and is displaying panicky vacillation along with other symptoms of *hypervigilance*. What the counselor can do is give realistic reassurances about what can be accomplished before the final deadline. Sometimes it is also appropriate to encourage the client to find out whether the deadline is negotiable, to see if he or she can obtain an extension without serious costs or risks.

More than one of these four general guidelines may be applicable to the same client as he or she moves through the successive stages of decision making. For example, the first one might be applicable at the outset if the client is ignoring a challenging threat. Later on, one or more of the other prescriptive hypotheses might become applicable as the client changes his or her answers to the key questions in response to new information obtained about probable losses, resources available for working out a good solution, and deadlines.

Of these four general guidelines, it is the third that is likely to be most relevant for most clients who seek help in making or adhering to vital decisions. Defensive avoidance appears to be an extremely frequent coping pattern that people display when confronted with the most serious dilemmas of their lives. This is the pattern that most often tends to be dominant among clients who come to counselors at times when they are demoralized and feel rather hopeless about the future.

ILLUSTRATIVE APPLICATIONS IN HEALTH COUNSELING

Clients showing the characteristic manifestations of defensive avoidance are encountered in all types of counseling practices but are seen most often by counselors in hospitals and medical clinics, where there are large numbers of patients who are in a dilemma about what to do about chronic illness, acute physical suffering, or threatened disabilities. Although defensive avoidance sometimes has positive value in enabling people to surmount a temporary crisis, "the long-term avoidance of real problems tends to be maladaptive" (Hamburg, Coelho, & Adams, 1974, p. 426). The pattern of defensive avoidance is likely to have detrimental effects that extend beyond the delay of medical treatment at the outset of a life-threatening disease, which I mentioned earlier. It underlies failure to complete the course of treatments or to adhere to the recommended medical regimen after the patients have decided to seek medical aid. The latter type of maladaptive behavior has frequently been observed among patients diagnosed as suffering from coronary heart disease who continue to smoke and overeat, do not get sufficient exercise, or do not take essential medications (see Kasl, 1975; Stone, 1979).

It has been widely observed that many patients who have undergone life-threatening illnesses, such as heart attacks, become depressed during the period of convalescence, worry about recurring attacks, lose hope of fully recovering, and feel discourage about being able to return to a normal life. Hackett and Cassem (1975) point out that this type of postcoronary depression can lead to unwarranted invalidism. To some extent, according to their account, such reactions are induced by physicians and others on the hospital staff who talk a great deal about the restrictions but say little about the favorable prospects for recovering and returning to a fairly normal way of life. They quote a young convalescent cardiac patient who commented on the onerous restrictions: "No smokes, no booze, low salt, low fat, low energy, low sex or no sex—I feel like a cardiological capon!" These authors urge the hospital staff to counteract the depression and anxiety that so often arise during convalescence following a coronary by giving patients the heartening news that most people can work, have sexual intercourse, and lead a normal life after a heart attack. According to the conflict-theory model, as presented in Figure 6.1, such information should reduce the tendency to resort to defensive avoidance in response to the life-threatening illness by building up the *hope* of arriving at a satisfactory outcome. By providing realistic information about positive outcomes, a counselor who works with medical patients, even in only very brief sessions, could have a significant impact if he or she builds up sufficient optimism to facilitate a vigilant coping pattern that leads to effective action.

Several studies indicate that patients with coronary disease who develop a reactive depression are less likely to adhere to the recommended medical regimen necessary for rehabilitation than are equally ill patients who show less depression and less anxiety (Gentry, Foster, & Haney, 1972; Hackett, Cassem, & Wishnie, 1968; McGill, 1975). These findings are sometimes interpreted as suggesting that denial is beneficial, because the heart patients who seem to deny their illness do better than those who do not. But "denial" may be a misleading term for characterizing those patients who are not depressed or discouraged or extremely worried. The crucial factor may be that they feel *hopeful* about surmounting the threat to their health and display a vigilant pattern of coping; they decide to do whatever is necessary to recover. In contrast, those who remain hopeless may display a pattern of defensive avoidance by procrastinating and bolstering a do-nothing stance, or by pinning all their hopes on an authority figure such as a physician. The same pattern of defensive avoidance has been observed in persons who feel helpless about resolving decisional conflicts concerning their career, marriage, or other personal dilemmas.

ADDITIONAL GUIDELINES

In addition to the general guidelines already discussed, other implications for counseling procedures are suggested by the questions in part B of Table 6.3 (p. 152). These questions can be raised by the counselor to encourage the client to engage in adequate search and appraisal. The counselor can use them to discover gaps in the client's knowledge about the possible consequences of the alternatives under consideration and then make recommendations about where to go to obtain the missing information.

The questions in Table 6.1 on the five stages can also be explicitly asked when they become appropriate during the successive stages of decision making, in order to help the client focus on pertinent issues before making a final choice. They can also be used in connection with recommendations to the client to deliberate about the decision at home.

The five stages of sound decision making, as outlined at the beginning of this chapter, are not likely to be carried out adequately unless the decision maker's dominant pattern is vigilance. Earlier I pointed out that the stages tend to be short-circuited when the client's dominant coping pattern is unconflicted adherence, unconflicted change, defensive avoidance, or hypervigilance. Consequently, the questions in Table 6.1 (and also those in part B of Table 6.3) should not become the focus of a counseling session until after the counselor has applied whichever of the four general guidelines for promoting vigilance appears to be necessary. In other words, if the decision is one that could have serious consequences for the client's future, the counselor should first help the client to adopt a vigilant coping pattern instead of defensive avoidance or whatever other defective coping pattern he or she may be displaying; after that the client can be guided through the essential stages of sound decision making.

The general guidelines for decision counseling presented in this chapter are compatible with the guidelines presented earlier (chaps. 2–5) for establishing an effective helping relationship. While helping clients to acquire and maintain a vigilant coping pattern, the counselor can elicit a moderate level of self-disclosure, give positive feedback, make explicit recommendations, and do all the other things suggested in Table 2.1 (p. 27).

The main point here is that along with doing whatever is necessary to function as an effective helper, decision counselors can use their motivating power to influence clients who are facing vital choices to counteract defective coping patterns. According to the conflict-theory model, clients will not be properly motivated to engage in the difficult cognitive tasks of search and appraisal required for sound decision making unless they develop the set of expectations that are crucial for becoming and remaining vigilant—the belief that the risks involved in the decision are serious, that a satisfactory solution can be found, and that there is sufficient time to do so.

7 Helping Clients Make Difficult Decisions: Five Special Procedures

The conflict-theory analysis of decision making, which provides the general guidelines for counselors presented in the preceding chapter, forms the basis for a number of special counseling procedures. This chapter describes five such procedures to foster vigilant problem solving when clients are required to make unusually distressing decisions. From the research that has been done so far, the procedures appear to be useful aids for improving the quality of decision making in clients who display defensive avoidance or other defective coping patterns when making vital choices or plans concerning their health, education, career, marital problems, parental responsibilities, or any other important aspect of their lives. The five interventions are: (1) a technique to counteract rationalizations that bolster a do-nothing stance; (2) emotional role playing to explore personal vulnerability to objective threats; (3) a balance-sheet procedure to examine the pros and cons of available alternatives; (4) outcome psychodrama to discover neglected consequences; and (5) stress inoculation to prepare clients to cope with postdecisional setbacks.

Each of these procedures is designed to be used during a particular stage of decision making. The first two techniques are applicable primarily during the initial stage of decision making, when the client is confronted with a challenging threat that may require a new course of action. The third procedure, which involves constructing a balance sheet, is applicable toward the end of the second stage (surveying alternatives) or during the third stage (weighing alternatives). The fourth procedure is best used during the fourth stage, when the client is deliberating about commitment after having tacitly selected what appears to be the best course of action. The last procedure is also intended for clients who are about to commit themselves, or else just after they have become committed, before they encounter negative feedback while implementing the new decision (Stage 5).

158

A TECHNIQUE TO COUNTERACT RATIONALIZATIONS

When people encounter objective threats that require them to make major decisions, their initial reaction is likely to take the form of denial along with other manifestations of defensive avoidance. As a result, many people fail to survey and appraise adequately the alternatives that are open to them and they also fail to meet one or more of the other criteria for sound decision making. This is especially so when people encounter warning signs of cancer or other serious diseases, but it also occurs with other types of warnings, including those pertaining to being fired from one's job, alienating one's spouse or close friends, becoming involved in serious legal difficulties, or undergoing heavy financial losses.

The combination of conflict and pessimism about finding an ade quate solution leads to the all-too-human tendency to escape from a dilemma by resorting to wishful thinking. Sometimes defensive avoidance takes the form of procrastinating, supported by rationalizations enabling the person to maintain the wishful belief that nothing will be lost by putting off a decision indefinitely. Another form of defensive avoidance involves shifting responsibility or "buck passing," supported by rationalizations in favor of the wishful belief that nothing will be lost by letting someone else make the decision. In still other instances, perhaps the most frequent, defensive avoidance takes the form of bolstering the least objectionable alternative with rationalizations that play up its merits and play down its defects by wishfully distorting the gains and losses to be expected. When a client appears to be relying on rationalizations to support any of these three forms of evading the need for seeking a good course of protective action in response to an objective threat, a counselor can take a few simple steps that might evoke a more vigilant approach. The very first steps, of course, consist of raising appropriate questions about the threat and responding to the client's answers in a way that follows the general guideline for counteracting defensive avoidance as described in chapter 6. These initial steps include giving realistic information along with encouraging suggestions that build up the client's optimism with regard to finding a satisfactory solution to his or her dilemma.

Among the questions to be asked at the outset are those that help a person to *screen* potential challenges in an objective way so as to determine whether they need to be taken seriously or can be safely ignored. Obviously, everyone is exposed to so many warnings from all sorts of sources about so many possible threats that it is essential to discriminate carefully between those potential challenges that are likely to lead to avoidable crises if ignored and those that are not. Wheeler and Janis (1980) point out that although no generalizations have as yet been validated as dependable rules for screening challenges, there are a few key questions that might be worthwhile for anyone to consider in trying to appraise warnings. The questions they propose as most useful fall into three main categories:

1. Credibility of the Warning Information
- Is the source of the warning someone who is in a position to know the truth?
- If so, is the source likely to be honest or dishonest? (For example, is the person trying to sell something or to make scare propaganda for selfish purposes?)
- Is any evidence given that makes the predicted threat seem plausible, and, if so, how good is the evidence?
- If there are serious doubts about the credibility of the information, is there a trustworthy source who could easily be consulted—someone who is an impartial expert or someone who would be willing to give inside information?

2. Importance of the Threat
- If there is some real danger, how likely is it to materialize?
- How likely is it to affect me or people I care about?
- How severe might the losses be?

3. Urgency
- If the danger is likely to materialize and lead to serious losses, might it happen soon or is it unlikely to occur for a long time to come?
- Even if it is likely to occur soon, will the danger develop gradually so that there would be ample time to plan protective actions if I wait to see what happens? Or is the danger likely to come on so suddenly that I will be caught short and unable to protect myself if I postpone doing anything about it?

- If some immediate planning of protective action is urgent, could I do just a part of it now and safely postpone the rest until the first signs of danger appear?

Ordinarily only a few of these questions are appropriate to any particular warning to which a client has been exposed. (It would probably be worthwhile for a counselor to go through the entire set of questions with a client only when the purpose of the counseling session includes giving training in sound decision-making procedures for dealing with problems that might arise in the future.) Raising two or three pertinent questions may occasionally prove sufficient to induce the client to take seriously a realistic threat that he or she has been defensively avoiding and to start considering what needs to be done. But psychological resistances usually are not overcome so easily. Even though the counselor asks all the pertinent questions about the threat, the client may continue to ignore impressive warnings that experts judge to be credible, important, and urgent enough to require the threatened person to do something.

Persistent resistances of this kind are often encountered among clients who come to clinics for help in carrying out difficult decisions such as cutting down on drugs, alcohol, smoking, or overeating. Many of these clients are not actually willing to commit themselves to a rigorous program of self-management recommended by the health professionals. In the presence of the counselor they usually pay lip service to the norms of the clinic, and they may claim that at home they are following all the behavioral prescriptions. But it soon becomes apparent that they are not taking the health hazards seriously and actually have no intention of taking protective action by changing their behavior in any significant way. They carry out the recommended daily rules only halfheartedly right from the start. Then, as they encounter the usual unpleasant consequences of self-imposed deprivations, they become even more perfunctory about following the recommended rules and soon give up altogether.

These resistant clients usually bolster their decision to reject the stringent demands made by the clinic with numerous rationalizations that minimize their vulnerability to cancer, heart disease, or other harmful consequences. Some people who smoke two or three packs of cigarettes a day, for example, rely heavily on rationalizations that explicitly minimize the chances of *their* becoming cancer victims ("It won't happen to me"). Others fully acknowledge the risk but adopt a fatalistic attitude or claim that their addiction is so entrenched that they can do nothing about it. All such rationalizations dampen the impact of credible information about health hazards, with the result that they do not take full account of the losses that could result from their present course of action, even though they are sufficiently motivated (often as a result of pressure from their families) to come to a clinic and go through the motions of attempting to cut down. As long as the defensive avoidance pattern is dominant, they are unlikely to commit themselves fully to the recommended program of self-regulation.

This impasse often persists despite the counselor's best efforts to raise all the pertinent questions and inform the client about what the experts say concerning the consequences of ignoring the threat. What can be done to help such clients when they say over and over again that they want to change their behavior but in practice manage to continue with the same old, unacceptable course of action?

In an antismoking clinic Harvey Reed and I (1974) developed an *awareness-of-rationalizations* procedure that helps to undermine some of the main rationalizations used by heavy smokers to bolster the decision to continue smoking. The counselor begins with an introduction that stresses the importance of "honest exploration and frank acknowledgment of basic, deep-down thoughts and feelings" about giving up smoking. The interviewer then presents the client with a list of evasive statements (referred to as "excuses") and asks if he or she is aware of using any of them. The list consists of eight typical rationalizations made by heavy smokers, selected on the basis of pilot work with a sample of about 50 heavy smokers:

1. "It hasn't really been proved that cigarette smoking is a cause of lung cancer."
2. "The only possible health problem caused by cigarettes that one might face is lung cancer, and you don't really see a lot of that."
3. "I have been smoking for a fairly long time now, so it is probably too late to do anything anyway."
4. "If I stop smoking, I will gain too much weight."

5. "Smoking just seems to be an unbreakable habit for me."
6. "I need cigarettes to relax; I will become edgy or irritable without them."
7. "If I prefer to smoke, I am only hurting myself and nobody else."
8. "So smoking may be a risk; big deal! So is most of life! I enjoy smoking too much to give it up."

To facilitate the subject's recognition of his or her tendency to resort to each rationalization, the interviewer asks as many of the following questions as are necessary to elicit a positive (acknowledgment) response:

1. "Have you ever said this to excuse your smoking?"
2. "Has this excuse ever occurred to you?"
3. "Do you think, deep down, that this just might be at least a reasonable or valid argument?"
4. "Have you ever heard anyone use this excuse?"

The counselor then plays a brief, tape-recorded lecture presenting factual information designed to refute each of the eight rationalizations, whether or not the client has acknowledged using it.

The effectiveness of this procedure was tested in a field experiment at the Yale Antismoking Clinic on a sample of 74 men and women who wanted to cut down on cigarette consumption (Reed and Janis, 1974). Half the clients were randomly assigned to the experimental group that was given the awareness-of-rationalizations procedure while the other half received a control treatment that included the same antismoking communications presented to the experimental group. The clients in both groups were given the lecture refuting the eight rationalizations followed by two dramatic documentary films, distributed by the American Cancer Society to promote their antismoking campaign. These films contain strong warning messages about the harmful effects of cigarette smoking.

We found that at the end of the session the smokers who had received the awareness-of-rationalizations treatment expressed greater feelings of susceptibility to lung cancer and emphysema. They also expressed stronger belief in the harmfulness of smoking and gave more complete endorsements of the antismoking films.

Follow-up interviews 2 or 3 months later revealed that, as far as the reported amount of smoking was concerned, the awareness-of-rationalizations treatment had a significant effect when given by one psychologist but not by the other. Hence it probably needs to be supplemented with additional procedures to bring about dependable changes in smoking behavior. But because this technique of inducing a decision maker to acknowledge tendencies to rationalize was found to have significant effects on feelings of vulnerability to lung diseases, it has considerable promise for reducing resistance to realistic warning messages.

When counselors are dealing with clients who are defensively ignoring other threats that require different kinds of protective action, they may find it useful to improvise a procedure modeled after the awareness-of-rationalizations procedure used with heavy smokers. Although a sizable percentage of clients may remain completely unaffected by claiming that they are not relying on any of the common "excuses" to evade a potential threat, a substantial percentage of them may be sufficiently responsive to become less defensive and correspondingly more vigilant.

EMOTIONAL ROLE PLAYING

Even more effective for counteracting defensive avoidance and stimulating vigilance is a psychodramatic procedure known as emotional role playing. It appears to be capable of bypassing the defenses of many clients, making them for the first time keenly aware of their own vulnerability (Janis & Mann, 1965; Mann & Janis, 1968). The counselor creates a scenario in which the client is confronted with an "as if" experience of being a victim of a specific disaster. For example, in our initial experiment, which was carried out with young women who were heavy smokers, we asked each subject to play the role of a lung cancer patient at the moment when she is receiving the bad news from a physician. We soon found that this disquieting psychodramatic experience could be so realistic that many heavy smokers would spontaneously acknowledge their personal vulnerability to the threat of lung disease and decide to make a conscientious effort to stop smoking.

The procedure starts with a brief introduction in which the counselor explains that role playing can be used to create life-like situations for the purpose of exploring a person's emotional reactions.

The client is then asked to imagine that the counselor is a physician treating her for a "bad cough that is not getting any better." She is told to make believe that this is her third visit to his office and that she has come this time to be informed of the results of X rays and other medical tests. She is also told that there will be five different scenes, which should be acted out as realistically as possible—the way she would actually respond if each scene were really happening. The counselor describes the first scene, asks the client to act it out, then goes on to each of the successive scenes in turn. The five scenes are as follows:

Scene 1. Soliloquy in waiting room: The client is asked to give her thoughts out loud, expressing worry while awaiting the doctor's diagnosis and feeling conflicted about whether or not to smoke a cigarette.

Scene 2. Conversation with the doctor as he gives the diagnosis: In acting out the standard script of the physician's role, the counselor informs the patient that he will tell her the whole truth, since this is what she has requested. He goes on to say that a definite diagnosis can now be made on the basis of the X ray and sputum tests and that, unfortunately, it is bad news. Pointing to an actual chest X ray, he explains that there is a small malignant mass in the patient's right lung and that immediate surgery is indicated. He encourages the patient to ask questions. In the course of this conversation the doctor again mentions that the patient had asked for all the facts and then states that there is only a moderate chance for a successful outcome from surgery for this condition.

Scene 3. Soliloquy while the doctor phones for a hospital bed: The patient is again asked to express aloud her thoughts and feelings about the bad news while the doctor is telephoning in a distant part of the room.

Scene 4. Conversation with the doctor concerning hospitalization: Continuing to act on the basis of the standard script, the counselor gives detailed information about reporting to the hospital the following morning and asks several questions about the patient's family and personal circumstances. Then he tells the patient to expect to be in the hospital for at least six weeks because surgery of the chest takes a long time to heal.

Scene 5. Conversation with the doctor about smoking as a cause of lung cancer: The doctor asks about the patient's smoking history and then asks if the patient is aware of the connection between smoking and cancer. The doctor discusses the urgent need to stop smoking immediately and encourages the patient to speak freely about expected difficulties in trying to give up the habit at this time, now that the patient knows it is essential.

While enacting the role of a cancer victim during the psychodrama, many clients become extremely emotional as they vividly express their feelings of personal vulnerability—so much so that it is difficult for an observer to judge whether they are merely playing the assigned role. This is well illustrated by what was said by a 20-year-old girl (who had been smoking about two packs of cigarettes a day) when she was improvising her soliloquy during the third scene, while the doctor was phoning to arrange for her to be hospitalized for surgery:

> Cancer . . . Oh, God! I can't believe this. . . . This can't be happening to me. Maybe it's nothing . . . maybe. Oh, God, if it's only just benign, that's all I ask for. *One out of three* [survive]! *Holy smokes,* with my luck I'll be one of the fatalities. Why did this have to happen to me . . . cigarettes . . . one out of three. . . . If I ever asked for anything, I asked for this. I've read all those reports and I just wouldn't believe them. Please, just make it be OK. . . . Tomorrow, I'll go in [to the hospital] tomorrow. . . . What will I ever do? How can I ever tell my parents [sob], "Come down and see me in the hospital next week—I might be dead the week afterwards." What a jerk! Nice going! Just deliberately set out and just smoke yourself to death. Why couldn't I have known before this? . . . Surgery? . . . There must be something else. I don't want him cutting into me and finding things wrong inside me. Why did I ever pick up that stupid habit? I know that it causes cancer. I'm not kidding anybody. I know it does. But I just thought—I was hoping that it would never happen to me. . . . I can't believe it—they're going to operate. I might not ever be able to breathe again. I might be dead. Why did I ever come to him? Why couldn't I die slowly without having to go through this? That cough was not so bad. . . . (Quoted in Janis & Mann, 1977, p. 351)

After the emotional role-playing ordeal, which usually takes about an hour for the five scenes, many clients continue to express a great deal of emotional involvement. Here are some typical statements made by four different women after the psychodrama was over:

"I felt after a while that I wasn't acting, it was really true."

"It makes it sound so near."

"I started to think, this could be me—*really.*"

"That just shook me up—it *does* scare me—it *does.*"

Such statements suggest that typical cognitive defenses and rationalizations, such as "No one in my family has had cancer so it can't happen to me" and "It is impossible for me to give up cigarettes," can be undermined by the procedure.

In the initial controlled experiment, we found that the women given the emotional role-playing procedure, as compared with equivalent controls (who merely heard the tape recording of someone else's enactment of the five scenes of the psychodrama), manifested a marked and significant increase in feelings of personal vulnerability to the threat of lung disease along with greater willingness to try to give up smoking (Janis & Mann, 1965). These results were based on what the women said on questionnaires and in interviews at the end of the session. Two weeks later, the women who had been randomly assigned to the role-playing condition reported that they were smoking significantly less than those who had been assigned to the control condition. A follow-up study, conducted as an independent health survey, showed that the sharp decrease in reported amount of smoking produced by emotional role playing was still persisting 18 months after the session (Mann & Janis, 1968). At the time of the follow-up study, some of the subjects spontaneously reported that it was the role-playing session a year and a half earlier that had led them to make their sustained decision to quite smoking. For example, one woman said that she had been in a study with a professor who "was doing this psychological thing . . . and that was what really affected me. . . . I got thinking what if it were really true and I had to go home and tell everyone that I had cancer. And right then I decided I would not go through this again, and if there were any way of preventing it, I would. And I stopped smoking. It was really the professor's study that made me quit."

Sufficient additional research has been done in antismoking clinics to show that emotional role playing can produce long-term changes in attitudes of personal vulnerability and in cigarette consumption among heavy smokers (see Janis & Mann, 1977, pp. 350–60). Some studies suggest that the technique may prove to be effective for other types of decisions as well—for example, inducing heavy drinkers to "go on the wagon" (Toomey, 1972). In general, the emotional role-playing technique may prove to be especially useful for clients who want to change their behavior but cannot mobilize or sustain the motivation necessary for doing so. The "as if" experience created by engaging in psychodramatic enactment of the threatening consequences that could result from the client's current course of action (or inaction) apparently can make the client vividly aware of his or her personal vulnerability and thereby provide a marked increase in motivation to change.

Any psychologically powerful technique is likely to have undesirable side effects and drawbacks that a cautious counselor must watch out for and try to prevent. In the case of emotional role playing, one of the main dangers is that the technique may occasionally be *too* successful in making a client aware of impending disaster. If there are signs that a client is becoming very upset the counselor must be prepared to provide essential reassurances and continue in a supportive role to help the client regain his or her emotional equanimity.

Despite the counselor's efforts to provide reassurance and supportive help, there are risks associated with the use of a technique that makes the challenge to change more potent by heightening clients' awareness of their personal vulnerability to a threat. Perhaps the best way for a counselor to prevent overreactions, such as hypervigilance, is to encourage the client to survey the available alternatives and evaluate them carefully. In short, once a client appraises and accepts a challenge to his or her current course of action, which is the first stage of effective decision making, the counselor must be prepared to guide the client through each of the successive stages. This may require the use of additional techniques, such as the one to be described next.

THE BALANCE-SHEET PROCEDURE

Several types of intervention have been developed specifically to encourage clients to adopt a vigilant approach to surveying and evaluating alternatives when they are making a vital decision. One such intervention is the decisional balance-sheet procedure, which requires a decision maker to examine carefully the available alternatives and to contemplate in a systematic way the major potential risks as well as gains that might otherwise be overlooked (Janis & Mann, 1977, pp. 377–79). In line with the conflict-theory analysis of coping patterns, this type of intervention is based on the assumption that when clients are displaying unconflicted inertia, unconflicted change, defensive avoidance, or hypervigilance, their defective coping pattern can be overcome or at least minimized to some extent if they are given guidance that promotes a vigilant approach.

The first step in the procedure is for the counselor to ask the client to describe all the alternatives he or she is considering and to talk about the pros and cons of each. During this initial part of the procedure the counselor might surmise that the client has not yet sufficiently surveyed the available alternatives. If so, the counselor suggests that the client spend some additional time generating more alternatives. (This can be given as a proposed homework assignment in preparation for carrying out the main part of the balance-sheet procedure in the next session.) While making the suggestion, the counselor can call attention to a number of rules-of-thumb in order to help the client arrive at additional alternatives, perhaps even better than the ones originally under consideration. These rules come from the brainstorming methods originally developed to promote creative problem solving among groups of executives in business organizations. Seven rules have been extracted from brainstorming techniques that can be applied by an individual who is trying to find potential solutions to personal problems:

Rule 1: Don't evaluate at the beginning. Think of possible choices and write them down without worrying about what is wrong with them.

Rule 2: Generate as many alternatives as possible. . . . It is always possible later to cut down the choices to a smaller, manageable set that contains the most promising choices.

Rule 3: Try to be original. Deliberately try to think up a few far-out choices to include on the list. The choices people find when they are looking for unusual possibilities frequently turn out to be more practical than they seemed at first.

Rule 4: Modify flawed alternatives. Use the alternatives that you have already generated as springboards for new ideas. The old ideas can be combined, broken apart, or shifted around to avoid their flaws.

Rule 5: Ask other people. . . . Combining ideas from several people produces a wider variety than any one person could have produced.

. . . It pays, of course, to consult an expert or someone with considerable personal experience that is relevant to the decision. Such people not only can supply useful information about the probable consequences of the alternatives that are under consideration but also can suggest new alternatives that the decision maker never thought of.

Rule 6: Use contemplation as a source of ideas. If you set aside some time to engage in free-floating contemplation of a decision you are facing, practically any train of thought or external stimulus can serve as a source of an idea. There is no need to try to be transcendental in these meditations. . . . Even just daydreaming about an ideal choice . . . can be helpful.

Rule 7: Avoid dichotomies. Many decisions seem to have only two alternatives, either *do it* or *don't do it.* Examples of either-or choices are getting married, getting divorced, accepting a unique job offer, moving to another city, accepting a social invitation, or going on a diet. Although the alternatives fall into two dichotomous classes, there are always different ways to do it and different ways not to do it. . . . [For example, one could] say "yes," but only on specified conditions. (Wheeler & Janis, 1980, pp. 43–48)

After the client appears to have made an adequate survey of the available alternatives, the counselor introduces the main steps in the balance-sheet procedure. The counselor shows the client a balance-sheet grid like the one illustrated in Table 7.1, except that the eight cells are empty. The four categories shown in the left-hand column are carefully explained to the client. The counselor's explanation includes examples of potentially positive and negative consequences selected from the client's own prior statements about the pros and cons of one of the alternatives he or she is considering. Then the client is asked to fill out a separate balance-sheet grid for each alternative.

The example shown in Table 7.1 is the balance sheet filled out by a production manager in a large industrial plant. He asked a decision counselor for help with a dilemma stemming from chronic dissatisfaction with his present job: should he stick with it or leave? As

Table 7.1. A manager's balance sheet. The grid lays out the pros and cons for staying with his present job. A balance-sheet grid would be filled out for each of the other alternatives as well—for example, whether to seek a lateral transfer within the company.

Expected consequences	Positive anticipations	Negative anticipations
Tangible gains and losses for *self*	1. Satisfactory pay. 2. Plenty of opportunities to use my skills and competencies. 3. For the present, my status in the organization is OK (but it won't be for long if I am not promoted in the next year).	1. Long hours. 2. Constant time pressures, short deadlines. 3. Unpleasant paper work. 4. Poor prospects for advancement to a higher-level position. 5. Repeated reorganizations make my work chaotic.
Tangible gains and losses for *others*	1. Adequate income for family. 2. Wife and children get special privileges because of my position in the firm.	1. Not enough time free to spend with my family. 2. Wife often has to put up with my irritability when I come home after bad days at work.
Self-approval or self-disapproval	1. This position allows me to make full use of my potentialities. 2. Proud of my achievements. 3. Proud of the competent team I have shaped up. 4. Sense of meaningful accomplishment.	1. Sometimes feel I'm a fool to continue putting up with the unreasonable deadlines and other stupid demands made by the top managers.
Social approval or disapproval	1. Approval of men on my team, who look up to me as their leader and who are good friends. 2. Approval of my superior who is a friend and wants me to stay.	1. Very slight skeptical reaction of my wife—she asks me if I might be better off in a different firm. 2. A friend who has been wanting to wangle a new job for me will be disappointed.

Source. Wheeler & Janis, 1980.

can be seen in the list of negative anticipations, he was keenly aware of all sorts of negative features, ranging from long hours and unreasonable deadlines to his own irritability at home, which he attributed to frustrations on the job. Nevertheless, after he examined carefully the grid he had just filled out for his present job and compared it with his entries in the grids for two alternatives (seeking a lateral transfer to a different managerial position in his own company and seeking a managerial position in a different company) he decided not to leave. Among his major reasons for arriving at this decision were the positive anticipations he had listed in the nonutilitarian categories. For example, while examining his balance sheet, he repeatedly pointed to the entries pertaining to friendship with his superior and with the men on his team, whom he did not want to let down by changing to another job. Although this manager decided to continue on the job, his listing of the negative aspects, including the stupidity and negligence of the top managers in his firm, did have a noticeable effect on his contingency planning. Along with his decision to stay put he announced that if his unit is broken up when the firm goes through another reorganization, he will definitely look for a position elsewhere.

As a standard part of the balance-sheet procedure, the counselor mentions—immediately after the client has finished filling out grids for the major alternatives—that there may be some gaps that need to be filled in. The client is asked to reexamine each cell, this time trying to think of additional pros and cons that might be important to consider, including consequences that may not be highly probable but could happen. In order to help the client discover pros and cons that are being overlooked, the counselor shows the client a list of various considerations that are usually taken into account by vigilant decision makers when they are making a choice of the kind that the client is facing. An example of such a list used in career counseling is shown in Table 7.2. The counselor suggests that the client focus especially on categories that have few or no entries in the grids the client has filled out. Very often the cells with fewest entries are in the category pertaining to anticipated disapproval from oneself, which includes violations of one's ethical or moral code and failure to live up to one's ego ideals.

The balance-sheet procedure was developed in a series of pilot

Table 7.2. List of considerations that might affect career choice, used in the balance-sheet procedure as tested with college seniors facing a decision about what to do after graduation

1. Utilitarian considerations: gains and losses for self
   a. income
   b. difficulty of the work
   c. interest level of the work
   d. freedom to select work tasks
   e. chances of advancement
   f. security
   g. time available for personal interests, e.g., recreation
   h. other (e.g., special restrictions or opportunities with respect to social life; effect of the career or job demands on marriage; type of people you will come in contact with)
2. Utilitarian considerations: gains and losses for others
   a. income for family
   b. status for family
   c. time available for family
   d. kind of environment for family, e.g., stimulating, dull; safe, unsafe
   e. being in a position to help an organization or group (e.g., social, political, or religious)
   f. other (e.g., fringe benefits for family)
3. Self-approval or self-disapproval
   a. self-esteem from contributions to society or to good causes
   b. extent to which work tasks are ethically justifiable
   c. extent to which work will involve compromising oneself
   d. creativeness or originality of work
   e. extent to which job will involve a way of life that meets one's moral or ethical standards
   f. opportunity to fulfill long-range life goals
   g. other (e.g., extent to which work is "more than just a job")
4. Approval or disapproval from others (includes being criticized or being excluded from a group as well as being praised or obtaining prestige, admiration, and respect)
   a. parents
   b. college friends
   c. wife (or husband)
   d. colleagues
   e. community at large
   f. others (e.g., social, political, or religious groups)

Source. Janis & Mann, 1977.

studies I carried out with Yale College seniors at a time when they were deciding what to do during the year after their graduation. In trial runs with 36 seniors, I found that the procedure was a feasible way to stimulate them to take account of favorable and unfavorable consequences that they had been overlooking. Many of the students thought of previously neglected consequences when confronted with the task of filling in major gaps in their decisional balance sheets, which influenced their final choice. I also observed that for people facing a vital decision the procedure was not a coldly intellectual exercise. Most of the students displayed affective reactions as they worked on their balance sheets. For some of them, the procedure had a profound emotional impact that led to psychological insights, as in the following case:

> One senior who originally was planning to go to a graduate business school for training to become an executive in his father's Wall Street firm was surprised at first when he discovered that the cells in the balance-sheet grid pertaining to self-approval or -disapproval were almost completely empty. After looking over the standard list of items to be considered in those categories, ... he was stimulated to write down several ways in which his career as a broker would fail to meet his ethical ideals or satisfy his desire to help improve the quality of life for people in his community. As he thought about these neglected considerations, he became worried and depressed. Then, while filling out the cells of the balance-sheet grid for his second choice—going to law school—he began to brighten up a bit. Eventually he became glowingly enthusiastic when he hit upon the notion that instead of becoming a Wall Street lawyer he might better meet his objectives by being trained for a career in a legal aid clinic or in public-interest law. Finally, his mood became more sober, but with some residual elation, as he conscientiously listed the serious drawbacks (parental disapproval, relatively low income, poor prospects for travel abroad, etc.) of the new career plan he had conceived. Afterward he thanked the interviewer for making him realize he had been on the wrong track and for helping him arrive at his new career plan, which, in fact, he had worked out entirely by himself in response to the open-ended nature of the balance-sheet procedure. (Janis & Mann, 1977, pp. 150–52)

After the pilot work with college seniors, several well-controlled field experiments were carried out to determine the effectiveness of the balance-sheet procedure. In one experimental study by Leon Mann (1972) the procedure was used to aid high school seniors make decisions about their choice of a college. In a second study, Colten and I (1982) found that the procedure contributed to success in dieting among clients who came to the weight-reduction clinic, as manifested by their weight loss. A field experiment by Hoyt and myself (1975) showed that the balance-sheet procedure was effective in helping healthy women who had decided to attend an early morning exercise class to stick with their decision, as shown by their attendance records. This study was replicated by Wankel and Thompson (1977) in an experiment with 100 women who were members of a physical fitness club but had become inactive. Taking account of comparisons with a control group, they too found that attendance rates were significantly increased for a group given the decisional balance-sheet procedure. But in a study by LaFlamme and Janis (1977) the balance-sheet procedure had no observable effect on the information-seeking activity of clients who came to a career counseling clinic, most of whom were in the early stages of deciding on a shift in career. It seems likely that the procedure is of value only in the later stages of decision making, after clients have already learned a great deal about the available alternatives, as in the case of college seniors for whom such procedures were found to be effective as aids for making career choices. All but the last of these experimental studies support the earlier research in indicating that the balance-sheet procedure is a useful intervention for improving the quality of clients' decision making. The bulk of the evidence indicates that it increases the stability of clients' decisions and decreases their postdecisional regret.

Why would it be beneficial for a decision counselor to ask a client to go through the laborious balance-sheet procedure after having already asked the client to talk about the pros and cons for each alternative? Several functions seem to be at least partly achieved by systematically filling out the balance sheet, which makes it something much more than a simple bookkeeping operation for recording what a client already knows. First of all, it often leads clients to realize that they need to obtain more information about consequences that they had not thought about before. Second, it usually increases their awareness of the need to work out detailed contingency plans, to be prepared for meeting the anticipated drawbacks they have listed in the minus column for the chosen alternative. Third, it helps clients to make a comprehensive evaluation of the alternatives. By reading over their entries on the balance-sheet grids, clients sometimes are able to differentiate more carefully between major and minor consequences, to notice possible tradeoffs that could make one alternative clearly superior to the others, or to use a more complex set of criteria in making their final choice rather than rely on oversimplified decision rules (such as selecting whichever job offers the highest initial salary). Another unexpected benefit, as I noted earlier, is that the procedure also helps some clients take into account their gut feelings.

> People are often concerned that if they work out a balance sheet of any kind, they will become so coldly analytical that their emotional reactions to the alternatives will be left out of the picture entirely. John Stuart Mill, the great nineteenth-century philosopher, said, "The habit of analysis has a tendency to wear away the feelings." But as an extraordinarily rational and analytical man, Mill may have underestimated the persistence of the emotions aroused when vital choices have to be made. A recent commentator points out that the reverse of what Mill said might be closer to the truth: "With most people, rather, it works the other way round; as long as their feelings are involved, they are incapable of analysis."
>
> We believe that it is a gross exaggeration to set up any such dichotomy, to assume that either you have strong feelings or you engage in rational analysis. Even when emotions run high, most people can adopt an analytical approach, at least for a short period of time, by following the simple procedures of filling out the entries in a balance sheet. Furthermore, they do not need to leave their emotional feelings out of the analysis and probably should not. Twinges of emotion, in fact, often occur while people are writing down specific entries. Vague feelings of uneasiness as well as more specific apprehensions about certain risks can be recorded in the balance sheet if the person expects that he or she will suffer that kind of subjective discomfort from choosing a particular alternative. Similarly, people can write down expected feelings of shame or guilt and take them into account as an important part of the overall picture while thinking analytically about the choice that would suit them best.
>
> Sometimes the emotional reactions people experience while filling

out the balance sheet can play a crucial role in making them realize that they must be leaving out something very important. A person may be surprised that he is still strongly attracted to an alternative that has relatively few pluses and many minuses in the balance sheet. It may induce him to ask, "Why do I feel that way? What am I leaving out of the picture?" The surprising reaction may be a strong "irrational" feeling of aversion toward the alternative that looks like it might be the best one. Either reaction shows that something important must be missing from the balance sheet or that the intuitive feelings are being influenced by some irrelevant factor. These discrepancies between one's gut feelings and the picture that emerges from the record of pros and cons can stimulate one to engage in intensive self-scrutiny or to talk about the conflict in a less inhibited way with close friends. This may lead to fresh discoveries of specific reasons for being attracted to one alternative or for being repulsed by another. Here we are referring to wishes and fears that psychologists describe as "preconscious" sources of conflict—considerations that people remain unaware of unless they are stimulated to think about the discrepancy between their conscious appraisals and their gut feelings. (Wheeler & Janis, 1980, pp. 70–71)

After a client has completed the balance-sheet procedure, the counselor can facilitate the beneficial effects by raising appropriate questions, such as the following:

- What information do you need that is still missing?
- Whom could you talk with to obtain the missing information? An expert? A friend?
- As you look over the balance-sheet entries, which alternative looks best?
- Does your tentative choice based on the balance-sheet entries agree with your gut feelings? If not, what might have been left out?
- Is the alternative that looks best *good enough?* Does it meet *all* your main objectives? If not, could it be modified in some way to satisfy your most essential requirements?
- Do you feel ready to commit yourself to the best alternative by allowing others to know your decision?
- What contingency plans do you need to make before starting to implement your decision?

OUTCOME PSYCHODRAMA

The purpose of this procedure is to induce clients to explore fully the nonobvious consequences of the leading alternatives, particularly when the client seems on the verge of making a final choice without having reviewed all the major consequences that might ensue (Janis & LaFlamme, 1982). Clients are asked to act out a scenario that involves projecting themselves into the future in order to explore a potential outcome as though it has actually occurred, such as "The decision has worked out badly." They are required to use their imaginations in order to improvise what specifically could happen, which may enable them to become more aware of expectations and attitudes not previously verbalized even to themselves. The psychodrama can be repeated to explore the potential consequences of each alternative under consideration.

> Outcome psychodrama as an intervention for use in decision counseling was developed by Janis in a series of pilot studies. He first used it in interviews with clients having serious marital problems who came to a marital counseling clinic for aid in making a decision about whether or not to seek a divorce. One woman, for example, who in three earlier interviews had consistently described her marriage as nothing but misery and seemed fully convinced that the only solution was to divorce her unfaithful husband, was asked to imagine that one year had gone by since she made her decision. Mrs. Stern, as we shall call her, was told that she would be asked to go through this procedure twice, once as if she had decided to obtain a divorce and a second time as if she had made a genuine effort to keep her marriage going. She was asked to imagine that she had come back to see the counselor for a follow-up interview, and to tell him what had happened during the interim year. Mrs. Stern chose to enact the divorce alternative first. After a brief warm-up period (in which she had to be encouraged to describe her feelings in the present tense instead of using conditional phrases such as "I suppose I would feel . . ."), Mrs. Stern began giving an imaginative account of what her life would be like after the divorce. During the first ten minutes, her statements merely repeated what she had already said in earlier interviews about relief from constant quarreling and other improvements in her daily life that she expected as a result of being rid of her husband. But when asked whether she now felt fairly contented living independently, she blurted out, "No, I feel lonely and miserable, I miss my husband terribly, my life is completely empty

now," and she burst into tears. This was the first time in any of the interviews that she displayed any intense emotion and the first time that she alluded to any affectionate feelings toward her husband.

During the second part of the procedure, devoted to enacting a follow-up interview a year after her decision to continue the marriage, Mrs. Stern continued to explore the positive aspects of her relationship with her husband, including (again for the first time) her exclusive sexual attachment to him and her fear of being frigid with any other man. In the final part of the interview, while reviewing what she had said during the psychodramatic enactments, she expressed her surprise at the strong feelings that had momentarily overwhelmed her and said, "I have so much reason to hate him I guess I hadn't been willing to admit to myself that I still love him and will miss him." Thus the psychodramatic enactments enabled Mrs. Stern to gain access to deep-seated emotional attitudes toward her husband that she had defensively avoided acknowledging to herself.

Once these formerly preconscious components became part of her conscious balance sheet, she could make a more thorough assessment of the alternatives and work out more realistic plans for implementation. As it turned out, Mrs. Stern felt convinced that despite her newly acknowledged attachment to her husband, his constant mistreatment of her was so intolerable that she should obtain a divorce. In a final session, one month after the psychodramatic enactments, Mrs. Stern spoke about a definite plan to avoid the loneliness of the separation by moving into an apartment with a girlfriend. It seems probable that this plan was at least partly shaped by the increased awareness she had gained from the psychodramatic enactments of the losses she would sustain from going through with a divorce. (Janis & Mann, 1977, pp. 380–81)

In marital counseling of six other women and two men, I observed similar indications that outcome psychodrama is of value for overcoming psychological resistances that interfere with the exploration of consequences that are distressing for the client to contemplate. The outcome psychodrama technique seemed to be helpful in promoting a more vigilant approach that enabled clients to uncover preconscious worries, aspirations, and other previously unverbalized feelings about the decision. Accordingly, I tried it out in another pilot study, this time with male college seniors who came for career counseling. Before the psychodramatic procedure was introduced, each student was given a preliminary interview concerning the pros and cons of the two career alternatives he most preferred. He was also asked to fill out a balance sheet for both.

> The seniors were then instructed to enact a 1-year follow-up interview for each of the two leading alternatives. However, such instructions did not seem fruitful in this setting until a revised psychodrama scenario was constructed which required the seniors to conceive of themselves as telling a *friend* about a *crisis* situation in which "everything that could go wrong had gone wrong." Additional pilot work in this setting on the positive scenarios appeared to be relatively unproductive. Consequently, the procedure that was finally adopted asked the seniors to focus exclusively on the crisis scenario, which required them to elaborate on the unfavorable consequences of each alternative. When this scenario was used, the seniors became aware of important entries for their balance sheets, which they had not mentioned earlier, as a result of the psychodramatic enactments. For 12 of the 15 seniors [in the final pilot study], new considerations emerged during the psychodramas that affected the final evaluation of their career alternatives. Four students were so impressed by the undesirable consequences that surfaced during their improvised performance of the psychodrama that they reversed their preferences. Other students became more convinced of the correctness of their original first choice. Practically all the seniors seemed to acquire a more realistic view of their main alternatives. (Janis & LaFlamme, 1982, p. 307)

The positive effects of outcome psychodrama in the pilot work in marital and career counseling clinics led me to expect that the technique could be a potentially useful supplement to the balance-sheet procedure, especially for counteracting defensive avoidance tendencies. But because the procedure makes the role players keenly aware of potentially disastrous outcomes, it could have a demoralizing effect on some clients which might adversely affect the quality of their decision-making procedures. Taking this into account, Donna-Maria LaFlamme and I (1977) carried out a large-scale field experiment to test the effectiveness of outcome psychodrama in career counseling. Eighty men and women who were undecided about whether to change their jobs or careers came to our career counseling clinic. Half of them (on a random basis) were given the outcome psychodrama as part of their interview and the other half were not. Unfortunately, the results were not what we had expected: the clients did not seem to benefit from the procedure. Worse yet, it appeared to have an adverse effect on some of them, lowering their self-confidence about finding a good solution and decreasing vigilant information seeking. Consequently, the procedure cannot be recommended for routine use in decision counseling.

The clients in the career decision counseling experiment differed from those in the pilot studies in one important respect: most of them were in an early stage of decision making: They were dissatisfied with their present occupations but had not yet obtained enough information to know very much about what alternatives specifically to consider and what the main pros and cons might be. Also, most of them felt quite insecure about contemplating any change in their careers even though they did not want to continue in their current occupations. For such clients, becoming vividly aware of unfavorable outcomes as a result of going through the psychodramatic enactments may have the adverse effect of making them less hopeful about finding an adequate solution, which fosters defensive avoidance. In contrast, the clients in the pilot work on the effects of outcome psychodrama in career counseling and in marital counseling were men and women who were in the *later* stages of decision making: They had already spent a great deal of time obtaining information and weighing specific alternatives.

Where does this leave us on the practical issue of when, if ever, outcome psychodrama should be used? Obviously, in view of the negative results from the LaFlamme and Janis study (1977) we cannot recommend outcome psychodrama for general use in decision counseling. Nevertheless, the promising results from the pilot studies suggest that the technique might prove to be useful with carefully selected clients if limited to those in the later stages of decision making who appear to be quite robust with regard to self-confidence about finding good solutions to their dilemmas. Counselors who think it is worthwhile to try out the procedure should, of course, use it with caution. They should be alert to possible signs of demoralizing effects, which may require additional steps to help the client regain a hopeful outlook. In any case we must await further systematic research to assess the effects of the procedure before formulating any definitive generalizations about when and with whom outcome psychodrama could be used effectively to increase vigilance with minimal risks of producing demoralization.

Before the LaFlamme and Janis experiment was carried out, we thought that the risk of demoralizing the client through the use of the outcome psychodrama would be very slight, especially since the images of unfavorable consequences are generated entirely by the client rather than supplied by the counselor. The unexpected negative findings remind us once again of the need for systematic evaluation before a new intervention procedure is applied on a large scale to clients who seek help from counselors. All too often, counselors rely exclusively on their clinical experience when it comes to using new procedures, which ultimately could prove to be detrimental rather than beneficial. Even very conscientious counselors who want to provide the best possible services to their clients will sometimes try out a new procedure with a series of cases to see if it looks promising (usually without bothering to do a systematic evaluation of changes). If an innovative clinician sees a series of cases in which a new procedure appears to be helpful, with no apparent detrimental effects, he or she is likely to apply it across the board to all types of clients and to recommend that it be widely used by other professional counselors. But, as the LaFlamme and Janis study shows, even after promising results have been obtained from a pilot study, a new procedure applied in a different context with a different type of client could prove to be ineffective or even harmful to the objectives of the counseling. The evidence of detrimental effects (with clients who sought help about their ill-defined career dilemmas) despite the positive results obtained in the initial pilot work (with college seniors who were dealing with clear-cut choices for which they were well informed) provides empirical grounds for being skeptical about applying new interventions before they have been carefully tested with samples of the population for which they are intended.

STRESS INOCULATION

Stress inoculation involves giving people preparatory communications that contain realistic information about anticipated dangers or losses, self-help recommendations, and reassurances to prepare them

to cope with an impending ordeal. I shall discuss this type of counseling in more detail than the others because considerably more
research has been done on its effectiveness and because I think there
is now sufficient evidence to warrant including it as an essential
component in decision counseling to prepare clients for anticipated
setbacks.

At present stress-inoculation procedures range in intensiveness
from a single 10-minute preparatory communication to an elaborate
training program with graded exposure to danger stimuli accompanied by guided practice in coping skills, which might require 15
or more hours of training. Any preparatory communication is said
to function as stress inoculation if it enables a person to increase
his or her tolerance for subsequent threatening events, as manifested
by behavior that is relatively efficient and stable rather than disor-
ganized by anxiety or inappropriate as a result of denial of real
dangers. Preparatory communications and related training procedures can be administered before or shortly after a person makes a
commitment to carry out a stressful decision, such as undergoing
surgery or a painful series of medical treatments. When successful,
the process is called stress inoculation because it may be analogous
to what happens when people are inoculated to produce antibodies
that will prevent a disease.

The underlying principle of stress inoculation is that accurate preparatory communications about an impending crisis and how it can
be dealt with gives decision makers the opportunity not only to make
contingency plans but also to develop reassurances and other self
statements that enable them to cope more adequately (see Janis,
1958, 1971; Meichenbaum, 1977; Meichenbaum & Turk, 1976). Stress-
inoculation procedures are especially applicable when a decision
entails moderate or severe short-term losses before substantial long-
term gains can be attained. Most decisions concerning personal health
problems belong in this category because they usually require the
person to undergo painful treatments and deprivations before physical well-being improves.

Stress inoculation for surgery, painful treatments, or other medical
ordeals is likely to be effective with initially uninformed patients.
Without it they would be quite unperturbed about agreeing to do
whatever the physicians recommend. They would continue to dis-

play a pattern of unconflicted change until the first setback occurs, for which they would be psychologically unprepared.

In recent years, a quite different type of psychological problem has frequently been encountered in clinics and hospitals as a consequence of new legal requirements: informed consent must be obtained from every patient before a risky medical treatment or surgery is administered. In some patients, anxiety is heightened, sometimes to the point of becoming hypervigilance, as a result of their being given detailed information about all the things that could go wrong. These unintended effects of obtaining informed consent might be prevented or at least somewhat alleviated by giving patients, at the same time, the reassuring components of stress inoculation.

Another group of patients for whom stress inoculation is probably especially effective consists of those who bolster their decision to undergo surgery or some other painful treatment with rationalizations based on wishful thinking, such as "There's really nothing to it" or "I won't feel a thing." This form of defensive avoidance occurs frequently among hospitalized patients. In many cases it appears to be replaced by a more reality-oriented coping pattern of vigilance when the patients are given a stress-inoculation procedure.

Research Findings

While studying stress reactions in a series of case studies of surgical patients during the early 1950s, I observed numerous indications suggesting that preparatory information could help people to cope more effectively with surgery and painful medical treatments. I was able to check on this idea by obtaining survey data from 77 young men who had recently undergone major surgery (Janis, 1958, pp. 352–94). The results indicated that those patients who had been best informed beforehand about what to expect were least likely to overreact to setbacks during the postoperative period. Although no dependable conclusions about the causal sequence could be drawn from these correlational results, they led to subsequent experiments on the effects of giving hospitalized patients preparatory communications.

Supporting evidence for the effectiveness of giving information about what to expect, especially when combined with reassurances and various coping suggestions, has come from a variety of controlled field experiments with adult surgical patients (e.g., DeLong, 1971; Egbert, Battit, Welch, & Bartlett, 1964; Johnson, 1966; Johnson, Rice, Fuller, & Endress, 1977; Vernon & Bigelow, 1974). Although some of these studies did not use adequate controls and there are some partial inconsistencies among the findings, all of them provide evidence indicating that when someone on the hospital staff gives preoperative information about the stresses of surgery and ways of coping with those stresses, adult patients show more favorable reactions after the operation. They display less anger, less postoperative regret, more adherence to the postoperative medical regimen, and sometimes better recovery from surgery.

Similar positive results on the value of giving psychological preparation have also been reported in studies of distressing medical procedures (Johnson & Leventhal, 1974) and in studies of childbirth (Breen, 1975; Doering & Entwhisle, 1975; Levy & McGee, 1975). Field experiments by Melamed and Siegel (1975), Moran (1963), and Wolfer and Visintainer (1975) with children on pediatric surgery wards have also shown positive effects of stress inoculation. At the other end of the age continuum, preparatory communications given prior to relocation of elderly patients to a new nursing home or to a hospital have been found to be effective in reducing protests and debilitation (Schultz & Hanusa, 1978).

Essentially the same adaptive cognitive and emotional changes have been noted in many case studies and in a few field experiments that focus on people who have encountered setbacks and losses when carrying out other decisions, including typical problems arising after choosing a career or shifting to a new job. For example, it has been found that if new employees are given realistic preparatory information at the time they are offered the job, or immediately after they accept it, they are more likely to stay with the organization (Gomersall & Myers, 1966; Wanous, 1973).

The various findings I have cited support the conclusion that many people will display higher stress tolerance in response to undesirable consequences if they have been given warnings in advance about what to expect, together with sufficient reassurances and coping suggestions so that anxiety does not mount to an intolerably high level. There are exceptions, of course, such as neurotic personalities who are hypersensitive to information about impending threats. But such considerations do not preclude the possibility that techniques of stress inoculation might be developed and used by decision counselors to help mitigate the impact of a wide variety of anticipated postdecisional setbacks, especially when the chosen course of action requires undergoing temporary losses in order to achieve long-term goals.

It seems likely that stress inoculation will prove to be a useful aid to practitioners not only in health counseling and career counseling, but also in marital counseling, although no systematic research has been done as yet with clients who seek help in making decisions concerning marriage or divorce. In counseling clients who were trying to decide whether to seek divorce, I have used stress inoculation to help them deal with setbacks arising from marital discord and separation. The following illustrative case study is based on my interview notes of five counseling sessions with a 35-year-old woman who still loved her estranged husband:

> About one month after her husband had moved out of the house, Mrs. Roberts (as we shall call her) decided to try to win him back by resuming sexual relations with him. He had left home after a big fight and had said he wanted a divorce. During the period of separation, he had acquired a mistress, with whom he was seen around town. He visited his wife only one evening a week, ostensibly to see their three children. Mrs. Roberts said that she treated him coldly and rejected his sexual advances. But she felt that this might not be the best way to deal with him, since she wanted to have him back. Before making the decision to resume sexual relations with her husband, she discussed with the counselor in considerable detail the potentially unpleasant consequences of this course of action. She focused on her concern about becoming deeply disappointed and enraged if, after resuming sexual relations with her husband, she were to find out that he was still seeing his mistress. That would be a terrible blow to her pride, she felt, because she was convinced that her husband had no interest in his mistress except as a source of sexual gratification.
>
> After the first week of implementing the decision, all seemed to be going well: she had enjoyed the lovemaking and felt that her husband's basic affection for her was still there. But the next day, her aunt (a chronic snooper) told her that she had seen the husband double-parked in front of the business office where his mistress was employed,

obviously to pick her up after work. Mrs. Roberts was very disappointed to hear that the outcome she feared had materialized, but she did not become enraged or depressed. She reassured herself with a plausible explanation she had worked out beforehand—that her husband might continue seeing his mistress for a while because he might break off that relationship gradually. This idea, Mrs. Roberts reported, enabled her to respond affectionately without recriminations when he came to sleep with her again, two nights later.

The following night her husband again returned and unexpectedly proposed that he move back some of his clothes and live part-time at home with her. He made it absolutely clear, however, that he wanted to do this only if he could have complete freedom to come home or stay away at night whenever he felt like it, without being required to give any advance notice or offer any excuses. This offer was very gratifying to Mrs. Roberts, because she saw it as a big step toward achieving her goal of attracting her husband back home permanently. Elated by her husband's renewed interest in returning to her, she promptly accepted his offer, without thinking over its potentially unfavorable consequences.

By the time Mrs. Roberts came to the counselor for her next session, she had already encountered a severe setback that made her regret the impulsive way in which she had made the second decision. In a highly agitated and depressed mood, she explained that after she had agreed to the new arrangement her husband came home on four successive nights and gave her intimate gifts. He told her that he was still hooked on her and that he might want to move back home on a full-time basis. But then came the weekend, and he did not show up at all until the following Monday night. With her hopes raised so high and her affectionate and sexual needs once again strongly aroused, she was bitterly disappointed and felt acutely depressed throughout the entire weekend. When he finally did appear and offered no explanation, she could not control her agitation and "spoiled her whole plan" by an angry outburst that provoked a bitter fight. Once again he stormed out, bellowing that the marriage was finished—she had broken their agreement, she could not respect a man's freedom, divorce was the only solution. He never returned.

Thus, following her first decision, when a setback occurred that Mrs. Roberts had anticipated beforehand, she was already prepared with a reassuring way of interpreting the cruel facts and was able to cope well. But when an unanticipated setback followed her second (impulsive) decision, as a result of her husband's using the freedom she had granted him, she was bitterly disappointed. Unprepared emotionally, she overreacted with extreme resentment and thus spoiled whatever prospects there were of reconciliation. If Mrs. Roberts had acknowledged to herself before making her second decision that there might be just such a setback she would have been better prepared to accept it as just another bump on the rocky road toward her goal of regaining her husband. Whether or not that road would have been a "good" choice in the long run is a separate question that the counselor had just started to take up with her when the whole issue was abruptly settled by her husband's decision to obtain a divorce.

Like the case studies of surgical patients, this case study of a marital decision suggests that one of the main functions of . . . [stress] inoculation is to tone down the decision maker's optimism about how beautifully everything is going to work out now that he or she has hit upon the best course of action. Preparatory information given shortly after a choice is made can prevent excessive bolstering of a new decision, so that instead of elatedly believing that "nothing bad will happen as a result of this choice," the decision maker becomes resigned to accepting a somewhat more pessimistic view of human enterprises, believing that "some bad things will probably happen but everything will still work out all right—and it's worth it." This differentiated view, unlike an oversimplified, Panglossian reassurance, moves the decision maker to worry about the bad consequences he is likely to encounter. . . . As a result, the decision maker develops supportive belief that are both realistic and reassuring, which help to mitigate the emotional impact of subsequent setbacks. (Janis & Mann, 1977, pp. 392–94)

Stress inoculation focusing on the anticipated effects of a broken home might also be beneficial for the large numbers of parents among the millions of couples who decide to divorce each year. In an intensive study of 60 divorcing couples and their children, Wallerstein and Kelly (1980) observed that the majority of the parents were not aware in advance of the hardships and heartaches that would beset them after the divorce—drastically lower income, loss of friends, hostility of the former spouse, feelings of loneliness, difficulties in functioning as a good parent, and perhaps most important, acute symptoms of emotional upset in the children. These authors surmise that the divorced parents would have been able to cope much better with the deprivational changes if they had been given psychological preparation by a counselor. Such preparation is especially needed, they point out, because many couples make the decision to divorce without reflection or planning. In some of their cases the decision was made without forethought after the husband or wife was directly advised to leave the spouse by a professional adviser, such as a psychotherapist or physician, who "took insufficient cognizance of the road ahead" and lacked "direct knowledge of the children involved" (Wallerstein & Kelly, 1980, p. 22). In line with their observations, the authors suggest that professionals who are consulted by embattled spouses should abstain from advising divorce and, instead, should adopt a neutral stance while devoting their efforts to helping the clients as parents think realistically about the expected effects of divorce on themselves and on their children. In order to implement this suggestion, psychotherapists, physicians, and attorneys who specialize in family law would need to develop skill in decision counseling, particularly in applying the procedures of stress inoculation.

Three Main Steps for Building up Stress Tolerance

Taking account of the data from my research and my case study observations, as well as other research findings, I have introduced a theoretical concept—"the work of worrying"—to refer to the process of mentally rehearsing anticipated losses and developing reassuring cognitions that can at least partially alleviate fear or other intense emotions when a crisis is subsequently encountered (Janis, 1958, 1971). The concept can be best understood by considering what happens when a person does *not* engage in the work of worrying.

Many observations of surgical patients and of people exposed to comparable stress situations suggest the following sequence:

Absence of anticipatory fear
↓
Absence of mental rehearsal of the impending danger
↓
Feelings of helplessness when the danger materializes
↓
Increased expectations of vulnerability and disappointment
in protective authorities
↓
Intense fear and anger

This sequence can be regarded as the major consequence of *failing to carry out the work of worrying*. Such failures are to be expected whenever a stressful event occurs under any of the following three conditions: (1) if the person is accustomed to suppressing anticipatory fear by means of denial defenses, by overoptimism, and by avoiding warnings that would stimulate the work of worrying; (2) if the stressful event is so sudden that it cannot be prepared for; and (3) if an adequate prior warning is not given, or if strong but false reassurances encourage the person to believe that he is invulnerable.

In order for the work of worrying to be complete, it seems that each source of stress must be anticipated and "worked through" in advance. This necessity is suggested by some outstanding instances of fright and rage observed in surgical patients who had displayed a moderate degree of anticipatory fear.

A young housewife, for example, had been somewhat worried before a lung operation and then, like most others in the moderately fearful group, showed excellent cooperation and little emotional disturbance throughout the postoperative period—except for one brief crisis she had not expected. She knew in advance about the acute incision pains and other unpleasant aspects of the postoperative recovery treatments, since she had undergone a similar operation once before and had asked her physician many pertinent questions about the impending second operation. But on the first postoperative day a physician entered her room and told her she would have to swallow a drainage tube, which she had never heard about before. She became extremely upset, could not relax sufficiently to cooperate, and finally begged the physician to take the tube away and let her alone. During an interview the following day she reported that she began to have extremely unfavorable thoughts about the physician at the time he made the unexpected demand; she suspected that he was withholding information about the seriousness of her condition, that he was unnecessarily imposing a hideous form of treatment on her, and that he was carrying out the treatment "so badly it was practically killing me." At no other time during the long and painful convalescence following the removal of her lung did she have any such doubts about this physician or any other member of the hospital staff; nor did she at any other time display any form of overt resistance. Evidently this was the one stressful event she had not anticipated and for which she had not, therefore, carried out the work of worrying.

This episode might help to explain why other patients who are caught by surprise display so much fright, anger, and uncooperative behavior. Those calm, seemingly stoic patients who do practically none of the work of worrying beforehand would be likely to encounter the same type of disruptive episode many times over during each day of their convalescence. (Janis, 1971, pp. 101–02)

The work of worrying is assumed to be stimulated by preparatory information concerning any realistic threat to one's physical, material, social, or moral well-being. It can be guided in a constructive direction by giving suggestions about how to cope with the threat together with reassuring information that fosters a hopeful outlook despite the anticipated losses.

This theoretical analysis emphasizes the importance of three main steps in the stress-inoculation procedure for people who initially ignore or deny any impending threat of suffering or loss (Janis, 1971, pp. 196–97): (1) giving "realistic information" in a way that challenges the clients' "blanket immunity reassurances" so as to make them aware of their vulnerability and to motivate them "to plan preparatory actions for dealing with the subsequent crisis"; (2) calling attention to reassuring facts about personal and social coping resources that enable the clients "to feel reasonably confident about surviving and ultimately recovering from the impending ordeal," in order to counteract "feelings of helplessness, hopelessness, and demoralization"; and (3) encouraging the clients to work out their own ways of reassuring themselves and their own plans for protecting themselves. The third step is important because in a crisis many people become passive and overdependent on family, friends, and authority figures, such as physicians or professional counselors. They need to build up cognitive defenses involving some degree of self-reliance instead of relying exclusively on others to protect them from suffering and loss.

The first two steps require careful administration of both distressing and calming information about what is likely to happen. For persons whose initial level of fear or grief is high, only the second and third steps would be used.

When carrying out the first step for clients who initially appear to be unperturbed or only moderately concerned about an impending ordeal, such as surgery, it is probably essential to include descriptive information that conveys a realistic picture of *the stressful occur-*

rences that the person is most likely to perceive. It probably does not help clients to mention unlikely occurrences, such as the dire complications and the potential risks that the surgeon needs to be concerned about. Giving clients information about all sorts of terrible things that might conceivably happen, as I pointed out earlier when discussing the legal requirements of informed consent, is likely to have unfavorable psychological consequences, inducing a state of hypervigilance and increasing the clients' sensitivity to anxiety-provoking events.

Clinical Uses in Treating Emotional and Physical Disorders

During the past decade stress inoculation has been extensively used by clinical practitioners who have developed the "cognitive-behavioral modification" form of therapy (see Goldfried, Decenteco, & Weinberg, 1974; Meichenbaum, 1977; Meichenbaum & Turk, 1976). In the research I have just reviewed, stress inoculation was introduced to *prevent* the damaging psychological consequences of subsequent exposures to stress, such as demoralization, depression, phobias, and psychosomatic disorders. In contrast, this new trend in clinical psychology uses stress inoculation to *alleviate* or *cure* the stress-related disorders from which patients are already suffering.

The procedures described by Donald Meichenbaum and his associates for clients suffering from phobic anxiety, such as excessive fear of needles used in injections and blood tests, include more than the three main steps I have just described. Again, the first step is to give preparatory information about the stressful situations that evoke the anxiety symptoms. Just as in the surgery cases, the client is told about (1) the negative features of the situations that arouse anxiety, including the possibility of high physiological arousal and feelings of being emotionally overwhelmed, and (2) the positive features that are reassuring and that can lead to the development of more effective ways of managing the situation. A major goal of this initial educational phase, which is usually conducted by means of a Socratic type of dialogue, is to help the clients reconceptualize their anxiety symptoms so that what they say to themselves when they are confronted with the phobic situation will no longer be self-defeating but conducive to effective action. Another somewhat related goal is to enable the client to grasp a more differentiated view of anxiety as comprising both cognitive appraisals of threat and physiological arousal. This differentiation sets the stage for the next phase.

The second phase is intended to help the client develop a new set of coping techniques that modify distressing cognitions and physiological arousal. The client is not only encouraged to make use of coping skills already in his or her repertoire but is also given training in new "direct action" skills, such as relaxation exercises that can be used to reduce emotional arousal in anxiety-provoking situations. A major goal of this phase is to prepare the client to react in a constructive way to early warning signs before the full onset of the anxiety symptoms. In addition to direct-action skills, cognitive coping skills are also discussed in collaborative interchanges designed to help the client work out coping strategies. The counselor gives suggestive examples of positive self-talk that might promote effective coping, such as "I can handle this situation by taking one step at a time." Some of the recommended self-talk is also likely to enhance the client's sense of self-efficacy after each successful trial—for example, "I can do it, it really worked; I can control my fear by controlling my ideas."

The third phase involves applying the new coping skills to a graded series of imaginary and real stress situations. The procedures used in this phase are based on the pioneering work of Seymour Epstein (1967), who emphasized the importance of "self-pacing" and exposure to small doses of threat in the acquisition of coping skills for mastery of stress among men engaged in dangerous activities, such as parachuting and combat flying. In the graduated practice phase of stress inoculation, the patient is given role-playing exercises and also a series of homework assignments involving increasingly demanding real-life exposures.

Favorable results from using this type of stress inoculation have been reported in clinical studies of clients suffering from emotional symptoms such as test anxiety and shyness (Meichenbaum, 1977). Essentially the same procedures have also been used successfully with patients suffering from certain kinds of physical ailments, most notably those involving sporadic or chronic pain (Turk & Genest, 1979). From the clinical research that has been done so far, it appears that a package treatment combining the various kinds of intervention that enter into this type of stress inoculation can sometimes be effective with some patients, but it is not yet known which interventions are essential and which are not. At present we are just starting to learn about the conditions under which giving preparatory information and administering any other components of stress inoculation are likely to succeed or fail.

When Preparatory Communications Fail

The fact is that preparatory communications are not always successful. Here and there in the prior research on stress inoculation one can discern a few rudimentary indications of the conditions under which it is ineffective. From the very outset of my research on surgery it was apparent that although preparatory communications are advantageous for many patients, they definitely are not for some of them (Janis, 1958, pp. 370–74). In numerous instances of failure the main source of difficulty seems to be that the message is too meager to influence the patients. Very brief preparatory messages that take only a few minutes to convey information about impending threats are usually too weak to change a patient's expectations or to stimulate the development of effective self-reassurances and therefore have no effect at all (Field, 1974; Langer, Janis, & Wolfer, 1975). At the opposite extreme, some patients receive very strong preparatory communications from their physicians and friends, which unintentionally stimulate anxiety and feelings of helplessness that decrease rather than increase stress tolerance. Like an overdose of antigens, an overenthusiastic inoculation attempt can produce the very condition it is intended to prevent. (For a review of research on the negative and positive effects of preparatory information given to surgical patients see Cohen & Lazarus, 1979.)

Other sources of detrimental effects have to do with the nature of the stress to which the person is subsequently exposed. For example, some of my observations suggest that medical practitioners elicit better cooperation if they give no preparatory information about a disturbing procedure of short duration, such as an enema or an injection, until they administer it, provided that they give the patients reassurances along with instructions about what to do (Janis, 1958, p. 394). In these instances the stress episode itself is relatively mild because the patients do not undergo acute pain or prolonged discomfort and an authority figure is present to reassure them that they are doing fine. Probably stress inoculation is most applicable for those episodes that are very painful and recurrent, or of long duration, and that are likely to occur at times when no one will be around to give reassurances.

When the anticipated threat is extremely severe and practically nothing can be done to mitigate it, as in the case of cancer patients who have little prospect of being cured, a practitioner should be very cautious about introducing a stress-inoculation procedure, especially with patients who appear to be dealing about as well as can be expected with the increasingly adverse circumstances as they arise. In such cases, a stress-inoculation procedure might interfere with effective denial defenses and benign illusions that might best be left intact (Lazarus, 1983; Taylor, 1982).

Until the effectiveness of a stress-inoculation procedure has been carefully tested in well-designed evaluation studies, we cannot be certain that it will work the way it is intended to. Consider, for example, the question of whether stress inoculation should be used for helping people to maintain self-control when they are trying to carry out a difficult course of action such as sticking to a diet. There is now some evidence that makes me very skeptical about the applicability of stress inoculation to dieters. Recently, I have collaborated with Donald M. Quinlan and Debra Kimes (1982) on three field experiments at the Yale Weight-Reduction Clinic to assess the effectiveness of various components of stress inoculation in helping dieters avoid backsliding. Our initial assumption was that stress-inoculation procedures of the type that had been found to be effective in research with surgical and medical patients would also be effective in preventing backsliding among overweight clients who commit themselves to adhering to a low-calorie diet. But the findings failed to support this assumption. We found in two of our field experiments that the standard type of stress inoculation, including two key components (giving preparatory information that calls attention to problems to be anticipated and presenting recommendations about ways of coping with those problems), was not effective in helping overweight clients adhere to the diet in the long run; we also found that neither of the two components alone was effective. In our third field experiment we used a related but different type of psychological preparation—a coping device that involves guided positive self-talk, which our prior research had shown was effective with surgical patients. The new findings indicate that it too failed to have the expected effect with dieters.

These three field experiments raise serious doubts about the efficacy of using stress-inoculation procedures with clients who seek help in losing weight. Currently such procedures are used by many clinical practitioners for dealing with all sorts of stresses on the basis of the positive findings from the surgery studies and other research cited. Cormier and Cormier (1979) in their textbook for counselors discuss the wide applicability of stress inoculation.

> The prevention aspect of stress inoculation is achieved by having clients apply the newly learned coping strategies to situations that may not be problematic now but could be stressful in the future.
>
> . . . Application of coping skills to other potentially stressful situations is accomplished in the same way as application to the specific problem areas. . . . The counselor might select a situation the client has not encountered, although the situation would require active coping for anyone who might encounter it. Such situations could include not receiving a desired job promotion or raise, facing a family crisis, moving to a new place, anticipating retirement, being very ill, and so on. (Cormier & Cormier, 1979, p. 384)

The unexpected negative findings from our three field experiments with dieters once again call attention to the need for separate empirical evaluation of stress inoculation for each type of stress situation to which it is thought to be applicable. As our field experiments show, even though a procedure has been found to be effective in several clinical settings, applying it in a different context or with a different type of client can prove to be ineffective and perhaps even detrimental. Our findings provide strong empirical grounds for skepticism about applying stress-inoculation and related coping procedures in new contexts before they have been carefully tested in the new settings.

What Are the Effective Components?

We have seen that most research findings indicate that stress inoculation works but that there are also a few findings that show it sometimes does not. Obviously the time has come to move on to a more sophisticated phase of research, to investigate systematically the conditions under which stress inoculation is effective and the conditions under which it is not. In this new phase of research, which has recently begun, the investigators' primary purpose is no longer to evaluate the overall effectiveness of stress-inoculation procedures, to find out whether one or another compound treatment program is successful in building up tolerance for one or another type of stress, but rather, to find out which are the *effective components* of the stress-inoculation treatments that have already been found to be at least partially successful and to determine the conditions under which each component has a positive effect on stress tolerance.

From prior studies, we have already obtained important clues about what could prove to be the crucial components that stimulate the kind of mental rehearsal necessary for the constructive work of worrying. One such promising component involves conveying preparatory messages that enable the clients to reconceptualize the anticipated stresses in a positive way so that they can engage in reassuring and hopeful self-talk when they think about the stresses beforehand and when the stresses are actually encountered. A coping device developed by Langer, Janis, and Wolfer (1975), which involves encouraging an optimistic reappraisal of anxiety-provoking events, was tested in a field experiment with surgical patients by inserting it in a brief preoperative interview conducted by a psychologist.

Each patient was given several examples of the positive consequences of his or her decision to undergo surgery (for example, improvement in health, extra care and attention in the hospital, temporary vacation from outside pressures). Then the patient was invited to think up additional positive examples that pertained to his or her individual case. Finally the patient was given the recommendation to rehearse these compensatory favorable consequences whenever he or she started to feel upset about the unpleasant aspects of the surgical experience. Patients were urged to be as realistic as possible about the compensatory features, so as to emphasize that what was being recommended was not equivalent to trying to deceive oneself. The instructions were designed to promote warranted optimism and awareness of the anticipated gains that outweighed the losses to be expected from the chosen course of action.

The findings from the controlled experiment conducted by Langer, Janis, and Wolfer (1975) supported the prediction that cognitive reappraisal would reduce stress both before and after an operation. Patients given the reappraisal intervention obtained lower scores on nurses' blind ratings of preoperative stress and on unobtrusive postoperative measures of the number of times pain-relieving drugs and sedatives were requested and administered.

Additional evidence of the value of encouraging cognitive coping strategies comes from a study by Kendall, Williams, Pechacek, Graham, Shisslak, and Herzoff (1977) on the effectiveness of stress inoculation for patients who had agreed to undergo cardiac catheterization. Stress tolerance for this extremely unpleasant and frightening procedure was assessed by self-ratings and by observers' ratings (made by medical technicians). The patients given a stress-inoculation procedure that encouraged them to develop their own cognitive coping strategies for reassuring self-talk showed higher stress tolerance during the cardiac catheterization than those given other preparatory treatments.

One cannot expect, of course, that every attempt to encourage positive thinking among patients facing surgery or distressing treatments will succeed in helping their recovery during convalescence. One such attempt with surgical patients by Cohen (1975), using different intervention procedures from those in the preceding studies, failed to have any effect on indicators of psychological and physical recovery.

Although few studies have been done among patients who are not hospitalized, there is some evidence suggesting that encouraging positive self-talk and related cognitive coping strategies might prove to be successful in other spheres of health care. In a controlled field experiment, a stress-inoculation procedure designed to encourage positive self-talk was found to be effective in helping patients reduce the frequency, duration, and intensity of muscle-contraction headaches (Holroyd, Andrasik, & Westbrook, 1977).

From the few systematic studies just reviewed, it seems reasonable to expect that recommendations about coping strategies may prove to be essential ingredients of successful stress inoculation. The evidence is particularly promising, as we have seen, with regard to increasing the stress tolerance of medical and surgical patients by encouraging them to replace self-defeating thoughts with positive coping cognitions. A similar conclusion is drawn by Girodo (1977) after reviewing the positive and negative outcomes of treating phobic patients with the type of stress-inoculation procedures recommended by Meichenbaum (1977). Girodo goes so far as to say that the only successful ingredients of stress inoculation are those that induce the person to reconceptualize the threat into nonthreatening terms and that all other ingredients are of limited value, merely serving to divert attention temporarily from threat cues. Any such generalization, however, gives undue weight to a limited set of findings and would be premature until we have well-replicated results from a variety of investigations that carefully test the effectiveness of each component of stress inoculation.

Two other key components are suggested by systematic research findings from a number of studies. One consists of *descriptive warning information* about whatever ordeals lie ahead, which increases the *predictability* of the stressful events so that the clients will know what to expect and not be caught by surprise. Another consists of *information and suggestions about specific coping actions* that could enable the clients to protect themselves from impending dangers or at least reduce the amount of suffering and loss. Some of the positive effects of making plans and developing adequate coping skills, both for handling the objective threats and for controlling one's own emotions, involve another important psychological variable, namely, *building up a sense of self-confidence* about being able to "take it" and to do whatever is required. Bandura (1977) has emphasized the crucial role of this variable—which he refers to as *feelings of personal efficacy*—as a major determinant of the positive behavioral changes resulting from counseling and psychotherapy.

Closely related to clients' attitudes of self-confidence are their beliefs about mastery in a stressful situation. Stress inoculation may change a client's *expectations of being in control* of a dangerous situation, with regard to both the external threats of being helpless to prevent physical damage and the internal threats of becoming panic-stricken and losing emotional control. The stress-inoculation procedures used with surgical and medical patients typically include statements designed to counteract feelings of helplessness and to promote a sense of active control (Janis & Rodin, 1979). For example, Pranulis, Dabbs, and Johnson (1975) redirect hospitalized patients' attention away from their own emotional reactions as passive recipients of medical treatments to information that makes them feel more in control as active collaborators with the staff. Perhaps many of the preparatory communications used for purposes of stress inoculation have essentially the same effect on the patients' perceived control over distressing environmental events, which could increase their self-confidence and hope.

Yet another psychological component that may contribute to the positive effects of stress inoculation is the *heightening of commitment*. As part of the stress-inoculation procedure for a new course of action, such as undergoing painful treatments, clients are induced to acknowledge that they are going to have to do something to cope with the anticipated stresses, which is tantamount to making commitment statements to the counselor.

Along with inducing increased commitment, stress inoculation also tends to *build up the client's sense of personal responsibility*. For example, after hearing about the unpleasant consequences to be expected from undergoing a prescribed medical treatment, the client is likely to realize all the more keenly that he or she is personally responsible for doing whatever is necessary to cooperate with the physician who is administering the treatment, rather than simply being a passive recipient of whatever the physician does. Each time a counselor makes a prediction about a stressful experience to be expected and offers a coping suggestion about how to deal with it, he or she implicitly conveys the theme, "this is a problem *you* must solve yourself; no one else can do it for you."

The last two variables—inducing commitment and a sense of personal responsibility—are among the 12 that were singled out as essential for an effective helping relationship according to the theoretical analysis presented earlier (Table 2.1, p. 27). In general, the theory and research presented in chapters 2–5 lead one to expect that clients will be most responsive to stress inoculation if the counselor follows the guidelines for including the other key variables as well, so as to build, use, and retain motivating power as a dependable enhancer of self-esteem. The same can be said, of course, for any special counseling procedures, including the ones discussed in earlier sections of the present chapter.

Taking Account of Individual Differences

Although a number of studies on the effectiveness of stress inoculation show positive results for many clients, no such procedure does so for all clients. For certain types of persons, stress inoculation has been found to have no effect at all and occasionally even an adverse effect. For example, two independent studies of surgical patients indicate that persons who display defensive avoidance tendencies, as assessed by personality tests of coping styles, do not respond well to standard preparatory communications that have a favorable effect on the postoperative recovery of other people (Andrew, 1970; DeLong, 1971). These and numerous other findings on personality factors related to responsiveness to stress inoculation call attention, once again, to the need for counselors to take account of individual differences. (See my review of the pertinent studies in Janis, 1983.) One client may show signs of ignoring the standard warning information about an anticipated ordeal, which may require the counselor to give a somewhat more elaborate descriptive account to induce at least some mild feelings of personal vulnerability. Another client may show signs of becoming upset by one of the specific threats mentioned in a standard warning communication and may need a specific form of reassurance to alleviate intense feelings of personal vulnerability. Still another client may display signs of demoralization in response to all the counselor's suggestions about how to cope with the anticipated stresses and may require considerable encouragement to build up attitudes of hope and self-confidence.

In short, counselors must be prepared to be flexible when using a stress-inoculation procedure. The counselor must use his or her best clinical judgment to select the appropriate components for each client, paying close attention to the client's personal reactions while presenting the preparatory communications so as to ascertain which components to emphasize and which ones to modulate. In this way the procedure can be hand-tailored to suit the individual needs of each client. It seems to me that this approach should be particularly emphasized for stress inoculation, and also for the awareness-of-rationalizations technique, emotional role playing, the balance-sheet procedure, and outcome psychodrama. An approach that takes account of individual differences is especially necessary because such procedures have the potentiality of temporarily undermining a person's psychological defenses and evoking acute affective distress. Although the guidelines for these counseling procedures are based on scientific research, applying them effectively remains more an art than a science.

References

American Psychological Association Task Force on Health. Contributions of psychology to health research; Pattern, problems and potentials. *American Psychologist,* 1976, *37,* 263–274.

Andrew, J. M. Recovery from surgery, with and without preparatory instructions, for three coping styles, *Journal of Personality and Social Psychology,* 1970, *15,* 223–226.

Atthowe, J. Behavior innovation and persistence. *American Psychologist,* 1973, *28,* 34–41.

Bandura, A. *Principles of behavior modification,* New York: Holt, Rinehart & Winston, 1969.

Bandura, A. Effecting change through participant modeling. In J. D. Krumboltz & C. E. Thoresen (Eds.), *Counseling methods.* New York: Holt, Rinehart & Winston, 1976.

Bandura A. Self-efficacy: Toward a unifying theory of behavioral change. *Psychological Review,* 1977, *84,* 191–215.

Bandura, A., Adams, N. E., & Beyer, J. Cognitive processes mediating behavioral change. *Journal of Personality and Social Psychology.* 1977, *35,* 125–139.

Bandura, A., & Simon, K. The role of proximal intentions in self-regulation of refractory behavior. *Cognitive Therapy and Research,* 1977, *1,* 177–193.

Baron, R., & Rodin, J. Perceived control and crowding stress. In A. Baum, J. E. Singer, & S. Valins (Eds.), *Advances in environmental psychology.* Hillsdale, N.J.: Erlbaum, 1978.

Barrett-Leonard, G. T. Dimensions of therapist response as causal factors in therapeutic change. *Psychological Monographs,* 1962, *76*(43, Whole No. 562).

Baudry, R., & Wiener, A. The pregnant patient in conflict about abortion: A challenge for the obstetrician. *American Journal of Obstetrics and Gynecology,* 1974, *119,* 705–711.

Beck, A. T. *Cognitive therapy and the emotional disorders.* New York: International Universities Press, 1976.

Becker, E. *The structure of evil.* New York: Braziller, 1968.

Bennis, W. G., Berlew, D. E., Schein, E. H., & Steele, F. I. Some interpersonal aspects of self confirmation. In W. G. Bennis et al. (Eds.), *Interpersonal dynamics* (3rd ed.) Homewood, Ill.: Dorsey, 1973.

Berne, E. *Transactional analysis in psychotherapy.* New York: Grove, 1961.

Berscheid, E., & Walster, E. *Interpersonal attraction* (2nd ed.), Reading, Mass.: Addison-Wesley, 1978.

Best, J. H., Bass, F., & Owen, L. E. Mode of service delivery in a smoking cessation program for public health. *Canadian Journal of Public Health,* 1977, *68,* 469–473.

Blackwell, B. The literature of delay in seeking medical care for chronic illnesses. *Health Education Monographs, No. 16: 3,* 1963.

Blechman, E. A. The role of problem solutions and problem solving in behavioral intreraction. Unpublished manuscript, Yale University, 1977.

Blechman, E. A., Olson, D., & Hellman, I. Stimulus control over family problem-solving behavior: The family contract game. *Behavior Therapy,* 1976, *7,* 686–692.

Brammer, L. M., & Shostrom, E. L. *Therapeutic psychology: Fundamentals of actualization counseling and psychotherapy.* Englewood Cliffs, N.J.: Prentice-Hall, 1968.

Breen, D. *The birth of a first child: Toward an understanding of femininity.* London: Tavistock, 1975.

Brehm, S. *The application of social psychology to clinical practice.* New York: Halsted Press (Wiley), 1976.

Broadhurst, A. Applications of the psychology of decisions. In M. P. Feldman and A. Broadhurst (Eds.), *Theoretical and experimental bases of the behavior therapies.* London: Wiley, 1976.

Brownell, K. D., Heckerman, C. L., & Westlake, R. J. Therapist and group contact as variables in the behavioral treatment of obesity. Paper presented at the annual meeting of the Association for the Advancement of Behavior Therapy, New York, December 1976.

Byrne, D. *The attraction paradigm.* New York: Academic Press, 1971.

Byrne, D., & Griffitt, W. Similarity and awareness of similarity of personality characteristics as determinants of attraction. *Journal of Experimental Research in Personality.* 1969, *3,* 179–186.

Carkhuff, R. R. *The art of helping.* Amherst, Mass.: Human Resources Development Press, 1972.

Carkhuff, R. R., & Pierce, R. M. *Trainer's guide: The art of helping.* Amherst, Mass.: Human Resources Development Press, 1975.

Carter, E. N., Rice, H. P., & De Julio, S. Role of the therapist in the self-control of obesity. *Journal of Consulting and Clinical psychology,* 1977, *45,* 503.

Cartwright, D., & Zander, A. (Eds.). *Group dynamics: Research and theory* (3rd ed.). New York: Harper & Row, 1968.

Chaiken, A. L., Derlega, V. J., & Miller, S. Effect of room environment on self-disclosure in a counseling analogue. *Journal of Counseling Psychology,* 1976, *23,* 479–481.

Chang, P. *The effects of quality of self-disclosure on reactions to interviewer feedback.* Unpublished doctoral dissertation, University of Southern California, 1977.

Cochran, D. J., Hoffman, S. D., Strand, K. H., & Warren, P. Effects of client/computer interaction on career decision-making processes. *Journal of Counseling Psychology,* 1977, *24,* 308–312.

Cohen, F. *Psychological preparation, coping, and recovery from surgery.* Unpublished doctoral dissertation, University of California, Berkeley, 1975.

Cohen, F. & Lazarus, R. S. Coping with the stresses of illness. In G. C. Stone, F. Cohen, & N. E. Adler (Eds.), *Health psychology.* San Francisco: Jossey-Bass, 1979.

Collins, B. E., & Raven, B. H. Group structure: Attraction, coalitions, communication and power. In G. Lindzey & E. Aronson (Eds.), *The handbook of social psychology* (Vol. 4). Reading, Mass.: Addison-Wesley, 1969.

Colten, M. E., & Janis, I. L. Effects of moderate self-disclosure and the balance-sheet procedure. In I. L. Janis (Ed.), *Counseling on personal decisions: Theory and research on short-term helping relationships.* New Haven: Yale University Press, 1982.

Conolley, E. S., Janis, I. L., & Dowds, M. M., Jr. Effects of variations in the type of feedback given by the counselor. In I. L. Janis (Ed.), *Counseling on personal decisions: Theory and research on short-term helping relationships.* New Haven: Yale University Press, 1982.

Cormier, W. H., & Cormier, L. S. *Interviewing strategies for helpers: A guide to assessment, treatment and evaluation.* Monterey, Calif.: Brooks/Cole, 1979.

Corsini, R. J. Counseling and psychotherapy. In E. F. Borgatta & W. W. Lambert (Eds.), *Handbook of personality theory and research.* Chicago: Rand McNally, 1968.

Cozby, P. C. Self-disclosure: A literature review. *Psychological Bulletin,* 1973, *79,* 73–91.

Darley, J. M., & Aronson, E. Self-evaluation vs. direct anxiety reduction as determinants of the fear–affiliation relationship. In B. Latane (Ed.), *Studies in social comparison.* New York: Academic Press. 1966.

Davis, M. S. Variations in patients' compliance with doctor's orders: Analysis of congruence between survey responses and results of empirical investigations. *Journal of Medical Education,* 1966, *41,* 1037.

Davison, G. C., & Valins, S. Maintenance of self-attributed and drug attributed behavior change. *Journal of Personality and Social Psychology,* 1969, *11,* 25–33.

DeLong, D. R. *Individual differences in patterns of anxiety arousal, stress-relevant information and recovery from surgery.* Unpublished doctoral dissertation, University of California, Los Angeles, 1971.

DeRisi, W. I., and Butz, G. *Writing behavioral contracts.* Champaign, Ill.: Research Press, 1974.

Deutsch, M., & Solomon, L. Reactions to evaluations by others as influenced by self-evaluation. *Sociometry,* 1959, *22,* 93–112.

Dittes, J. E. Attractiveness of the group as function of self esteem and acceptance by the group. *Journal of Abnormal and Social Psychology,* 1959, *59,* 77–82.

Doering, S. G., & Entwhisle, D. R. Preparation during pregnancy and ability to cope with labor and delivery. *American Journal of Orthopsychiatry,* 1975, *45,* 825–837.

Dowds, M. M., Jr., Janis, I. L., & Conolley, E. S. Effects of acceptance by the counselor. In I. L. Janis (Ed.), *Counseling on personal decisions: Theory and research on short-term helping relationships.* New Haven: Yale University Press, 1982.

Edwards, W. The theory of decision making. *Psychological Bulletin,* 1954, *51,* 380–417.

Egan, G. *The skilled helper: A model for systematic helping and interpersonal relating.* Monterey, Calif.: Brooks/Cole, 1975.

Egbert, L., Battit, G., Welch, C., & Bartlett, M. Reduction of post-operative pain by encouragement and instruction. *New England Journal of Medicine,* 1964, *270,* 825–827.

Ellis, A. Psychotherapy and the value of a human being. In A. Ellis & R. Grieger (Eds.), *Handbook of rational-emotive therapy.* New York: Springer, 1977a.

Ellis, A. Sex and love problems in women. In A. Ellis & R. Grieger (Eds.), *Handbook of rational-emotive therapy.* New York: Springer, 1977b.

Ellis, A., & Grieger, R. (Eds.). *Handbook of rational-emotive therapy.* New York: Springer, 1977.

Erickson, M. H., & Rossi, E. L. *Utilizing ideodynamic processes in hypnotherapy: An exploratory casebook.* New York: Wiley, 1979.

Ewart, C. *Behavior contracts in couple therapy: An experimental evaluation of quid pro quo and good faith models.* Unpublished doctoral dissertation, Stanford University, 1978.

Fellner, C. H., & Marshall, J. Kidney donors: The myth of informed consent. *American Journal of Psychiatry,* 1970, *126,* 1245–1251.

Festinger, L. A theory of social comparison processes. *Human Relations,* 1954, *7,* 117–140.

Field, P. Effects of tape-recorded hypnotic preparation for surgery. *International Journal of Clinical and Experimental Hypnosis.* 1974, *22,* 54–61.

Fish, J. M. *Placebo therapy.* San Francisco: Jossey-Bass, 1973.

Fiske, P. W., Hunt, H. F., Luborsky, L., Orne, M. T., Parloff, M. B., Reiser, M. F., & Tuma, A. H. The planning of research on effectiveness of psychotherapy. (Report of workshop sponsored and supported by Clinical Projects Res. Rev. Comm., NIMH). *Archives of General Psychiatry,* 1970, *22,* 22–32.

Frank, J. The bewildering world of psychotherapy. *Journal of Social Issues,* 1972, *28,* 27–44.

Franks, C. M. (Ed.). *Behavior therapy: Appraisal and status.* New York: McGraw-Hill, 1969.

French, J. R., & Raven, B. The bases of social power. In D. Cartwright (Ed.), *Studies in social power.* Ann Arbor: University of Michigan Press, 1959.

Garfield S. L. Research on client variables in psychotherapy. In A. E. Bergin and S. L. Garfield (Eds.), *Handbook of psychotherapy and behavior change.* New York: Wiley, 1971.

Garfield, S. L., & Bergin, A. E. (Eds.). *Handbook of psychotherapy and behavior change: An empirical analysis* (2nd ed.). New York: Wiley, 1978.

Gentry, D., Foster, S., & Haney, T. Denial as a determinant of anxiety and perceived health in the coronary care unit. *Psychosomatic Medicine,* 1972, *34,* 39.

Girodo, M. Self-talk: Mechanisms in anxiety and stress management. In C. Spielberger & I. G. Sarason (Eds.). *Stress and anxiety.* Vol. 4. Washington, D.C.: Hemisphere, 1977.

Goldfried, M. R., Decenteco, E. T., & Weinberg, L. Systematic rational restructuring as a self-control technique. *Behavior Therapy,* 1974, *5,* 247–254.

Goldsen, R. K., Gerhardt, P. T., & Handy, V. H. Some factors related to patient delay in seeking diagnosis for cancer symptoms. *Cancer,* 1957, *10,* 1–7.

Goldstein, A. P. Relationship-enhancement methods. In F. H. Kanfer and A. P. Goldstein (Eds.), *Helping people change.* New York: Pergamon Press, 1975.

Gomersall, E. R., & Myers, M. S. Breakthrough in on-the-job training. *Harvard Business Review,* 1966, *44,* 62–72.

Greene, L. R. Effects of the counselor's verbal feedback, interpersonal distance, and clients' field dependence. In I. L. Janis (Ed.), *Counseling on personal decisions: Theory and research on short-term helping relationships.* New Haven: Yale University Press, 1982.

Greenwald, H. *Decision therapy:* New York: Wyden, 1973.

Hackett, T. P., & Cassem, N. H. Psychological management of the myocardial infarction patient. *Journal of Human Stress,* 1975, *1,* 25–38.

Hackett, T. P., Cassem, N. H., & Wishnie, H. A. The coronary care unit: An appraisal of its psychological hazards. *New England Journal of Medicine,* 1968, *279,* 1365.

Hackman, R., & Morris, C. G. Group tasks, group interaction process, and group performance effectiveness: A review and proposed integration. In L. Berkowitz (Ed.), *Advances in experimental social psychology* (Vol 8). New York: Academic Press, 1975.

Hamburg, D. A., Coelho, G. V., & Adams, J. E. Coping and adaptation: Steps toward a synthesis of biological and social perspectives. In G. V. Coelho, D. A. Hamburg, & J. E. Adams (Eds.), *Coping and adaptation.* New York: Basic Books, 1974.

Hamilton, E. *Three Greek plays—translated with introductions by Edith Hamilton.* New York: Norton, 1958.

Hare, A. P. *Handbook of small group research* (2nd ed.). New York: Free Press, 1976.

Harris, J. E. The computer: Guidance tool of the future, *Journal of Counseling Psychology,* 1974, *21,* 331–339.

Helmreich, R. L., & Collins, B. E. Situational determinants of affiliative preference under stress. *Journal of Personality and Social Psychology,* 1967, *6,* 79–85.

Henderson, J. B., Hall, S. M., & Lipton, H. L. Changing self-destructive behaviors. In J. C. Stone, F. Cohen, & N. E. Adler (Eds.), *Health psychology.* San Francisco: Jossey-Bass, 1979.

Holland, J. L., Magoon, T. M., & Spokane, A. R. Counseling psychology: Career interventions, research, and theory. *Annual Review of Psychology,* 1981, *32,* 279–305.

Holroyd, K. A., Andrasik, F., & Westbrook, T. Cognitive control of tension headache. *Cognitive Therapy and Research,* 1977, *1,* 121–133.

Horan, J. J. "In vivo" emotive imagery: A technique for reducing childbirth anxiety and discomfort. *Psychological Reports,* 1973, *32,* 1328.

Hoyt, M. F., & Janis, I. L. Increasing adherence to a stressful decision via a motivational balance-sheet procedure: A field experiment. *Journal of Personality and Social Psychology,* 1975, *31,* 833–839 (Reprinted in I. L. Janis [Ed.], *Counseling on personal decisions: Theory and research on short-term helping relationships.* New Haven: Yale University Press, 1982.

Hunt, W. A., & Bespalec, D. A. An evaluation of current methods of modifying smoking behavior. *Journal of Clinical Psychology,* 1974, *30,* 431–438.

Hunt, W. A., & Matarazzo, J. F. Three years later: Recent developments in the experimental modification of smoking behavior. *Journal of Abnormal Psychology,* 1973, *81,* 107–114.

Janis, I. L. *Psychological stress.* New York: Wiley, 1958.

Janis, I. L. Group identification under conditions of external danger. In D. Cartwright & A. Zander (Eds.), *Group dynamics: Research and theory* (3rd ed.). New York: Harper & Row, 1968.

Janis, I. L. *Stress and frustration.* New York: Harcourt, Brace, Jovanovich, 1971.

Janis, I. L. (Ed.). *Counseling on personal decisions: Theory and research on short-term helping relationships.* New Haven: Yale University Press, 1982a.

Janis, I. L. *Final progress report: Stress inoculation and adherence to health decisions.* Submitted to Behavioral and Social Sciences Research Branch, Public Health Service, HHS, ADAMA. (Mimeo). 1982b.

Janis, I. L. Improving adherence to medical recommendations: Prescriptive hypotheses derived from recent research in social psychology. In A. Baum, J. E. Singer, & S. E. Taylor (Eds.), *Handbook of medical psychology.* Vol. 4. New York: Erlbaum. In Press.

Janis, I. L. Stress inoculation in health care: Theory and research. In D. Meichenbaum & M. Jaremko (Eds.), *Stress reduction and prevention.* New York: Plenum, 1983.

Janis, I. L., & Hoffman, D. Facilitating effects of daily contact between partners who make a decision to cut down on smoking. *Journal of Personality and Social Psychology,* 1970, *17,* 25–35.

Janis, I. L. & Hoffman, D. Effective partnerships in a clinic for smokers. In I. L. Janis (Ed.), *Counseling on personal decisions: Theory and research on short-term helping relationships.* New Haven: Yale University Press, 1982.

Janis, I. L., & LaFlamme, D. M. Effects of outcome psychodrama as a supplementary technique in marital and career counseling. In I. L. Janis (Ed.), *Counseling on personal decisions: Theory and research on short-term helping relationships.* New Haven: Yale University Press, 1982.

Janis, I. L., & Mann, L. Effectiveness of emotional role playing in modifying smoking habits and attitudes. *Journal of Experimental Research in Personality,* 1965, *1,* 84–90.

Janis, I. L., & Mann, L. *Decision making: A psychological analysis of conflict, choice, and commitment.* New York: Free Press, 1977.

Janis, I. L., & Quinlan, D. M. What disclosing means to the client: Comparative case studies. In I. L. Janis (Ed.), *Counseling on personal decisions: Theory and research on short-term helping relationships.* New Haven: Yale University Press, 1982.

Janis, I. L., Quinlan, D. M., & Kimes, D. *Effects of stress inoculation designed to help dieters: Negative results from three field experiments*. Mimeo, Yale University, 1982 (To be published).

Janis, I. L., & Rodin, J. Attribution, control and decision-making: Social psychology in health care. In G. C. Stone, F. Cohen, and N. E. Adler (Eds.), *Health psychology*. San Francisco: Jossey-Bass, 1979.

Janoff-Bulman, R. Self-blame in rape victims: A control-maintenance strategy. Paper presented at American Psychological Association Meetings, Toronto, 1978.

Johnson, J. E. The influence of purposeful nurse–patient interaction on the patients' postoperative course. *A.N.A. Monograph series No. 2: Exploring medical-surgical nursing practice*. New York: American Nurses' Association, 1966.

Johnson, J. E., & Leventhal, H. Effects of accurate expectations and behavioral instructions on reactions during a noxious medical examination. *Journal of Personality and Social Psychology*, 1974, *29*, 710–718.

Johnson, J. E., Rice, V. H., Fuller, S. S., & Endress, P. Sensory information, behavioral instruction, and recovery from surgery. Paper presented at annual meeting of the American Psychological Association, San Francisco, 1977.

Jonas, G. Profiles: Visceral learning I. Dr. Neal E. Miller. *New Yorker Magazine*, 1972, *48*, 34–57.

Jones, E. E. *Ingratiation: A social psychological analysis*. New York: Appleton-Century-Crofts, 1964

Jourard, S. M. *Disclosing man to himself*. Princeton: Van Nostrand, 1968.

Jourard, S. M. *The transparent self* (Rev. ed.). New York: Van Nostrand Reinhold, 1971.

Kahneman, D., & Tversky, A. Prospect theory: An analysis of decision under risk. *Econometrica*, 1979, *47*, 263–292.

Kanfer, F. H., Cox, L. E., Greiner, J. M., & Karoly, P. Contracts, demand characteristics, and self-control. *Journal of Personality and Social Psychology*, 1974, *30*, 605–619.

Kanfer, F. H., & Karoly, P. Self-control: A behavioristic excursion into the lion's den. *Behavior Therapy*, 1972, *3*, 398–416.

Kanfer, F. H., & Phillips, J. S. *Learning foundations of behavior therapy*. New York: Wiley, 1970.

Kaplan, K. J., Firestone, I. J., Degnore, R., & Moore, M. Gradients of attraction as a function of disclosure, probe intimacy and setting formality: On distinguishing attitude oscillation from attitude change—study one. *Journal of Personality and Social Psychology*, 1974, *30*, 638–646.

Kasl, S. V. Issues in patient adherence to health care regimens. *Journal of Human Stress*. 1975, *1*, 5–18.

Kasl, S. V., & Cobb, S. Health behavior, illness behavior, and sick role behavior. *Archives of Environmental Health,* 1966, *12,* 246–266, 531–541.

Kazdin, A. E. Developing assertive behavior through covert modeling. In J. D. Krumboltz & C. E. Thoresen (Eds.), *Counseling methods.* New York: Holt, Rinehart & Winston, 1976.

Kendall, P., Williams, L., Pechacek, T. F., Graham, L. E., Shisslak, C., & Herzoff, N. The Palo Alto medical psychology project: Cognitive-behavioral patient education interventions in catheterization procedures. *Journal of Consulting and Clinical Psychology,* 1979, *47,* 49–58.

Kiesler, C. A. (Ed.). *The psychology of commitment* New York: Academic Press, 1971.

Kiesler, C. A., & Sakumura, J. A test of a model for commitment. *Journal of Personality and Social Psychology,* 1966, *3,* 349–353.

Kirscht, J. P., & Rosenstock, I. M. Patients' problems in following recommendations of health experts. In G. C. Stone, F. Cohen, & N. E. Adler (Eds.), *Health psychology.* San Francisco: Jossey-Bass, 1979.

Knapp, M. L. *Nonverbal communication in human interaction.* New York: Holt, Rinehart & Winston, 1972.

Kohut, H. *The restoration of the self.* New York: International Universities Press, 1977.

Krumboltz, J. D. (Ed.). *Revolution in counseling.* Boston: Houghton Mifflin, 1966.

Krumboltz, J. D., Becker-Haven, J. F., & Burnett, K. F. Counseling psychology. *Annual Review of Psychology,* 1979, *30,* 556–602.

Kutner, B., Makover, H. B., & Oppenheim, A. Delay in the diagnosis and treatment of cancer: A critical analysis of the literature. *Journal of Chronic Diseases,* 1958, *7,* 95–120.

LaFlamme, D., & Janis, I. L. *Effects of the balance-sheet and the outcome psychodrama procedures on career decision-making processes.* Unpublished study, Yale University, 1977.

Labov, W., & Fanshel, D. *Therapeutic discourse.* New York: Academic Press, 1977.

Lando, Harry A. Successful treatment of smokers with a broad-spectrum behavioral approach. *Journal of Consulting and Clinical Psychology,* 1977, *45,* 361–366.

Langer, E. J., Janis, I. L., & Wolfer, J. Reduction of psychological stress in surgical patients. *Journal of Experimental Social Psychology,* 1975, *1,* 155–166. Reprinted in I. L. Janis (Ed.), *Counseling on personal decisions: Theory and research on short-term helping relationships.* New Haven: Yale University Press, 1982.

Lazarus, A. *Multi-modal behavior therapy*. New York: Springer, 1976.

Lazarus, R. S. The costs and benefits of denial. In S. Breznitz (Ed.), *The denial of stress*. New York: International Universities Press, 1983.

Lester, D., & Brockopp, G. W. (Eds.). *Crisis intervention and counseling by telephone*. Springfield, Ill.: Thomas, 1973.

Leventhal, H., & Cleary P. D. The smoking problem: A review of the research and theory in behavioral risk modification. *Psychological Bulletin, 1980, 88*, 370–405.

Leventhal, H., & Niles, P. A field experiment on fear arousal with data on the validity of questionnaire measures. *Journal of Personality, 1964, 32*, 459–479.

Levin, F. M., & Gergen, K. J. Revealingness, ingratiation, and the disclosure of self. *Proceedings of the 77th Annual Convention of the American Psychological Association, 1969, 4* (Pt. 1), 447–448.

Levinger, G., & Breedlove, J. Interpersonal attraction and agreement: A study of marriage partners. *Journal of Personality and Social Psychology, 1966, 3*, 367–372.

Levy, J. M., & McGee, R. K. Childbirth as crisis: A test of Janis' theory of communication and stress resolution. *Journal of Personality and Social Psychology, 1975, 3*, 171–179.

Lichtenstein, E., & Danaher, B. G. Modification of smoking behavior: A critical analysis of theory, research, and practice. In M. Hersen, R. M. Eisler, & P. M. Miller (Eds.). *Progress in behavior modification* (vol. 3). New York: Academic Press, 1976.

Luborsky, L. Helping alliances in psychotherapy: The groundwork for a study of their relationship to its outcome. In J. L. Claghorn (Ed.), *Successful psychotherapy*. New York: Brunner/Mazel, 1976.

Mahoney, M. J. Research issues in self-management. *Behavior Therapy, 1972, 3*, 45–63.

Mahoney, M. J. *Cognition and behavior modification*. Cambridge, Mass.: Ballinger, 1974.

Malan, D. H. *The frontier of brief psychotherapy*. New York: Plenum Medical Book Company, 1976.

Mann, L. Use of a "balance sheet" procedure to improve the quality of personal decision making: A field experiment with college applicants. *Journal of Vocational Behavior, 1972, 2*, 291–300.

Mann, L., & Janis, I. L. A follow-up study on the long-term effects of emotional role playing. *Journal of Personality and Social Psychology, 1968, 8*, 339–342.

Maracek, J., & Mettee, D. R. Avoidance of continued success as a function of self-esteem certainty and responsibility for success. *Journal of Personality and Social Psychology,* 1972, 98–107.

Marlowe, D., & Gergen, K. J. Personality and social interaction. In G. Lindzey & E. Aronson (Eds.), *The handbook of social psychology* (Vol. 3, 2nd ed.). Reading, Mass.: Addison-Wesley, 1969.

Marston, M. V. Compliance with medical regimens: A review of the literature. *Nursing Research,* 1970, *19,* 312–323.

May, R. *Love and will.* New York: Norton, 1969.

McClean, P. D. Depression as a specific response to stress. In I. G. Sarason and C. D. Spielberger (Eds.), *Stress and anxiety* (Vol. 3). New York: Wiley, 1976.

McFall, R. M., & Hammen, L. Motivation, structure, and self-monitoring: Role of nonspecific factors in smoking reduction. *Journal of Consulting and Clinical Psychology,* 1971, *37,* 80–86.

McGill, A. M. Review of literature on cardiovascular rehabilitations. In S. M. Weiss (Ed.), *Proceedings of the National Heart and Lung Institute Working Conference on Health Behavior.* Washington, D.C.: DHEW (Publication No. NIH 76-868), 1975.

Meichenbaum, D. H. *Cognitive-behavior modification: An integrative approach.* New York: Plenum, 1977.

Meichenbaum, D. H., & Turk, D. C. The cognitive-behavioral management of anxiety, anger, and pain. In P. O. Davidson (Ed.). *The behavioral management of anxiety, depression and pain.* New York: Brunner/Mazel, 1976.

Melamed, B. C., & Siegel, L. J. Reduction of anxiety in children facing hospitalization and surgery by use of filmed modeling. *Journal of Consulting and Clinical Psychology,* 1975, *43,* 511–521.

Miller, D. W., & Star, M. K. *The structure of human decisions.* Englewood Cliffs, N.J.: Prentice-Hall, 1967.

Miller, J. C., & Janis, I. L. Dyadic interaction and adaptation to the stresses of college life. *Journal of Consulting Psychology,* 1973, *3,* 258–264.

Miller, N., & Dworkin, B. R. Critical issues in therapeutic applications of biofeedback. In G. E. Schwartz & J. Beatty (Eds.), *Biofeedback: Theory and research.* New York: Academic Press 1977.

Moran, P. A. *An experimental study of pediatric admission.* Unpublished master's thesis, Yale University School of Nursing, 1963.

Mulligan, W. L. Effects of self-disclosure and interviewer feedback: A field experiment during a Red Cross blood donation campaign. In I. L. Janis (Ed.), *Counseling on personal decisions: Theory and research on short-term helping relationships.* New Haven: Yale University Press, 1982.

Nay, W. R. *Behavioral intervention.* New York: Gardner, 1976.

Newcomb, T. M. *The acquaintance process.* New York: Holt, Rinehart & Winston, 1961.

Nisbett, R., & Ross, L. *Human inference: Strategies and shortcomings of social judgment.* Englewood Cliffs, N.J.: Prentice-Hall, 1980.

Nowell, C., & Janis, I. L. Effective and ineffective partnerships in a weight-reduction clinic. In I. L. Janis (Ed.), *Counseling on personal decisions: Theory and research on short-term helping relationships.* New Haven: Yale University Press, 1982.

Okun, B. F. *Effective helping: Interviewing and counseling techniques.* North Scituate, Mass.: Duxbury Press, 1976.

Perls, F. S. *Gestalt therapy verbatim.* Lafayette, Calif.: Real People Press, 1969.

Polansky, N. A. On duplicity in the interview. *American Journal of Orthopsychiatry,* 1967, *37,* 568–579.

Pranulis, M., Dabbs, J., & Johnson, J. General anesthesia and the patient's attempts at control. *Social Behavior and Personality,* 1975, *3,* 49–54.

Quinlan, D. M., & Janis, I. L. Unfavorable effects of high levels of self-disclosure. In I. L. Janis (Ed.), *Counseling on personal decisions: Theory and research on short-term helping relationships.* New Haven: Yale University Press, 1982.

Quinlan, D. M., Janis, I. L., & Bales, V. Effects of moderate self-disclosure and amount of contact with the counselor. In I. L. Janis (Ed.), *Counseling on personal decisions: Theory and research on short-term helping relationships.* New Haven: Yale University Press, 1982.

Radloff, B. What is the next thing I want to do with my life? *Carnegie Quarterly,* 1977.

Radloff, R., & Helmreich, R. *Groups under stress: Psychological research in Sealab II.* New York: Appleton-Century-Crofts, 1968.

Rae-Grant, Q. The art of being a failure as a consultant. In J. Zusman and D. L. Davidson (Eds.), *Practical aspects of mental health consultation.* Springfield, Ill.: Charles C Thomas, 1972.

Raiffa, H. *Decision analysis.* Reading, Mass.: Addison-Wesley, 1968.

Reed, H. B., & Janis, I. L. Effects of a new type of psychological treatment on smokers' resistance to warnings about health hazards. *Journal of Consulting and Clinical Psychology,* 1974, *42,* 748.

Richmond, J. B. *Healthy people: The surgeon general's report on health promotion and disease prevention.* (DHEW PHS Publication No. 79-55071). Washington, D.C.: U.S. Government Printing Office, 1979.

Rimm, D. C., and Masters, J. C. *Behavior therapy: Techniques and empirical findings.* New York: Academic Press, 1974.

Riskind, J. H. The clients' sense of personal mastery: Effects of time perspective and self-esteem. In I. L. Janis (Ed.), *Counseling on personal de-*

cisions: Theory and research on short-term helping relationships. New Haven: Yale University Press, 1982.

Riskind, J. H., & Janis, I. L. Effects of high self-disclosure and approval training procedures. In I. L. Janis (Ed.), *Counseling on personal decisions: Theory and research on short-term helping relationships.* New Haven: Yale University Press, 1982.

Rodin, J. Cognitive-behavioral strategies for the control of obesity. Paper presented at conference on cognitive-behavior therapy: Applications and issues, Los Angeles, September 1978.

Rodin, J., & Janis, I. L. The social power of health-care practitioners as agents of change. *Journal of Social Issues,* 1979, *35,* 60–81.

Rogers, C. R. *Client-centered therapy.* Boston: Houghton Mifflin, 1951.

Rogers, C. R. *On becoming a person.* Boston: Houghton Mifflin, 1961.

Rogers, C. R. (Ed.). *The therapeutic relationship and its impact.* Madison: University of Wisconsin Press, 1967.

Rogers, C. R., & Dymond, R. F. (Eds.). *Psychotherapy and personality change.* Chicago: University of Chicago Press, 1954.

Romanczyk, R. G. Self-monitoring in the treatment of obesity: Parameters of reactivity. *Behavior Therapy,* 1974, *5,* 531–540.

Rubin, Z. *Liking and loving.* New York: Holt, Rinehart & Winston, 1973.

Sackett, D. L. The magnitude of compliance and noncompliance. In D. L. Sackett & R. B. Haynes (Eds.), *Compliance with therapeutic regimens.* Baltimore: Johns Hopkins University Press, 1976.

Sackett, D. L., & Haynes, R. B. (Eds.). *Compliance with therapeutic regimens.* Baltimore: Johns Hopkins University Press, 1976.

Schachter, S. *The psychology of affiliation.* Stanford, Calif.: Stanford University Press, 1959.

Schachter, S. Recidivism and self-cure of smoking and obesity. *American Psychologist,* 1982, *37,* 436–444.

Schein, E. H. *Process consultation.* Reading, Mass.: Addison-Wesley, 1969.

Schultz, R., & Hanusa, B. M. Long-term effects of control and predictability enhancing interventions: Findings and ethical issues. *Journal of Personality and Social Psychology,* 1978, *36,* 1194–1201.

Schwartz, G. E. Biofeedback and the self-management of disregulation disorders. In R. B. Stuart (Ed.), *Behavioral self-management: Strategies, techniques, and outcome.* New York: Brunner/Mazel, 1977.

Seligman, M. E. P. *Helplessness: On depression, development, and death.* San Francisco: Freeman, 1975.

Shaw, M. E. *Group dynamics.* New York: McGraw-Hill, 1971.

Shewchuk, L. A. Special report: Smoking cessation programs of the American Health Foundation. *Preventive Medicine,* 1976, *5,* 454–474.

Simmons, R. G., Klein, S. D., & Simmons, R. L. *Gift of life: The social and psychological impact of organ transplant.* New York: Wiley-Interscience, 1977.

Simon, H. A. *Administrative behavior: A study of decision-making processes in administrative organization.* (3rd ed.). New York: Free Press, 1976.

Singer, J. L. *Imagery and daydream methods in psychotherapy and behavior modification.* New York: Academic Press, 1974.

Smith, A. D. Effects of self-esteem enhancement on teachers' acceptance of innovation in a classroom setting. In I. L. Janis (Ed.), *Counseling on personal decisions: Theory and research on short-term helping relationships.* New Haven: Yale University Press, 1982.

Stachnik, T. J. Priorities for psychology in medical education and health care delivery. *American Psychologist,* 1980, *35,* 8–15.

Stekel, S., & Swain, M. The use of written contracts to increase adherence. *Hospitals,* 1977, *51,* 81–84.

Stone, G. C. Patient compliance and the role of the expert. *Journal of Social Issues,* 1979, *35,* 34–59.

Stone, G. L., & Gotlib, I. Effect of instructions and modeling on self-disclosure. *Journal of Counseling Psychology,* 1975, *22,* 288–293.

Stone, G. L., & Morden, C. J. Effect of distance on verbal productivity. *Journal of Counseling Psychology,* 1976, *23,* 486–488.

Strong, S. R. Counseling: An interpersonal influence process. *Journal of Counseling Psychology,* 1968, *15,* 215–224.

Strong, S. R., & Matross, R. Change processes in counseling and psychotherapy. *Journal of Counseling Psychology,* 1973, *20,* 25–37.

Strong, S. R., & Schmidt, L. D. Expertness and influence in counseling. *Journal of Counseling Psychology,* 1970, *17,* 81–87.

Stuart, R. B., & Davis, B. *Slim chance in a fat world: Behavioral control of obesity.* Champaign, Ill.: Research Press, 1971.

Taylor, S. E. *Adjustment to threatening events: A theory of cognitive adaptation.* The tenth Katz–Newcomb lecture delivered at the University of Michigan, April 28, 1982.

Tedeschi, J. T., & Lindskold, S. *Social psychology: Interdependence, interaction, and influence.* New York: Wiley, 1976.

Thibaut, J. W., & Kelley, H. H. *The social psychology of groups.* New York; Wiley, 1959.

Toomey, M. Conflict theory approach to decision making applied to alcoholics. *Journal of Personality and Social Psychology,* 1972, *24,* 199–206.

Truax, C. B., & Carkhuff, R. R. *Toward effective counseling and psychotherapy.* Chicago: Aldine, 1967.

Truax, C. B., & Mitchell, K. M. Research on certain therapist interpersonal skills in relation to process and outcome. In A. E. Bergin & S. L. Garfield (Eds.), *Handbook of psychotherapy and behavior change.* New York: Wiley, 1971.

Turk, D. C., & Genest, M. Regulation of pain: The application of cognitive and behavioral techniques for prevention and remediation. In P. Kendall & S. Hollon (Eds.), *Cognitive-behavioral interventions: Theory, research and practices.* New York: Academic Press, 1979.

Vance, B. Using contracts to control weight and to improve cardiovascular physical fitness. In J. D. Krumboltz & C. E. Thoresen (Eds.), *Counseling methods.* New York: Holt, Rinehart & Winston, 1976.

Vernon, D. T. A., & Bigelow, D. A. Effect of information about a potentially stressful situation on responses to stress impact. *Journal of Personality and Social Psychology,* 1974, *29,* 50–59.

Wallerstein, J., & Kelly, J. B. *Surviving the breakup: How children and parents cope with divorce.* New York: Basic Books, 1980.

Walster, E., Berscheid, E., & Walster, G. W. New directions in equity research. In L. Berkowitz and E. Walster (Eds.), *Advances in experimental social psychology* (Vol. 9). New York: Academic Press, 1976.

Wankel, L. M., & Thompson, C. Motivating people to be physically active: Self-persuasion vs. balanced decision making. *Journal of Applied Social Psychology,* 1977, *7,* 332–340.

Wanous, J. P. Effects of a realistic job preview on job acceptance, job attitudes and job survival. *Journal of Applied Psychology,* 1973, *58,* 321–332.

Wessler, R. A., & Wessler, R. L. *The principles and practice of rational-emotive therapy.* San Francisco: Jossey-Bass, 1980.

Wheeler, D., & Janis, I. L. *A practical guide for making decisions.* New York: Free Press, 1980.

Winnicott, D. W. *Therapeutic consultations in child psychiatry.* London: Hogarth Press, 1971.

Wolfer, J. A., & Visintainer, M. A. Pediatric surgical patients' and parents' stress responses and adjustment as a function of psychologic preparation and stress-point nursing care. *Nursing Research,* 1975, *24,* 244–255.

Wolpe, J. *The practice of behavior therapy* (2nd ed.). New York: Pergamon Press, 1973.

Wylie, R. C. *The self concept.* Lincoln: University of Nebraska Press, 1961.

Zimbardo, P. G., & Formica, R. Emotional comparison and self-esteem as determinants of affiliation. *Journal of Personality,* 1963, *31,* 141–162.

Name Index

Subject Index

acceptance: contingent, 20, 30–31, 33, 35–37, 40, 76, 113; noncontingent, 23–25; by counselor, 27, 28, 47, 68, 70, 71, 85–115; mutual by partners, 66; how conveyed by counselor, 85–115
acceptance statements, appropriate formulations of, 113–14
acquired motivating power. *See* motivational power of counselor
"addictive-appetitive disorders," prognosis for, 6
addicts, counseling of, 3
adherence to a decision, xi, 4, 36, 55, 59, 77–79, 139–40; problem of in health counseling, 4–7, 41, 154–55, 161, 185; and internalization of counselor's norms, 22, 39, 69; and positive vs. neutral feedback from counselor, 32, 76, 87, 104, 108–11, 114–15, 116; and self-disclosure, 32, 116, 121, 122, 123; and commitment, 72, 73, 75; and approval training, 79, 132–33; and self-esteem enhancement, 107; and decisional balance sheet, 175. *See also* backsliding; stress inoculation
affiliation motivation of persons in stressful dilemmas, 22–23
Agamemnon, 11
Alcoholics Anonymous, 22, 62
alternative courses of action, techniques for thinking of, 169–70
ambiguity in counselor's feedback, 32, 108
ambivalence toward counselor, 92–102, 124–31
American Cancer Society film, 65, 163

American Cancer Society pamphlet, 64
American Psychological Association Task Force on Health Research, 56, 57, 60
amount of contact with the client and counselor effectiveness, 27, 56–61, 78
approval training via psychodrama, 76–77, 79, 132–33
"art of being a failure as a consultant," by Raé-Grant, 11–13
assertiveness training, 44, 46
attorneys as counselors, 4, 8, 22, 40, 41, 189
attributing recommendations to a respected secondary group, 37, 43, 71, 75
audio system used in counseling, 88
authoritarian-directive approach to counseling, 8, 70
aversion therapy, 61–62
awareness-of-rationalizations procedure, 159–64, 201

backsliding, 6, 25, 39, 40, 51, 54, 55–57, 66, 68, 72, 195. *See also* adherence to a decision
balance-sheet procedure. *See* decisional balance-sheet procedure
behavioral disorders, treatment of, 52
behavior modification technique, 19, 81, 82–83
behavior-therapy approach, 1, 21, 40, 42–45, 46, 47, 57, 61–62, 70, 73
biofeedback treatment, 1, 40–41, 43–44
bolstering self-esteem. *See* self-esteem enhancement by a counselor